beds are burning

Mark Dodshon's varied career has included work as producer/director of a daily music show, *JAM*, for Australia Television; creator and presenter of a weekly international radio program, *The Big Backyard*, which was distributed by the Department of Foreign Affairs and Trade to 500 radio stations worldwide; national campaign manager for the Nuclear Disarmament Party for the 1984 federal election; presenter and researcher of a weekly music show, *Edge of the Wedge*, on ABC TV; full-time househusband and child-carer; high-school history teacher; presenter/producer on JJJ radio and long-time host of *The Australian Music Show*; and freelance journalist for newspapers and magazines including the *Sydney Morning Herald* and *Rolling Stone*. Most recently he has been a strategist and designer with Balance Design, a multimedia company that specialises in web sites for the music industry. Mark lives in Sydney with his wife and son.

I asked Bobby Dylan
I asked the Beatles
I asked Timothy Leary
But he couldn't tell me either
They call me the seeker
I've been searching low and high
I won't get to get what I'm after
Till the day I die

'The Seeker' – Pete Townshend, 1970

Midnight Oil: the journey

BEDSAREBURNING

mark dodshon

VIKING
an imprint of
PENGUIN BOOKS

For my mother and father, my three brothers,
my wife, and my son – I love you all

VIKING

Published by the Penguin Group
Penguin Group (Australia)
250 Camberwell Road, Camberwell, Victoria 3124, Australia
(a division of Pearson Australia Group Pty Ltd)
Penguin Group (USA) Inc.
375 Hudson Street, New York, New York 10014, USA
Penguin Group (Canada)
10 Alcorn Avenue, Toronto, Ontario, Canada M4V 3B2
(a division of Pearson Penguin Canada Inc.)
Penguin Books Ltd
80 Strand, London WC2R 0RL, England
Penguin Ireland
25 St Stephen's Green, Dublin 2, Ireland
(a division of Penguin Books Ltd)
Penguin Books India Pvt Ltd
11 Community Centre, Panchsheel Park, New Delhi – 110 017, India
Penguin Group (NZ)
Cnr Airborne and Rosedale Roads, Albany, Auckland, New Zealand
(a division of Pearson New Zealand Ltd)
Penguin Books (South Africa) (Pty) Ltd
24 Sturdee Avenue, Rosebank, Johannesburg 2196, South Africa

Penguin Books Ltd, Registered Offices: 80 Strand, London, WC2R 0RL, England

First published by Penguin Group (Australia), a division of Pearson Australia Group Pty Ltd, 2004

10 9 8 7 6 5 4 3 2 1

Text copyright © Mark Dodshon 2004

The moral right of the author has been asserted

All rights reserved. Without limiting the rights under copyright reserved above, no part of this publication may be reproduced, stored in or introduced into a retrieval system, or transmitted, in any form or by any means (electronic, mechanical, photocopying, recording or otherwise), without the prior written permission of both the copyright owner and the above publisher of this book.

Cover and text designed by Nikki Townsend © Penguin Group (Australia)
Cover photograph of band © Midnight Oil Ents Pty Ltd (photograph by Andrzej Liguz/moreimages.net)
Cover photograph of Peter Garrett © Nick Laham/Getty Images
Typeset in 12.25/18pt Fairfield Light by Post Pre-Press Group, Brisbane, Queensland
Printed and bound in Australia by McPhersons Printing Group, Maryborough, Victoria

National Library of Australia
Cataloguing-in-Publication data:

Dodshon, Mark, 1952– .
Beds are burning: Midnight Oil: the journey.
Includes index.
ISBN 0 670 04163 7.
1. Midnight Oil (Musical group). 2. Rock groups – Australia – Biography.
3. Rock musicians – Australia – Biography. I. Title.
782.421660922

www.penguin.com.au

contents

	acknowledgements	vi
prologue	time to talk	1
one	patrick's typewriter	7
two	is it now?	54
three	instant relief	95
four	crossing the bridge	140
five	hear the time clock sing	173
six	into the black	211
seven	kiss that girl	249
eight	outbreak of love	292
nine	eyes of light	330
epilogue	as big as U2	377
	discography	387
	references	395
	index	397

acknowledgements

Special thanks to:
Rob Hirst
Peter Garrett
Jim Moginie
Martin Rotsey
Wayne Stevens – Bones Hillman
Peter Gifford – Giffo
Andrew James – Bear
Gary Morris

Thanks also to Connie Adolph, David Fricke, Paul Gilding, Denis Handlin, Salomon Hazat, Nick Launay, Michael Lippold, Warne Livesey, Rhonda Markowitz, Chris Moss, Mason Munoz and John Watson.

I would also like to acknowledge the help and support of Damian Trotter, Stephanie Lewis, Bruce Elder, Glad Reed, Arlene Brookes, Robert Hambling, Adrienne Overall, John Dauth, Glen Preece, Nikki Townsend, Katie Purvis, Robert Sessions and Rosemary Creswell.

Thank you to Midnight Oil and Sony Music for permission to reprint the following song lyrics: 'Don't Wanna Be the One' (pp. 8–9; Hirst/Garrett/Rotsey/

Moginie); 'Read About It' (pp. 10–11; Hirst/Moginie/Garrett); 'Sometimes' (p. 23; Midnight Oil); 'Put Down That Weapon' (pp. 28–9; Midnight Oil); 'If Ned Kelly Was King' (p. 143; Moginie/Garrett); 'Jimmy Sharman's Boxers' (p. 144; Hirst/Moginie); 'Kosciuszko' (p. 144; Hirst/Moginie); 'Beds Are Burning' (p. 169; Midnight Oil); 'Who Can Stand in the Way' (p. 264; Moginie/Garrett); 'Bells and Horns in the Back of Beyond' (pp. 264–5; Midnight Oil); 'Blossom and Blood' (p. 269; Hirst/Moginie); 'King of the Mountain' (p. 270; Hirst/Moginie); 'Forgotten Years' (p. 271; Hirst/Moginie); 'Truganini' (pp. 278–9; Hirst/Moginie); 'Kiss That Girl' (p. 290; Hirst/Garrett); 'Common Ground' (p. 349; Midnight Oil); 'Home' (p. 350; Midnight Oil); 'Redneck Wonderland' (pp. 358–9; Midnight Oil); 'I'm the Cure' (p. 364; Moginie); 'Say Your Prayers' (p. 365; Moginie); 'Golden Age' (p. 375; Moginie/Hirst/Garrett). Thank you to Neil Murray and Universal Music Publishing Australia for permission to reprint lyrics from 'Circumstances' (pp. 352–3), and to Pete Townshend and Fabulous Music/Cromwell Music Australia for permission to reprint lyrics from 'The Seeker' (p. ii).

Every effort has been made to trace and acknowledge copyright material, but this has not always been possible. The author and publisher would be pleased to hear from any copyright holders who have not been formally acknowledged in the book.

prologue

time to talk

Rob Hirst telephoned at a very un-rock'n'roll hour to say he had discovered another box of Midnight Oil archives, and invited me to pick them up at my convenience. I had already spoken with all the other members of the band, except Martin Rotsey, but Rob was proving difficult to tie down for an interview. He seemed to want the last word, and a bit more time to consider what that word might be. It was time for me to try again.

I grabbed my recorder and drove directly to his house. It was about 9 a.m. As I walked through his garden gate a cowbell rattled loud enough to alert the neighbourhood, and as I stood at the front door some time passed before it was opened. 'Is Rob here?' I asked his wife, Lesley.

'You've just missed him,' she said, indicating over her shoulder. Down in the little bay below their house on the edge of Sydney Harbour was Rob, rowing a little dinghy rapidly in the opposite direction.

This is not *the* history of Midnight Oil; it is *a* history. True, the band – lead singer Peter Garrett, guitarists Jim Moginie and Martin Rotsey, drummer Rob Hirst and all three bass players from the band's long career (Bear, Giffo and Bones) – have cooperated to varying degrees, but this is not the authorised version of their story. The band's long-time manager, Gary Morris, has been alternately revered and reviled for his vice-like control of the band's business and media relations, and for a while he seemed determined to make his cooperation conditional on the right to check the final manuscript. Once that was ruled out, he gave 'Gary copy' – a virtually uninterruptible monologue – down the telephone line from his camp site in the bush till my ears burned. Needless to say, this is not altogether how Gary would have written the tale.

I am a friend, and a fan, and have been an occasional employee of Midnight Oil. I was also a music journalist during their career. I make no apologies for what follows except to the band members themselves. Once again someone is exposing them to largely unwanted public scrutiny – which means any scrutiny that deals with subjects other than their music. 'Get over it,' you say, 'these guys are in the entertainment industry – anything goes.' However, the band see themselves in the *music* industry and that is way bad enough. Privacy is a major concern for all of us, but it is particularly precious to people for whom being in public is a necessary part of their job.

If you're looking for marriage details or descriptions of the band members' lives at home, you won't find them here. Midnight Oil have never been disposed to reveal those sorts of details, partly because of their irrelevance to the band's core business of music making, partly due to an instinct to keep something for themselves, and partly, I suspect, because deep down they know that the truth of the non-musical parts of their lives could never match any mythology or gossip. In any case, there is enough reality about the band without knowing the extent of the members' individual ordinariness! They are all personable, friendly and capable of entertaining conversation, but only Rob or Bones could ever be described as the life of the party. Despite their undeniable musical talents and substantial achievements, they all remain overwhelmingly modest and unassuming. I have respected their ongoing wish to protect their private lives by noting personal details only where they add to or intersect with songs or career moves. Instead, I concentrate on their music and the political and social connections that have been part of it.

Jim was the most enthusiastic about the idea of a book – no saintly presentation, he insisted, no hagiography, but a warts-and-all account. He sat in my shed and told me lots of things I didn't know. Jim had only ever been interviewed once before about the band, and had plenty he wanted to say. That previous interview, in 1993, had got him into trouble with Gary. 'I said, "Well, it's just a band." I mean, to me it always was – if it doesn't work as a band, it doesn't work. We can have all the messages in the world, but if the grooves aren't there and the music's not there no one's gonna wanna hear it.'

When Peter's turn came, he spread himself out on a couch in his suitably super-sized living room by a big window looking across the yellowing-green countryside. He seemed drawn to what might be described as the Ringo Starr approach: 'It was all woonderful!' He answered every question, some more enthusiastically than others, but avoided speculating and tended to resist analysis.

Rob also chose his words carefully, when we eventually spoke on his harbourside veranda. His measured but detailed account of events was augmented by the mixed chirping and scrawking of local bush and sea birds.

Martin remains opposed to the idea of a book about the band. He steadfastly resisted my various invitations to contribute via an interview, although he did lurk outside my shed for a two-hour chat over a cup of tea – without a tape recorder running.

Wayne Stevens, better known as Bones Hillman, was as relaxed as anyone might be sitting beside a beautiful pool in the garden of his studio apartment. He was emphasising the tragi-comic perspective of the band's career when one of the prized posters he'd been showing me was blown into the pool.

The two earlier bass players were also keen to contribute. Andrew 'Bear' James wrote his memories down for me in fascinating detail, and Peter 'Giffo' Gifford munched on an apple while he reminisced on the phone from the headquarters of his thriving bikini business in Byron Bay.

So it's the story of these guys, and how they've seen their life as Midnight Oil. It's concerned primarily with the music they have made and how they created it, and the career they've had and how they managed it, but also with something of the impact that being Midnight Oil has made on the world and on them as people.

Pete: 'It was always a remarkable exercise in tolerance, and compromise, and wilfulness, and sort of walking the wire, to hold the Oils in one place at one time – even here in Australia it was pretty hard work. And if we could do it, then great, because we knew when we got up on stage we had this band that could set fire to a town and leave again with something other than burnt cinders to show for it – with a little bit of light in people's hearts, a little bit of thought in their heads. But holding it together for the long run, particularly to the level of being a global touring band, was always going to be our biggest challenge.'

Most people have heard the band's biggest hit, the 'Beds Are Burning' single from the late eighties, but there are some dedicated fans who know every one of the approximately 140 songs Midnight Oil have recorded and released. When a band write their music they are looking, often unconsciously, for the link between the idiosyncratic and the universal. How universally a personal sound or turn of phrase can resonate beyond the composer's consciousness can be the difference between the success and failure of a song. How far can a song about Aboriginal land rights communicate? Across national boundaries? Across cultures? Success in international pop music is notoriously fleeting – even one 'hit' song is considered a successful career. However, *survival* in the world of international pop music is another thing, and every story is different. Did a band's solitary hit song take years to achieve? Did they survive the acclaim? Maybe it was the band's very first effort – and maybe they went on to make many more hit records.

By the time Midnight Oil had their one true international hit, they had done ten hard years. There were six albums and two EPs and close to 1000 live rock'n'roll performances behind them. Since 'Beds Are Burning' there have been another five studio albums, two live releases and a compilation – and at least another 1000 shows. They have often dealt with difficult issues in their songs, confronting ideas and expressing their thoughts through words and music. Artists share their search for truth or beauty, and push forward in a way that sometimes helps us all push forward and perhaps see new ways of looking at things. In Midnight Oil's case, they actually have a message that was unlike the rock'n'roll stereotype they inhabited. It was not alienated, but it was born out of punk; it was not unrealistic, although it was a natural offshoot of the hippy movement; and it was not escapist, even though at their heart Midnight Oil are a surf band. They are about honesty in all its manifestations and, as unfashionable and naive as that sounds, they genuinely and conscientiously strive to be true to themselves and true to their fans above all else.

one

patrick's typewriter

The final run of concerts at Sydney's Hordern Pavilion was surreal and exhausting and exhilarating. With the end of Pete's campaign to be a senator for the Nuclear Disarmament Party in sight, and with only six home shows to do, it looked like we might actually make it to the finish line. The Hordern was packed. It was night six and the band were in the midst of the irresistible delirium of their final song, 'Don't Wanna Be the One'. Hundreds of outstretched hands were up, thousands of dancing heads and bodies. Near the stage the shirts were off as sweaty bodies stomped and surged to the music, and from the back to the front the crowd was at maximum sing-along intensity. They were raging.

The band were raging, too, but still relentlessly building to that inevitable cathartic finish. Pete had already spun like a dervish and staggered like a boxer during the powerhouse middle section of the song when the bass drives everyone's heart to breaking point and the guitars and keyboard cut slices through you. 'I don't wanna be the one, I don't wanna be the one, I – don't – wanna – be – the – ooooooooooooooooooooone,' screamed Pete until his breath ran out, followed by a weaker but still defiant scream, 'Eeeeayarrrr!', and then an exhausted, grunted 'Aaaaaarr' as he fell backwards from the microphone and stumbled towards side stage.

The effect of Pete's scream was, as always, spine-tingling. Never less than a howl from the deepest recesses, it froze you and freed you at the same time. For a few tantalising seconds, although it seemed longer, part of your brain was released from burdens unknown. Tonight the scream had all that and more, delivering a last-gasp quality that carried all the awful truths of pain unspecified. Pete was wrecked, in pain, soaking wet from top to toe, and barely able to make the few metres to the side-stage curtain. Rob was on his drum stool raining drumsticks onto his kit amidst swirling feedback and an ecstatic roar from the crowd. They hadn't had time to whoop and holler yet, let alone applaud or cheer or whistle. It took several more seconds before that started happening, and another half-minute before being joined by the sound of thousands screaming, crying and chanting for more. 'Oy-YERLS, Oy-YERLS, Oy-YERLS,' went the relentless call. The crowd was stunned, and stuffed. No one was going anywhere; they were just stuck to their spots, standing and yelling and looking towards the stage.

I'm an innocent victim, I'm just like you
We end up in home units with a brick-wall view
I can't believe the perfect families on my colour TV
If I don't make it to the top it'll never bother me

And I don't wanna be the one
And I don't wanna be the one

> *I'm an innocent bystander caught in the path*
> *Waiting out the back while the corporate attack*
> *Assaults the senses with relentless scenes of passion and delight*
> *I cut up all the options and went running for my life*

Pete just made it through the curtain before collapsing against my shoulder. I was instantly soaked down my entire left side and immediately dropped a folder of notes as I realised he was relying on me for support. He put a cupped hand over his mouth and somewhere someone said, 'Oxygen.' A canister with plastic tube and face mask appeared in an instant. Pete went to the ground where he sucked at the oxygen with his eyes shut, looking like death. Someone wanted to put a blanket over him, but he seemed way too hot for that. His whole system seemed at breaking point as he lay there, ashen-faced and shaking. I'd never seen him this bad before.

Meanwhile, the band had exited from the stage and some concern was being shown, but Pete had needed oxygen almost every night of the tour and the others were still holding their instruments in automatic anticipation of the encore. The sound of the roaring, chanting crowd was like a train going full speed through an underground station, except it didn't stop. The band members shifted their weight from foot to foot, towelling off themselves and their instruments. Rob also looked pretty bad, but at least he was still on his feet. After what was probably a minute and a half someone said, 'Encore?'

The band looked at each other and then at Pete. He lifted his hand with a finger raised. I thought the shaking finger meant 'Not this time', but the band interpreted it as 'Only the one song' and there was a short discussion followed by the roar of the crowd doubling in volume as one by one they walked back out onto the stage. Shortly the sound of Martin's softly strummed introduction to 'Wedding Cake Island' brought a massive and grateful cheer. The band's classic instrumental, inspired by the view from Coogee Beach, calmed and quietened the crowd. They were soon lost in the song, until a few shrieks from the front rows indicated that Pete was on stage again. Down the back, in the relative dark next to Rob's drum riser, he was sipping from a cup and towelling himself. He had a dry shirt on.

Jim's shimmering keyboard ending to the song, evoking nothing less than sunshine sparkling off the water, had barely finished echoing into the ether when firstly Rob's fast single-cowbell beats, then Jim's familiar guitar pattern, then finally Martin and Giffo with Rob's full drum-kit attack really crash-started the band's closer – the biting account of global media control, 'Read About It'.

Hammer and sickle
The news is at a trickle
The commissars are fickle but the stockpile grows

Bombers keeping coming
Engines softly humming
The stars and stripes are running for their own big show

Another little flare-up
Storm brewed in a tea cup
Imagine any mix-up and the lot would go

Nothing ever happens
Nothing ever matters
No one ever tells me so what I am to know

You wouldn't read about it
Read about it

I don't know how Pete made it through. It's one of the band's classics, fast and hard with a rousing sing-along chorus, which remained a live favourite twenty years after its recording. It's a rollercoaster of a song, with a false ending during which the stage goes dark and silent for several seconds. That night the blackout seemed to last forever. Suddenly the chorus and lights kicked back in simultaneously, accompanied by the crowd's surprised and appreciative roar. There was one final round of an extended, exhausting chorus for audience and band alike before it was lights out again and the band were gone. The feedback was eventually clicked off, leaving just the sound of the crowd chanting, chanting, chanting. There wouldn't be another song tonight, but the crowd, despite sensing this fact and hearing some after-show music on the PA, chanted for a further ten minutes. One by one, small group by small group, they gave up the call. Only then did they look left and right, reacquaint themselves with their neighbours, and start to think about dispersing.

Backstage an hour later, sometime after midnight, Pete was still just in a towel looking pale and drawn, but he had showered, or at least sat under a shower on a stool, and was weakly attempting to go through the folder full of NDP business I had retrieved from where it had fallen. We had things to do and there was correspondence he needed to deal with. Then we realised – the tour was over, the campaign was over, the toughest time, mentally and physically, of our respective lives was over. We had reached a point we had barely been able to envisage six weeks earlier. Today was election day.

'Not to be a republican at twenty is proof of want of heart; to be one at thirty is proof of want of head' – so said François Guisot (1787–1874). My father used to quote a version of this statement in the hope, no doubt, of dousing my enthusiasm for political change. Guisot was a French monarchist statesman, and his variously updated opinion has caused much soul-searching among those in their twenties. His implication that idealism is merely a rush of youthful blood and that conservatism – common sense – will eventually return is as contentious now as it was then. A slightly later version by George Clemenceau replaced 'republican' with 'socialist', and in the twentieth century the concept was overly simplified to 'If you're not a liberal when you're young you have no heart; if you're not a conservative when you're old you have no brain.'

To presume that idealism dies with the arrival of older age and responsibilities presumes way too much. Arguably we become more selfish, or more aware of the need for personal survival, but beyond that can be a greater awareness that what is good for society as a whole is in the longer run good for individuals as well. In truth, we are all capable of mixed philosophies and find room for conservative views on some things and radical views on others.

Midnight Oil has the outsider mentality that exists in all rock bands. It's a combination of that alienation born of adolescent frustrations and the natural distrust of authority exhibited by most artists. Collectively the band members share many ideals – all the big ones – but as individuals they come at their philosophies and answers from different directions. In broad terms, Rob and Pete are of the political left and Jim is a humanist. Martin seems to contribute the cynicism and feigned disinterest of an anarchist. They have made an intellectual commitment to judge things by their own sense of reality – in the way they make their music, deal with the music industry and relate to their fans and the rest of the planet.

It is, on the surface, a relatively unholy intersection of the magic world that is music with the profoundly non-magic world of politics. In that alone Midnight Oil are a rare band with relatively few, if any, direct precedents. Within the band there is a distrust of the political process and an indignation at the role of media and big business, and they made a conscious decision to engage with and get involved in the issues and causes they believed in. Pete: 'I certainly had always believed that we needed to put out in other ways, to express what it was we were singing about. I felt that was absolute: Midnight Oil was as much what it did as what it said. It's all part of making the word into the action, because actions *do* speak louder than words.'

They are educated guys who talk about issues, and there is a commitment to full and rigorous debate that often leads to marathon meetings before agreement is reached. Rob studied history as part of an Arts degree at Sydney University and completed an Honours paper in Economic History on the subject of wages and living conditions of American blues and jazz musicians. Martin didn't quite get to finish his Arts or

Architecture courses but he is a quiet thinker, too, and Jim's degree in Science led to research work at the CSIRO. Pete has a degree in Arts from the ANU and a Law degree from the University of New South Wales.

The band were not particularly politically active as individuals. To Jim, politics wasn't part of his life at all. 'I was a science student. I went to uni. I had an umbrella. I also had a briefcase. I didn't know anything about politics at all. I just wasn't interested in it.' They were non-aligned, you might say, and relatively free thinkers. They were from a generation politicised and disillusioned in a local sense through Australia's growing opposition to its involvement in the Vietnam War, and globally by the anti-apartheid movement. They had their eyes opened as to how politics can work positively when the National Service policy was overturned within days of the newly elected Whitlam Government taking office in 1972. Pete was only a few months short of deciding whether or not to register for national service and so avoided the birthday ballot that decided who went to training – and possibly off to war – and who missed out. The other guys were a couple of years younger.

Midnight Oil have often been described as a 'radical' band – meaning 'politically active' rather than 'revolutionary'. They have supported many causes over their career and actively promoted a range of ideas and endeavours, some of which could even be described as conservative. After all, the conservation movement is conservative by its very nature, even though the plan to retain forests or to return to clean air or clean water may require radical action.

When Pete was helping drive the process to save Jervis Bay, south of Sydney, from becoming an armaments depot and the new base for the Australian Navy, the action the band decided to take was direct. The Save Jervis Bay Committee was funded and operated out of Midnight Oil's office in Glebe in 1988 and 1989 and its coordinator, Paul Gilding, recalls the extent of the tactics. 'The defining action was when we occupied the Beecroft peninsula, the bombing range at Jervis Bay. It was a piece of direct-action activism – which Pete was particularly in favour of. We actually occupied the bombing range during a major military exercise and held it for five days and totally fucked up the exercise and they had to cancel it. They couldn't find us.'

Paul later went on to head Greenpeace International and continued his association with Pete by recommending him as a board member of that organisation in 1993. Midnight Oil had a longstanding connection to Greenpeace and other conservation groups, from their days of saving the whales and the seals in the seventies to the more contentious campaigns for forests and anti-nukes in the eighties. The list of benefit concerts is extensive and the issues supported broad, and every one of them required a contribution of time and effort and money from the band, and a big logistic effort from Gary, as Rob recalls. 'There was an enormous amount of endless, grinding bureaucratic work to do to make those tours, but particularly the benefits, work. And usually Gary, knowing that most other managers or promoters would fuck up, took it upon himself to do it. So it wasn't just Midnight Oil, he'd organise the whole damn thing, coordinate all the bands, a *huge* job. Most of the time people just complained at the end about how Gary was to deal with, without seeing that he'd done all the work, along with Diana Lindsay and Stephanie Lewis and Arlene Brookes, and all the staff – Wayne Willis, Craig Allen, all the office people put in – not to mention the crew and the work they did. From the nuclear disarmament concerts to the Open Family Foundation, the environmental causes, everything that the band generally and Pete specifically wanted to do, as an adjunct to a band already heavily playing, touring, recording and rehearsing. On top of all that workload Gary facilitated – to use his word – all the benefit concerts. These were things that were superimposed on the normal demands of touring and he could easily have rejected them as being outside his portfolio, but he rarely did. I think most of those big benefit concerts may have added to the band's reputation for putting our money where our mouth was, or as altruists or philanthropists or whatever, but Gary probably saw our regular touring and what he had planned for the band in terms of tours and stuff as what was really making our name.'

'It should be said that they were always Midnight Oil issues, not just Peter issues,' comments Paul Gilding. 'It was very clear that the band was a cohesive group in term of the politics of what they were doing. And the commitment to it was absolute – the amount of money they gave away was enormous! I know at some stage pretty early in the piece it was like a million bucks plus – not just to Jervis Bay but across all the issues. It was like a machine in there [the Midnight Oil office] in terms of the support it gave to the movement, and not just the environmental movement, also to youth groups and so on. They were an enormously powerful influence on homeless kids and on so many organisations. It was not only their ability to leverage their fame and influence to give hope and encouragement to people, but also the fact that they put their money behind that – cold, hard cash.'

When the band started doing financially well and demands on their time became international as well as local, the organising and playing of benefit concerts became much harder to do. Direct monetary donations were seen as a way of helping more people. The band established a donation register as a way of keeping track of who needed money and who they were able to help. It had always been their practice to allocate money from particular projects to specific causes, but as things became more frantic and fruitful – Pete refers to them as 'the honey years' – the band would take a percentage of tour income for giving away. Amounts varied from hundreds to many thousands, and although they went mainly to political and environmental activist groups, they managed to help a wide range of projects. There were always plenty of requests for help to choose from, but individual members of the band would suggest particular organisations for a portion as well. Film and book ideas as well as homelessness projects and research for innovative technical ideas were supported, and there were direct donations to the Open Family Foundation, the Salvation Army, the ACF and the Constable Care road safety campaign, among many others.

The band's support for cleaner beaches and surfing conditions along Australia's coastline was a constant during their career, prompted by Pete's first-hand revulsion at the state of things when he went for his regular workout in the waves along Sydney's northern beaches. Clean water was at the heart of one of their best-known activist actions, when they staged a hit-and-run performance on a truck top in New York City in May 1990 as a protest about oil company Exxon's inaction in dealing with the massive spill from their ship the *Exxon Valdez* at Prince William Sound in Alaska. The six-song concert opposite Exxon's global headquarters featured on news reports around the world and drew attention to the company's slowness in cleaning up the environmental disaster.

People had been putting oil in the fountain outside the Exxon building at the Rockefeller Center since the spill had happened in March 1989. The germ of the idea about a band protest came from Sony Records executive Mason Munoz, who had just been given responsibility for Midnight Oil within the company. He thought they should see that there were Americans who were prepared to support the band in their political standpoint. 'I had read a Rob Hirst interview where he talked about when they were in America their bus was like a cocoon that shielded them from all this bullshit, all this ugly terrible stuff that was all around them. And I've got to be honest, I took it as an affront. It was like during the previous year when I was going around Europe everybody was giving me a heap of crap because Ronald Reagan was the president, like every American was Ronald Reagan! That was really the genesis of the Exxon thing. I don't think the band realised there were people in America who understood what they were trying to do, and respected and cherished them because they maintained that agenda. And at some point in the next couple of weeks I thought of this idea to stage an event in front of the Exxon building. I remember calling Gary. I'd never met him, and everyone in New York who knew him said, "This guy is really scary, really scary. Be very careful. You can't do anything, suggest anything. Just watch out! BE CAREFUL." And I remember flying this idea by Gary over the phone and the next thing I know it's getting closer and closer and closer. It was an absolutely amazing time.'

Gary took to the idea immediately and, together with the band and Mason, he set up a joint action with Greenpeace. Mason did much of the work getting permissions and arranging logistics, and the ensuing performance was the result of much forethought, precise planning and a twist of fortune. Chris Moss was from Sony in Australia and responsible for the marketing of Australian artists internationally. He had become close to the band and managed to be in New York at the time. 'The plan was to play on Sixth Avenue, in front of the Exxon building, and the only way they could perform was to be on the back of a truck. If you just rolled up and started playing you'd get chucked out straight away and it would all be over before it began. The "Trojan horse" was to apply to film a picture. In New York everybody loves a movie. They love things to be filmed there and it's great for tourism, so if you go to the council and ask for permission to film a movie they'll give you a permit that covers all the Winnebagos and trucks you've got to park, the cameras and everything else.'

Apart from the permit from the council, there were also permits from the fire brigade, the ambulance service and the police that had to be secured. Everything was coming together but, as Chris remembers, 'There was all sorts of grief starting to happen. The day before the show the Rockefeller Center got wind of what was really going on and their lawyers started getting into the Sony lawyers with "We don't want any part of this – shut the whole thing down." The Sony lawyers shat themselves and requested a meeting with Peter and Gary. They had the meeting in the Sony offices where they basically said, "OK, if you are going to go ahead and do this then here's a document that says any liability that exists with this thing is your responsibility." Peter just said, "Fuck you, that's your problem, not ours," and walked away. So the lawyers then tried to go to Mason and say, "This isn't going to happen. We don't want the liability. We don't want to know about it. This is bigger than anything we want to deal with." But Mason, all power to him, just charged on.'

The night before the event, after performing at Radio City Music Hall, the band set their gear up on the back of a semi-trailer in a warehouse down in Greenwich Village. They did a rehearsal in the early hours of the morning before heading to their hotel for some sleep. The air was portentous. Finally the morning arrived and it was raining. All the trucks, vans and camera gear had to be moved in at daylight to make sure they got the planned position. Mason: 'I got to the site at seven o'clock in the morning and there was a police captain from midtown south asking to see my permits. I took him up to the record company building and he said, "I'm going to shut this thing down." And I said, "You can't shut it down. I've got the permits." "You don't have a sound permit." I said, "Well, the Mayor's Office on Film told me I didn't need it. I've got a permit to be filming out there. I don't need a sound permit." And he said, "I don't care what they told you. If anyone plays an instrument we're going to arrest everybody." I said, "With all due respect, piss off! If they have to play acoustic, they'll play acoustic." And he went, "You're not listening to me. Anybody plays a note on that flatbed, we're going to arrest you all."'

Before long they were joined by the fire chief and someone from the council and an argument developed over permits and jurisdiction. Chris: 'All the relevant government bodies for New York were arguing against each other because each one thinks that they have the ultimate authority. In the end each one agreed it should go ahead because they wanted to do the others over, they wanted to prove their higher authority on the issue. It was completely bizarre. It was a "Fuck you!" "No, fuck *you*!" thing.'

There is also an unconfirmed story that Tommy Mottola called somebody and reminded them that the record company had made a big donation to the Police Athletic Fund, which may also account for the police captain's change of mind. Mason: 'All of a sudden this captain is saying to me, "You can go ahead and do it, but you're going to have to go on an hour earlier than announced. It's got to happen at midday or not at all."'

After all the debating, this decision was taken sometime after eleven o'clock. Meanwhile, the band were back at the Parker Meridian Hotel with tour manager Willie MacInnes, hanging around, quite relaxed, having breakfast and thinking they had to be there at one o'clock. Chris: 'I got elected to run down Sixth Avenue as fast as I could. I barrel into the Parker Meridian and there's everyone, "Hi Mossy, what's up?" And I said, "You've got to get there NOW! Otherwise it's not gonna fuckin' happen! Quick, quick, quick! Willie, get everybody together. Jim, get Martin out of the toilet. Go. NOW!" So everybody jumps up and rushes and gets into cabs. But I've already headed off, running back up to the plaza to say, "They're on their way, everything's happening, we're going to be OK."'

Rob: 'I remember Willie and Chris freaking out and saying, "We've got to get there *now!*" We were halfway through breakfast. No one was in their stage gear so we went in our civvies – not that there's much difference.'

The traffic was shocking, and after a few minutes when the band didn't arrive Chris realised that due to New York's network of mainly single-direction avenues, the band were stuck in cabs that had first to go down Fifth Avenue a couple of blocks before they could turn to go back up to the Exxon building on Sixth. It was an unavoidable U-shaped route in bumper-to-bumper traffic. Chris: 'I called and managed to get one of them on a phone and said, "Get out of the fucking cab!" I then had to run down the street, in the traffic, in the middle of Fifth Avenue, trying to find the cabs they were in, get them out of the cabs, back to the plaza, and straight up onto the back of the truck.'

By that time it was 12.15. The rain had stopped half an hour earlier, the sun had come out, and suddenly the band arrived, instruments in their hands, and just leapt up onto the stage. Martin's only comment was, 'It would have been nice to twiddle a few knobs before we started.'

And Jim: 'I was too bloody asleep when we did that to even know what we were doing, just got outta bed. There was no wake-up call, everyone got up really late, we ran down to the gig to jump on stage, and Gary was screaming, "Where the fuck were you?"'

The band just plugged in and ripped into their six songs beneath the banner 'Midnight Oil makes you dance, Exxon Oil makes us sick'. There were hundreds, then thousands, watching as the lunch-hour crowd joined the 'in the know' fans. Alternative New York radio station WDRE had been giving cryptic hints about a Midnight Oil 'thing' during the morning, saying, 'Be around Rockefeller Plaza at one o'clock. Don't ask any questions, just be there.'

Some of the film footage can be seen on a video released by Sony called *Black Rain Falls* and in the 'King of the Mountain' video clip. The band delivered adrenaline-charged versions of 'Progress' and 'Sometimes', but during 'Sometimes' Pete fell a couple of metres from the top of one of the big speaker boxes. He managed to climb back up in time to deliver the next line and in doing so inadvertently illustrated the 'never say die' theme of the song: 'Sometimes you're beaten to the call/Sometimes you're taken to the wall/But you don't give in'. There was also a powerful and poignant 'River Runs Red', a breakneck 'Dreamworld', and a cover of John Lennon's 'Instant Karma'.

Rolling Stone music editor David Fricke was covering the event and had dropped in early at the Parker Meridian. He was swept into a taxi with Pete in the dash for the Rockefeller Center. 'It was very rare to see them do covers. I remember Peter was actually going over the lyrics in the car on the way to the gig. "Instant Karma" is a song about what are you going to do for yourself – and for everybody else. It's about taking action on everybody's behalf – and if you don't, it's gonna get you. Plain and simple and a perfect metaphor for everything the Oils did. When they came to America they were never like "We're going to roll you over". Not like the Clash, who were like "I'm so bored with the USA". The Clash were at war with American cultural imperialism, they were at war with their record company, all the things that the Oils were, but the Oils were never at war with their audience. The Oils didn't have to do that. The thing you got from the Oils was that we're in this together. It was like "You're going to roll with us". And that was a very critical and important difference. It's something that was true of every Oils show I've ever seen – even when they played that day out front of the Exxon building. When they were playing for the executives up in the ivory tower the message was "You guys *could* be down here with us if you wanted to be. You don't have to be up there."'

Mason only just managed to get through the day. 'It was a spectacular day and I knew then that, no matter what, those guys knew they had friends in America, and they had allies in the record company, because otherwise it never would have happened. There was more at stake there, some people rolled the dice and it was a pretty cool thing.'

In the end a crowd of 10 000 saw the show. Chris: 'It completely jammed the heart of New York, stopped it dead. The police just shut all the traffic at both ends, the people came out onto the footpath, the buildings were full of people at windows, up in trees, definitely a moment in my life that – well, it was incredible!' Several million more managed to hear it on radio as WDRE relayed it live out of a truck straight back to the station. But, more importantly, the global media coverage of the event was extensive, with renewed pressure on Exxon to move more quickly on cleaning the massive mess their oil spill had created.

In Australia the band was inextricably connected to politics, but their profile in the US was not predominantly political. In America they were associated with Indigenous issues because of the success of the *Diesel and Dust* album and the widely seen videos for 'The Dead Heart' and 'Beds Are Burning' singles. They had brought the newly formed Arnhem Land band Yothu Yindi with them on tour and also included Native American band Grafitti Man on the bill. They had an anti-nuclear profile too, having taken part in an enormous nuclear disarmament benefit in New York's Central Park and in small fundraising functions, like the night they performed for a local surfing anti-nuke group at a club in North LA right after a gig at the legendary Fillmore.

But the band's American publicist, Rhonda Markowitz, says she used to emphasise their musical impact, not their politics. 'I would say, "This is a band. This is rock'n'roll the way it ought to be. And if you don't want to listen to the politics you don't have to, because basically they will just pulverise you with the force of the music. If you want to ignore the politics they won't be happy about that, but you don't have to deal with them, I do."'

Rhonda had joined the team after what was for her a unique experience. 'I had to go through an audition – first time that ever happened! I had to go to a hotel and meet with Gary Morris, who wanted to know what I knew about nuclear disarmament, the environment and many other issues, and I said, "Actually, I know a lot about this. I just did some free publicity for the Muse concerts, the No Nukes concerts, in New York; we did all of Live Aid dealing with Bob Geldof; and I've been marching in Washington and so on for many years." And then I had to be interviewed by Peter! He peppered me with much the same sort of questions.'

David Fricke: 'I think sometimes people were confused by their political view. They weren't radical; they were commonsensical. Everything they said, if you thought about it, you'd go, "My God, how stupid am I? Of course!" Their point about the environment was not "Screw Exxon", it was like, "How do you behave responsibly?" I think if the Oils had been considered anything in this country, and it's an unfortunate term because it has so many bad connotations, they would be, in a sense, "liberal". In the sense that they were not telling you what to do, they were saying, "This is how we feel, these are some of the notions we've come up with, here's some pretty serious honest research, we'd like to share it with you." In the song "Blue Sky Mine", "This particular company screwed these people, just as you are probably being screwed by such and such corporation or the Pentagon or – fill in your own personal nemesis here." They didn't want to upset the established order, they wanted to change it. They didn't want to just tear it down and put in something new, they were more like "This is the situation we face on this planet in our respective societies, with our respective governments. These are things that are worth changing. Democracy is a good idea." You don't throw democracy out and take anarchy: they were not punk rock in that sense, and they were certainly not nihilists. They were about celebrating life, celebrating nature, celebrating those moments when you're together in a bar or a club, rockin' out.'

In Australia there was no confusion about Midnight Oil's politics: they were lefties and greenies. In the same week that their first record came out in November 1978 they played an anti-nuke benefit at the Sydney Town Hall. The night was a major event for the band and the movement. One of the volunteers at the Town Hall that night was Paul Gilding. 'I hung around with a bunch of BLF [Builders' Labourers Federation] blokes in the Australian Independence Movement before I became a BLF organiser. We were on security and Midnight Oil were playing. As far as I was concerned, they were this extremely loud heavy metal band that I'd never heard of. But of course when I listened to them I went, "Hang on, they're not really like that at all! They're actually quite a good band, playing serious music." That was long before I knew Pete.'

Over the next few years Midnight Oil's records dealt with many social and political issues, and among people with a commitment to political change and a love of modern music their records and performances were keenly followed. The lyrics were often collectively arrived at but usually originated from Jim and Rob, with later rewrites and additions by Pete. From the first few records came songs like 'Stand in Line', 'Armistice Day', 'Written in the Heart' and 'Kosciuszko', which set new standards for political content and impact. Then the release of the *10,9,8,7,6,5,4,3,2,1* album, which, in addition to setting Australian chart records during 1982 and 1983, contained their most biting lyrics to date. 'Short Memory' set a new benchmark for stinging rhetoric and, due to its uncharacteristically slow pace, found its way into many a non-rock lover's collection. 'Read About It' trashed the press, while 'US Forces' was as timely then as it is now in its condemnation of American foreign policy. 'Maralinga' continued the band's anti-nuke stance and 'Power and the Passion' attacked Australia's cultural and political submissiveness to America, among other things.

As part of the tour celebrating the release of the *10,9,8, 7,6,5,4,3,2,1* album, the Oils were the first local band to play at the Sydney Entertainment Centre. They did three sold-out nights, and segments were filmed by producer/director John Duigan for a scene in his apocalyptic *One Night Stand* movie set on Sydney Harbour. The band continued to contribute to the anti-nuke cause, notably when they took themselves to London in May 1983 to play for the newly formed Campaign for Nuclear Disarmament. But their contributions locally were regular and getting larger. The Stop the Drop gig earlier that year at the Myer Music Bowl in Melbourne, which they headlined and co-organised, helped raise $45 000 for Australia's People for Nuclear Disarmament. Later that year, along with the producers of the subsequently simulcast concert on Channel 10 and 3EON FM, they received a United Nations Media Peace Prize.

Thanks to George Orwell's book, 1984 was the first year to be famous ahead of time; 2001 was next. Nineteen eighty-four had loomed as a symbolic warning of how dangerously and recklessly human beings could treat each other. Yet here we were actually living in it and it wasn't quite as Orwell predicted – it was arguably far worse. Why would you worry about personal freedoms when the whole planet was about to become uninhabitable because of nuclear irresponsibility?

And if we think about it
And if we talk about it
And if the skies go dark with rain
Can you tell me does our freedom remain?

Put down that weapon or we'll all be gone
You can't hide nowhere with the torchlight on
And it happens to be an emergency

Some things aren't meant to be
Some things don't come for free

The word 'overkill' reached new levels of meaning. Both the main protagonists of the day, the USSR and the USA, were engaged in a strategy described as MAD – mutually assured destruction. Each was the evil empire to the other, and if symbolism, in the form of the threats and manoeuvring, the covert activities and the name-calling, made it seem like it could be just cultural and political posturing, then the reality of leaks and meltdowns and malfunctions and close calls and pits full of nuclear waste made the short-sighted 'MAD'-ness of it all too real.

Australia had been involved in the Vietnam War since 1962 and reluctant soldiers were still being sent there until Gough Whitlam ended conscription when he was elected prime minister. The Labor Party's brief three-year turn at the helm made significant differences to many core elements of people's lives – health and welfare, the arts, Indigenous affairs – and in ending the call-up. The government was loosening old strangleholds, and the sheer possibilities for progress and change seemed just a matter of how hard you tried – with a touch of how long you waited. Things that had been set in stone were now crumbling and the real world seemed full of possibilities.

Then Malcolm Fraser and the Liberal Party, with the aid of Governor-General John Kerr and maybe Uncle Sam, snatched back the power they had so steadfastly held in Australia for the quarter of a century before Whitlam. As far as Midnight

Oil were concerned – and many progressive Australians, too – the bad old days were with us again. Fraser became the devil incarnate for those of us who had tasted the change and progress of the Whitlam years and wanted more. (Needless to say, the current version of Malcolm Fraser as a progressive liberal champion on humanitarian issues is welcomed, but François Guisot would not have been impressed.) Nineteen seventy-six and 1977 were the formative years of the band, and they wrote some very angry songs through the Fraser Government's term of office, peaking in 1982 with the frontal attack of the material on the *10–1* album. In 1983 Fraser was beaten by Whitlam's successor, Bob Hawke, but those who presumed that the momentum of Whitlam's reforms would return instantly misjudged Hawke's pragmatism. The nuclear issue was still with us, and Australia's tie-in to the United States war machine through intelligence gathering at Pine Gap, North West Cape and Nurungah made it more likely that America's enemies saw a big, fat target in the centre of Australia.

In July 1984 the New Zealand Labour Party was elected with a strong anti-nuclear policy after a prolonged period in opposition. A surge of mainstream anti-nuclear politics seemed to be occurring around the globe, particularly with the Greens in Europe. Following the band's arrival home from a long spell recording in Japan, Pete was officially approached to be a candidate when the newly formed Sydney NDP branch committee heard advice that a glamour candidate was needed. Pete said he needed to consult the band. Jim: 'He came round to each of our rooms individually and said, "What do you reckon?" And we all said, "Yep, you should go for it." It wasn't enough to just be in a rock band and be out there treading the stages of the world; there was another thing in him that had to come out.'

The band were in Japan for June, July and August of 1984, recording the *Red Sails in the Sunset* album. It is one of their most eccentric recordings, and the time in Japan was strange and stimulating for the band members. The cultural glamour of their Tokyo surrounds was both inspiring and disorientating, and Pete had the added dimension of knowing he was likely to be called on by the NDP to run for the Senate if a federal election was called. This was unsettling for all of them, as Rob recalls. 'I was concerned about the future of the band because I felt a band that had to rehearse between Senate sittings might be a band that quickly folded in frustration. At the same time, it was clear that this was something Pete *had* to do. It's easy to forget how passionate Pete, and the band, and people in general were about the possibility of nuclear incineration. It was a huge issue and people ardently believed that the Mexican standoff between the Cold War opponents was going to end in a nuclear winter.'

'We supported him,' remembers bass player Peter Gifford (who had replaced Bear in 1980), 'but we'd made plans if he won his seat to the point where we were quite prepared to lose the band. We knew if Pete got his seat then "Goodbye Midnight Oil as we know it". We backed him because it was an issue we were all supporting as young blokes, and I guess someone had to get up and have a go, and he did it.'

Rob also recognised the value of the 'have a go' philosophy of politics. 'Real change happens as a result of people power, and people singing songs, it actually does. It changes the course of history on a daily basis. The other way of changing history is to grab the reigns of power and "giddy-up" – that's what Pete felt like he had to do, and what he feels he has to do now.'

'They may have thought it was a good way of burning up some of my extra energy,' says Pete, but adds, 'It was consistent with what we had been doing as songwriters and performers.'

There was some fuss within the ranks of the NDP as to whether Pete would be first or second on the ticket, but he won the support of many conservative elements of the anti-nuke movement, including ex-Liberal member of parliament Ted St John, who noted in his diary: 'Yesterday I spoke with him [Pete] for an hour . . . He is a very tall, highly intelligent, well-informed, shaven-haired young man. We got on well. He is dedicated to the cause, has been for years. He may do well. I am impressed by his grip of the issue and his political acumen.'

Pete did get the number one spot, just in time to hear Hawke announce the anticipated election for 1 December – which meant a national political network had to be set up from scratch and then an eight-week campaign had to be run. The band, meanwhile, were committed to a nationwide tour supporting the release of *Red Sails in the Sunset*, which had just joined *10,9,8* in the charts. They were fully committed, yet somehow Pete had to fit the daily campaigning of speeches, interviews and meetings into his already exhausting schedule of huge nightly shows in all the major cities, and media duties for the new record.

I was involved in the campaign as the NDP's campaign manager but was barely able to keep up with Pete as he dived headlong into the fray. He fitted all manner of public appearances into his ridiculously busy touring schedule. He was all over the country and all over the newspapers. He went to schools, spoke to peace groups, stirred up rallies, visited the Everleigh Railway Workshop to address the workers. He also did every bit of media he could possibly manage, with daily, if not hourly, commitments to explain himself and the issue, and to respond to shifts in opposition tactics as the campaign progressed. His radio interviews were almost non-stop. His first TV interview was for the blue-rinse set watching morning TV, and although Pete delivered the message well, he created too many distractions for the viewers. My rudimentary advice after that first appearance was 'Not so much "mate", try not to scratch your head so much, and don't sit on your foot – otherwise, great!' He was actually very engaging and the facts came across clearly. He also finished with a perfect closer for the interviewer: 'Look, I think we've got a good show, it's a really important issue and I'll be giving it my best shot.'

In the days and weeks that followed, Pete became a truly national figure. Everyone knew who he was. There was graffiti in the trains, 'Pete for PM', and young people gathered all over the country to help make the campaign happen. He must have done over 100 interviews with radio, magazines, newspapers and TV stations. People would go virtually anywhere to catch him for a one-on-one. Karina Kelly, a journalist from Channel Seven, came to my front yard to secure a sit-down interview with Pete for her nightly TV news program. Others made a similar effort to catch him in outdoor settings, which were always our preference as a way of figuratively and literally keeping the natural world part of the bigger picture. The music press were brilliantly supportive, with attempts leading up to the election to persuade young people to register to vote and then features on the issue, then total support for an enormous music industry benefit night at Selinas that raised several thousand dollars for the campaign. There was also significant support from pensioner groups, and even from some unlikely corners: the gun lobby tried to convince us to add 'the right to bear arms' to the platform, forgetting for a moment that all of the NDP's pacifist constituency would have disappeared if we'd done so!

Some stalwarts of the Australian left, like celebrated author Patrick White, took longer to be convinced. During the campaign I visited Patrick in Sydney's St Vincent's Hospital to discuss the campaign and try and win him over to our 'glamour' candidate. Patrick was propped up in bed in a pair of blue-and-white pyjamas and expressed an interest in meeting Pete. A few days later I left the two of them alone for half an hour in Patrick's hospital room to chew matters over. According to Pete, Patrick wanted to talk tactics rather than issues and, despite having several suggestions, was basically satisfied with the NDP's progress.

Later Patrick acknowledged to me that he was over his earlier doubts as to Pete's suitability as a candidate. He made several generous financial contributions to the NDP, but perhaps more significant than his money was the gift of his typewriter. Other than its obvious signs of wear and tear, it was a totally nondescript black item, but various wordsmiths hunched over it during the long days and nights of the campaign, not least of them filmmaker John Duigan, but also academic Alex Carey, lawyer Sean Flood, Ted St John, Pete and others. Rarely was it not in use. There were position papers to be written, attacks to be refuted, messages to be conveyed, press releases to be composed and various combinations of all of these tasks. Patrick's typewriter was practical but also symbolic.

The campaign went like a dream (or was that a nightmare?): so many volunteers, so much to do, so little time, so much apparently at stake. We had great people on the team right from the start, and although fellow NDP Senate candidate Gillian Fisher expressed initial reservations about Peter and his team of 'clever young men' dominating the campaign, these fears quickly evaporated as we were engulfed in something we all felt was important and significant. We were part of a worldwide protest movement and were surrounded by good and talented people wanting to help.

One call came from a guy in Brisbane who wanted to donate some money but asked to speak to Pete first. (There were plenty of those 'conditional' calls. Sometimes it was people wanting a 'brush with fame' experience, but often they wanted additional verification that he wasn't the wild rock freak that some people feared. They all had to be treated gently – money was useful – but Pete's time was extremely precious and in huge demand.) The call was put through to my cubicle. The immediate donation was a figure in the tens of thousands, but far more would be available if 'Peter and his band' could play at a concert for world disarmament as part of a global TV broadcast. The caller was offering to organise it and the venue had to be a certain rugby club in Brisbane. All the money to cover the cost of the event would come from the USA. So who was this guy? He said he worked for a US Republican senator, whose name and telephone number he supplied. The money, he said, was US government money earmarked for promoting its interests.

Not surprisingly, since President Ronald Reagan appeared at the time to be one of the guiltiest parties in the whole nuclear landscape, I pushed for further explanation. 'The "agency" works on an agenda that the politicians don't always admit to,' he said. 'Reagan is deeply *anti*-nuclear.' According to the caller, Reagan was merely waving the big stick with his plans for the Star Wars defence system in his first term of office, but he planned to dismantle and disarm in his second.

'Can this really be true?' I was thinking. After extracting some relatively plausible details about intercontinental TV link-ups and possible participating networks, I told him that the band were in fact already on tour with a full itinerary, and logistics could well prevent the project from getting to first base. At this hint that the idea was being considered he repeated that money would be no object and said he would call back at 5 p.m. I spoke to no one about the call until I next saw Pete, some hours later. I had barely started to relate the call's contents when he dismissed the whole thing out of hand.

'Absolutely not.'

'So you don't want me to check the senator's telephone number?'

'No. We don't need their money; let them support their own peace group.'

'What will I tell him when he calls back?'

'Tell him we're not interested.'

'What about the donation?'

'Next item!' Pete may have been instinctively rejecting a plan that was already sounding complicated and philosophically problematic due to its US connections, and decidedly shadowy. Or his decision may simply have been made with the knowledge that the band's tour agenda was already full. Either way, he decided it was a waste of precious time even to consider it further. This offer of help came with too much baggage.

In any case, we had our own spooks to worry about, clattering about on the telephone lines firstly at the band's headquarters on the corner of Glebe Point Road on Broadway and then at the NDP's temporary premises under the YWCA in Commonwealth Street, East Sydney. There were many stairwell and parking-lot conversations, and while we regularly spotted the unmarked vehicles that shadowed Pete's movements we wondered about those that we didn't identify. Pete found the cars parked with their engines running outside his house at 3 a.m. unsettling but wasn't paranoid about them – he *was* being followed and observed. Later, in conversation with Gillian Fisher for her book about the campaign, *Half-Life*, Graham Richardson, ex-Labor senator and hard man of the party's right wing, conceded, 'There were still some diehard elements in there [ASIO, the government's security and intelligence organisation] that might have decided Peter was an evil communist who had to be stopped or something – that's quite possible.'

It was mid-campaign when the NDP realised the ramifications of its umbrella nature, open as it was to members of other parties. We had been infiltrated – either that or every single member of every branch of the Socialist Workers Party had simultaneously had the idea to join the NDP and start campaigning. Their commitment to the issue was not in question, but their longer-term agenda was not shared by most

NDP members, including Pete. In one room – literally – we had conservative stalwarts like Ted St John working hand in hand with sworn radicals from the SWP. There were also Labor Party members, some Liberals, a smattering of Democrats and various otherwise apolitical folk, but the SWP was different, as people found out when the NDP went beyond the 1984 election and slowly imploded due to SWP takeover tactics, losing Pete and Senator Jo Valentine in the process.

But our primary battle was with the government. It was their policy that needed changing. Prime Minister Hawke was reported as saying, 'You can sing all the songs you like, write all the slogans, but you won't change government policy.' We could tell that the NDP surprised him with the strength of its campaigning and the broad public support. And even though all the cartoonists were having a field day depicting Pete and the NDP as Hawke's worst nightmare, the prime minister himself refused to get drawn directly into discussion about the potential threat posed by our little party. Instead, he sent in Bill Hayden.

Mike Willesee's nightly Channel Nine current affairs show, *Willesee*, had been pushing for a debate between Pete and a government representative, and the foreign minister, Bill Hayden, seemed to be considering it. But Pete versus anyone seemed like ratings gold to the media. Radio Double Jay also wanted Pete versus Hayden, the ABC's *PM* program wanted Pete versus the founder of the Democrats, Don Chipp, and TV's *Today* show wanted mining company boss Hugh Morgan to debate him.

We first knew Hayden was seriously considering the Willesee debate when a request came from his office for a copy of Pete's speech from the NDP launch. Pete accepted the invitation with the proviso that a time limit be put on answers. Meanwhile Hayden was saying there were no secrets about the US bases in Australia – he knew everything that was going on.

Midnight Oil were performing on the Gold Coast when details of the debate and Hayden's participation were confirmed. Pete found that he would barely make the drive from the Gold Coast to the Brisbane TV studio in time. He researched for the confrontation as the car sped up the coast, but when he arrived he found Hayden in another capital city studio, already seated, chatting in a matey fashion off-air with the host. He was waiting, totally prepared and ready to stretch the truth in a last-minute attempt to sabotage the NDP's campaign.

Pete managed, but only just. Days later, after disgusting us with the brazen nature of his misleading and arguably inaccurate utterances – but still failing to do any major damage to the NDP's momentum – Hayden attempted even more misinformation. He announced that the Australian government was to host a global disarmament summit to be attended by the USA and the USSR. This was big news to everyone and potentially crippling to our campaign – even though for anti-nuclear activists it was, on the surface, a wonderful and momentous initiative. However, the following day the *New York Times* refuted the story in no uncertain terms, quoting State Department officials: 'There is no intention of having the Australian government mediate between Moscow and Washington.' The backfire continued in the next paragraph: 'The Labor Party is being challenged by a new party, the Nuclear Disarmament Party, which has done surprisingly well in the polls.'

The NDP vote was polling as high as 20 per cent in some surveys and, with normal distribution of preferences by the parties, this was a vote high enough to guarantee that Pete and perhaps other NDP candidates would be elected. But one final act of political duplicity by the Labor Party in the last week of campaigning killed off any chance of electoral victory: they gave their ballot preferences to their oldest and deadliest enemy, the Liberal Party. Anything, it seemed, rather than having this loose cannon called Garrett join the boys' club in Canberra.

Peter Carey wrote our slogans, Brett Whiteley, Martin Sharp, Gary Shead and others donated paintings to auction, the media gave us unprecedented support, the young and old came out of the woodwork to help in a hundred different ways, and Patrick White donated his typewriter – it was a stellar cast. But still we didn't win. The trade of preferences between the Labor and Liberal parties meant that the counting of votes was complicated, and close, and took a long time. It was almost a week before we learned Pete definitely hadn't won the seat. Of course, the major parties ultimately did him a favour – going to Canberra was the last thing he really wanted to do at the time. The issue was everything to Pete, and to that end we succeeded beyond our wildest dreams. It was on the front page of every paper and discussed around breakfast tables right across the country. Then again, twenty years later we still have (unconfirmed) nuclear vessels visit our ports, there is still some uranium mining going on, and those bases at Pine Gap and elsewhere are still sitting ducks for the enemies of the USA.

In January the next year, at ex-Sex Pistol John Lydon's

Australian press conference for a tour by his new band, Public Image Limited, someone asked what he thought of Peter Garrett. 'He's the skinhead that ran for parliament, right? I think he's fucking mad.' Politics at that level *is* madness, and the members of the band were pretty much unanimous in their assessment of the experience: never again. Ten years later, talking to Gillian Fisher for her book, Pete said, regarding the NDP campaign, 'It had the tremendous benefit of being idealistically and morally based. It was inevitably going to come in contact with hard politics, but it campaigned professionally. I don't see it as a failure at all. I see it as another step towards the new politics in Australia.'

Graham Richardson recalled: '[Garrett] was a worry, always. He gave them [young people] a quality-of-life argument that I think they essentially believed. And only he could do it.' When Gillian asked if Richardson would have liked to see Pete join the Labor Party, he said, 'Oh, always. For me it would have been a pain . . . because he would have been in the left [of the party]. I'd have had to fight him then. But even so I wouldn't have minded, because he would have given us an extra dimension that we never had. And of course, eventually, when I discovered how right he was on the environment, I wouldn't have fought with him anyway. It would have been a great strength to us. But Peter would never accept the rigidity of party discipline . . . that's why we didn't ask him.'

In March 1985, during the band's first-ever European dates, they performed with the Clash at a big outdoor concert in Brittany. Rob impressed the crowd by making an anti-nuclear statement from the stage: 'Faites cesser la pollution nucléaire dans la Sud Pacifique' ('Stop nuclear pollution in the South Pacific'). Rob had continued his French studies to university level and had been a regular casual visitor to France during the band's spells in England, and as such was the obvious choice to write and deliver the band's message. The audience was a rock crowd rather than a greenie one, so it was not necessarily 100 per cent partisan on the issue, but the overwhelming cheer indicated that even those who may not have agreed with the band's point of view gave Rob extra marks for speaking their language.

After more touring of the USA and UK during the year they returned to Paradise Studios in Sydney and recorded the *Species Deceases* EP in less than a week, with all royalties going to a trust fund for promoting peace and disarmament. In November they announced a twenty-six-date local tour, their first local gigs for the year. The tour started in Dubbo with Gondwanaland supporting and ended at the Sydney Entertainment Centre. All profits from band merchandising went to selected local youth refuges and programs for unemployment. Pete and the rest of the band also took the opportunity to meet with other activists as the tour made its way across the country.

Midnight Oil had an ongoing participation in campaigns to save forests everywhere. There was financial support for the South East Forests Coalition of NSW and the Australian Forest Action Network. They made a big commitment to the national campaign to save the Lemonthyme Forest of Tasmania with funding and public appearances and by securing the involvement of other artists, notably Dire Straits, at the time one of the biggest bands in the world. They were also involved with the US Rainforest Action Network. At the final date of the tour, at the Sydney Entertainment Centre, they raised funds to save the Daintree rainforest from the bulldozers, specifically to provide money for final submissions to the Australian government to list the Daintree Tropical Rainforests of North Queensland for World Heritage protection.

Silverchair manager John Watson was a teenage fan of the Oils in the early eighties, and vividly recalls the band coming to Rockhampton to do an amphitheatre show. 'It was still Joh Bjelke-Petersen era Queensland,' he says, referring to the long years that maverick of the extreme right wing was the state's premier. On stage Pete invariably mentioned local issues in freewheeling political and social raves disguised as song introductions, but Joh was a regular target even when the band weren't in Australia's version of the Deep South. 'Garrett was doing the Garrett thing between songs and he said something about Joh. Now half the guys at the show had never given more than five minutes' thought to politics in their life. Their dad liked Joh; they liked Joh. They didn't really know what that stood for particularly. So when Garrett mentioned Joh they went, "Yeah! Good on you, Joh!" – that sort of thing. Pete turned around and clearly was shocked at the fact that this Midnight Oil crowd had a significant portion who reacted positively to the mention of Joh's name. But he just went after them, and when Joh was mentioned the next time the same portion of the crowd booed! Now I'm not saying those people then went away and voted green for the rest of their lives but I guarantee you it was one of the first times that anybody who they respected had ever questioned Joh Bjelke-Petersen. It didn't bring down the Queensland government, but it pushed the rock up the hill. That's got to mean something.'

In 1986 Pete was the only Australian invited to contribute a rap to the Sun City single, a project encouraging fellow musicians to resist the big money being offered to play at Sun City, South Africa's most prestigious music venue. It was produced by Artists United Against Apartheid and featured a cast of global artists organised by Steve Van Zandt from the Bruce Springsteen band. Pete's lines were: 'Relocation to phoney homelands/Separation of families I can't understand'. And he joined in the chorus: 'Ain't gonna play Sun City no more/No, no, no'.

Pete also became the first Australian civilian allowed entry to Pine Gap when he delivered a notice from the people of Australia saying we intended to terminate the Americans' lease – it was renewed by the Australian government a few months later. He was appointed to the Advisory Committee on Individual and Democratic Rights – part of the government's commission to review Australia's constitution. He wrote columns for Melbourne and Hobart papers, some of which were published as a collection of essays titled *Political Blues*. Then there was the unholy alliance with the right wing (people who had things to hide!) in a campaign to prevent the government introducing a national ID card. The Australia Card coalition included broadcaster Alan Jones and required enormous political tact and discipline to succeed, which it eventually did. The Oils even lent their 'hand' logo to the campaign propaganda.

During most of 1988 – Australia's 'celebratory' bicentennial year – the band were overseas playing the world their songs from the *Diesel and Dust* album. They deliberately avoided bicentennial events and rejected all offers to participate as a way of sympathising with the Indigenous view that 1788 was invasion year and its anniversary was nothing to celebrate.

Pete did manage to join leading Aboriginal activist Gary Foley as MC at Bondi Beach for the conclusion of the Long March for Justice, Freedom and Hope, in which 4000 people converged from Indigenous communities around the state. To honour this commitment the band turned down an appearance at the Grammy Awards in Los Angeles at the very peak of their 'Beds Are Burning' success, much to the consternation of their record company. Sony Australia's CEO, Denis Handlin: 'I got this call from Al Teller, who was running the US company, and Al said, "The great news is, the boys are going to be on the Grammys! We've got them on the Grammys!" And I said, "That's amazing." Because the audience! I spoke to Gary and then I spoke to Peter, and the Grammy date clashed with an event they had with an Aboriginal cause on Bondi Beach. And Peter said to me, "It's great the company is committed to us, but I'm not real comfortable about playing in front of a bunch of suits, and it's really important to me that I stay committed to this event for these people here on Bondi Beach." It was a very interesting phone call that I had to make back to the States! Millions and millions of people globally, over a few thousand on a beach. But I supported the band on it even though at the time I was thinking, "Boy, the potential of this massive audience with a smash, smash record." I actually tell that story to people now and again as a sign of the respect I have for the band.'

In 1989 Pete was appointed President of Australia's peak environment organisation, the Australian Conservation Foundation. (His predecessors in the position had all been substantial establishment figures – men of letters like H. C. 'Nugget' Coombs or judges like Hal Wootten and Murray Wilcox. The first president was Prince Philip, the Duke of Edinburgh.)

Over the next four years, both Coronation Hill in Kakadu and Shoalwater Bay in Queensland were protected from mining companies and significant results for many other threatened areas of the Australian environment, including Jervis Bay, followed. On one lovely day Prime Minister Hawke opened the new ACF building in Melbourne and announced that the government had finally scrapped the Navy's move to Jervis Bay.

The same year Pete joined the ACF, the band's Jervis Bay campaigner Paul Gilding joined Greenpeace Australia, and he became head of the organisation a few months later. According to Paul it was Pete who played the most significant role in pulling the various strands of the environmental movement together, and then forward, during that time. The issue of whether to protect Coronation Hill in Kakadu National Park from uranium mining has been described as a watershed moment in Bob Hawke's prime ministership, and the days leading up to the crucial Cabinet vote saw frantic lobbying and head counting within the Labor Party. Paul: 'When Phillip Toyne was director of the ACF and Pete was the president and Bob Hawke was doing Kakadu, that was the most extraordinary height of power of the movement. I was in the Oils' office one day when Hawke rang up after the Kakadu Cabinet meeting. His office rang up and got Pete to talk to him, to give him a pep talk to sort of give him encouragement that he'd done the right thing.' Some time later Pete and his family went and met the prime minister's family at an informal afternoon tea on the lawns of Kirribilli House.

Paul has some reservations about the longer-term benefits of the close relationship the ACF had with the government at this time. It survived well enough with Hawke's successor, Paul Keating, but has faced major hurdles since the Liberals were returned to power in 1996 with John Howard. 'It was an enormously influential period for the movement, but it was closely aligned with the Labor Party. They achieved extraordinary things. A whole bunch of very substantive policy changes were driven by Keating and by Hawke – and Pete and Phillip were the major influences. We had nothing to do with it at Greenpeace. It was all around Pete and Phillip. They played the game consummately in terms of power and influence, and I think it remains the defining period in the history of the Australian environmental movement in terms of achieving substantial change of a very profound nature.'

When Keating took over the Labor leadership and prime ministership from Hawke, Pete's access continued. In the book *Memoirs of a Bleeding Heart* Keating's speechwriter, Don Watson, notes the regular appearance of 'bald-headed rock singers' in the prime minister's private rooms. Pete admired Keating a lot and felt him to be more of a kindred spirit than Hawke. Maybe it was because Keating had managed a rock band in his pre-parliamentary life.

Pete and the band were not unknown in other high places, either. I had occasion to meet Rosalynn Carter when her husband, Jimmy, was American president. When she asked me if I could recommend any new Australian music to take home for their daughter Amy and I suggested Midnight Oil, she replied, 'Oh, we already have their records.' Bill Clinton was also aware of the band's status. In a speech given in Sydney's Royal Botanic Gardens in 1996, the president praised Australia's cultural impact overseas and included Midnight Oil in a stellar list of local artists. The reference, however, reveals him not to be a fan: 'This is a remarkable community and a remarkable nation. In this new global culture that we're all experiencing, Australia's contribution has been far out of proportion to its population – in modern art, in learning, in music, in theatre, in opera, in the cinema. The novels of Patrick White, Thomas Keneally, David Malouf; the paintings of Sidney Nolan, Russell Drysdale, Utopia artists; the films of Baz Luhrmann, Peter Weir, and so many others. Dame Joan Sutherland, James Morrison. And according to the young people in my group, bands like Midnight Oil and Silverchair.'

Despite Pete's responsibilities as the president of the ACF, the band maintained its commitment to international environmental matters. In 1992 Chris Moss saw the band go on stage at the huge Earth Day concert at Foxboro Stadium in Boston in below-freezing conditions. 'The day before it was 25 degrees Centigrade but the day of the concert it hit five below zero. The whole audience of fifteen to twenty thousand in the stadium all looked like Michelin men.' The band did as well, and Rob says he felt like he was drumming like a wind-up monkey, he was so restricted. Jim and Martin both wore fingerless gloves. Support act Grafitti Man encouraged them to 'Turn the ice into fire!' as they headed for the stage.

Before long the unavoidably international nature of Midnight Oil's career helped convince Pete to resign as ACF president, and in 1993 he took up Paul Gilding's offer to join Greenpeace's international board. The band continued their long history of joint actions with Greenpeace, including one in Brazil where they sat at an intersection in the centre of São Paulo with face masks on as part of an air pollution protest.

They were also invited to join a blockade to help prevent the clear-felling of the forests of Vancouver Island in Canada, particularly at Clayoquot Sound. Some of the trees there are 1000 years old. Pete had written to Chief Francis Frank of the Tla-o-qui-aht Band – one of five bands or tribes in the area defending a land claim by the Nuu-chah-nulth Nation – several months earlier offering Midnight Oil's support. Jim: 'There was always a little bit of suspicion from certain quarters [in the band] about those sorts of actions, but I know at the end of the day everyone was really proud of what we did.'

They flew to Vancouver Island, but because of a mix-up regarding whether the band's wives were going too the plane wasn't big enough. Rather than leave their wives at the airport some of the band didn't get on the plane. Gary: 'Willie [MacInnes, the band's tour manager] ended up flying back to Vancouver to get them. It cost an extra $1000 and put the action at risk.'

Bass player Bones Hillman (who replaced Peter Gifford in 1987) remembers a bit of friction between the band and Gary before the show. 'It almost didn't happen. It was a pretty fragile and shaky gig. We went up there and played in this clear-felled area. It was about ten in the morning, on a makeshift stage with a tiny PA, playing acoustic guitars.'

The audience was mainly made up of anti-logging activists and supporters of the local Indian cause, but it certainly wasn't a straightforward celebration. Jim: 'There were a few loggers there too, with their arms crossed – very heavy. I felt the music was sort of our shield at that one, but that was about all we had.'

Bones continues: 'Then it got quite hostile. The loggers were throwing dead fish down to where the protesters were camping to attract grizzly bears. When we tried to drive out people were trying to turn the van over and smashing copies of our records on the windscreen. It got very nasty. That's the first time I experienced people protesting about what we were trying to do. Usually people say, "Oh yeah, you're great", with arms open. But here there were loggers' grandmothers and they didn't like us. We felt like the minivan was about to roll down the side of the cliff and we would be killed. It was a turbulent twenty-four hours.'

Playing in South Africa had been an ongoing debate within the band but finally, once Nelson Mandela had been elected president, they accepted an offer. In October 1994 they left for South Africa via Perth, arriving at 6.05 a.m. local time to a contingent of enthusiastic local political and music press keen to catch up with a band whose records and attitudes were well known despite their having actively boycotted the country. 'We got really strong offers and pressure from South Africa to tour before the end of apartheid,' says Rob. 'We would have been playing up at Sun City – or Sin City. I felt sure that we shouldn't go, and I made a big deal about it. The other camp was "They are inviting you over as a land-rights band – you'll represent the disenfranchised blacks of this country". That was the way it was put. The reality was that you'd be playing to a whole bunch of wealthy white Afrikaners in Sun City with black gardeners and servants. And the albums that you would sell would be to *them*, and to the white neighbourhoods of Johannesburg and Cape Town and Durban, but not to the black servants who would never hear about you. That was the reality of it. But it was put as being "You should come and expedite the process of reconciliation in this country", which is the way they sucked in a lot of bands who went away realising that they were the ones who had been exploited. So I fought tooth and nail against playing in

South Africa and it's one of those things, when you look back at your career, that you're really glad you stuck out for something. Eventually when we did go, about a year after Mandela came in, it was magnificent, it still rates as one of the most amazing shows I think we've ever done. It was to a mixed-race audience, with a mixed South African line-up, and us, and Sting.'

In 1998 while recording *Redneck Wonderland*, Pete resigned from the international board of Greenpeace, six months after Paul Gilding's departure from the top job. Paul's time as chief executive had been fraught with problems, including a bit of ideological friction due to his opposition to Greenpeace's resolutely anticorporate stance. 'I said we should work with corporations that were doing the right thing and attack corporations who were doing the wrong thing. There was a bit of controversy about that internally. And there were some governance issues. There was a lot of money floating around Greenpeace that wasn't under adequate control as far as I was concerned – there was nothing corrupt going on, people weren't misusing the money at all, but it wasn't under appropriate governance for a nonprofit organisation. There was a lot of internal politics and Pete was very deeply involved in it because he was seen as the only member of the board who was able to have a rational discussion.'

Paul and Pete were friends, but they were caught up in a major ethical wrangle where each had separate responsibilities. 'Pete is very formal on this kind of stuff. He is very conservative in a lot of ways – in ways that the older I get the more I agree with. He had a formal role as a board member and as such wouldn't betray the confidential discussions of the board and so on. So he was very careful to do that sort of stuff properly, and that was good and appropriate.'

Pete even put off his departure from the board for the sake of Greenpeace's public profile. Paul: 'He was very careful to go quietly and not make a big fuss, otherwise it would have looked bad if both the Australians had left at the same time after this big internal conflict. That's what he said to me at the time – he wanted to leave straight away, but didn't feel it was appropriate in terms of the external perception.'

Pete's departure from the Greenpeace board and his acceptance of a new term as ACF president also reflected the reduced nature of the band's international engagement and his growing desire to focus his attention on home-grown rather than overseas environmental problems. With Pete as president once again, and a new director, Don Henry, the ACF has grown strongly. It has consolidated the groundbreaking relations with Australian farming organisations and has forged strong links with progressive elements of the corporate community. Neither of these groups has traditionally been regarded as 'greenies'. The ACF has also expanded significantly into areas of Indigenous environmental concern in the Top End.

In one of the conversations I had with Patrick White in his hospital room he expressed reservations about the likelihood of green issues ever having mainstream support. Ironically, he was agreeing with the conservatives' view that the environment movement was intrinsically one of the Left. When I pointed out the linguistic connection between 'conservation' and 'conservative' he replied with mock offence, 'I've certainly never considered *myself* a conservative.'

Australia's Nobel Prize-winning author may not have been

a conservative, but he was certainly old – and still very much an idealist. If idealism and optimism are just a rush of youthful blood, as François Guisot implied, then Midnight Oil would have stopped writing songs and being activists twenty years ago. They could have made a difference by doing nothing beyond writing their songs. After all, spreading seeds in fertile minds is also a potent way of effecting change. People may have been listening without necessarily hearing the themes in the band's songs, but the ideas were being introduced into the heads of teenagers and twenty-somethings all across the planet. The band didn't need to be doing anything else. 'Well,' says Pete, 'if the story is only what you created then it applies as much to people who didn't do anything as it does to those who did. But if the story is what you create, and then what you do, and then what people take from it, it's a different story. And the Midnight Oil story is a different story because of that.'

My mother used to say, 'Do good by stealth and blush to find it known', and although much of the good work the band did was deliberately very public as an act of solidarity with frontline activists, there was a lot of good work done away from the glare of the publicity spotlight that only those who were helped would know about. The band's overt social and political attitude influenced many others, not just fans and activists, but also other bands. There was a point in time when it became acceptable, important almost, to have something meaningful to say about the country you lived in. But that era seems to have passed. There are still musicians expressing social opinions but very few of them exist as part of mainstream culture, and none are part of the public discourse of a country in the way that Midnight Oil were in Australia.

two

is it now?

In the late seventies Midnight Oil's shows at the Royal Antler Hotel became must-see events for the Northern Beaches crowd. There was an abundance of atmosphere even before entering the venue. As you arrived there was the immediate, strong salty smell of the sea, followed by an awareness of the pounding surf, then maybe the feel of an off-shore breeze. There was also the sound of vehicles and excited chatter as hundreds of people converged on the venue.

Rob, Jim, Martin and Bear entered the hotel via the back bar and passed quietly and unacknowledged through a scene normal in every way for a suburban Saturday night at the local pub. The room was occupied by several old regulars, mainly men in shirts and shorts slouched on stools by the bar. A handful more – men and women – are scattered down the side of the room around small tables, doing their best to keep the drink mats wet and the ashtrays full. Most of them are successfully ignoring the growing level of activity and noise just outside in the parking area.

Panel vans with the back doors open are popular, but any

vehicle will do for the slightly rushed spirit consumption and not-so-sly herbal prepping. When these are satisfactorily completed it's onto the real action, around the other side of the hotel in the main bar facing the sea. Inside there are close to 1000 surfers and local music fans shoulder to shoulder, shouting at each other, trying to communicate over an excessively loud PA. Many are shirtless, some faces are red, some skin is peeling and many bodies are already dripping wet. Some have their T-shirts wrapped around their heads like Pete often does when he first arrives on stage. Some are carrying three or four glasses of beer above their heads, trying to make their way back through the multitude to their mates while spilling as little as possible on the crowd on the way through. Some are standing ten deep at the bar hoping their timing will be lucky – you didn't want to be there when the band came on, and that could be any time. Meanwhile, in the back bar, where the old folk play, Pete enters and makes his way between the tables and the bar. One of the old regulars looks up: 'Well, if it isn't Captain Midnight himself!' There's a chorus of knowing grunts and a muted mumbling of 'We know, we know.'

The Royal Antler was a magic venue for the band, but it wasn't long before conditions became almost impossible to tolerate. Bear: 'We began taking oxygen with us, to be available for Peter or Rob, whose energetic antics needed oxygen, a commodity in scarce supply at venues such as the Narrabeen Antler. We would tune up in the next-door section and walk through the bar to the stage. By the time we got there, our guitars were already out of tune and dripping with condensation. I had to towel my bass between songs. We had several large air conditioners blowing stale air onto the stage – normal fans didn't move air fast enough – and oxygen tanks at the side of the stage. There certainly wasn't much oxygen in the venue by that time, with all the smoking and breathing that over 1000 fans had done for several hours before our performance in a venue licensed to admit 300.'

For Bear this was more than uncomfortable, it was also unhealthy, and it had an air of aggression he found hard to relate to. He also had difficulties with what was expected from a member of the band. 'I used to have arguments with Rob about when I was on duty and when I was off duty. Rob considered that the life had to be led twenty-four hours a day, with clothing, attitude and action. I could never understand what was "in" and what was "out", whether beanies and shorts and long hair or black skin-tight jeans and short hair were in or not. I let the band dictate what I was to wear on stage, but I considered what I wore off stage to be my concern. Rob thought I was letting the image down by not wearing the "uniform" all the time. And bringing a mini-esky with food and drinks was not "rock" and was frowned upon.'

Rob tells the story of a gig in the days the band was known as 'Farm' playing one of the Christmas tours. 'It was somewhere down the south coast, Tarthra School of Arts maybe, or Pambula Country Women's Association. We played 'Soul Sacrifice', sort of like the version Santana played at Woodstock, but quite inept, to be honest! I had this big drum-solo part and Bear by then had got it timed roughly how long this would last. It wasn't that long, probably four or five minutes. Maybe on that occasion I just cut it short. Anyway, Bear had got it timed for a three-minute egg – so that he could go and actually boil an egg in three minutes and then eat it. Why he was doing it you'd have to ask Bear, maybe he needed the protein. So I finished early and neither Bear nor his Sunburst Rickenbacker were back on stage. And it was only then that we found out where he'd been disappearing to for the last week of gigs. Apparently I'd interrupted his three-minute egg – it wasn't ready!'

Midnight Oil have had three bass players over their history, most recently Bones Hillman – who filled the post from 1987 to 2002. Prior to him was Peter Gifford – 'Giffo' – who lasted seven years. And before him was Andrew James, known as 'Bear' or 'the Bear', who played with Midnight Oil for four years but had been the original bassist who jammed and played with Jim and Rob in Farm and under other monikers before that. Giffo puts it like this: 'I joined just after smoko and kicked arse through lunch to afternoon tea. Then Bones got in for dinner; he did that shift. The spark of it, in the morning, was the Bear.'

Pete's professional association with band mates Jim Moginie, Rob Hirst and Bear goes back thirty years to St Cecilia's Day, 22 November, 1973. The patron saint of music (and of the blind) may have foreseen a time when the music made by their future band would reach around the planet, but Jim and Rob and Bear certainly didn't. Their aim on that particular day was to find a lead singer for their band's proposed tour of various small coastal towns to the south of Sydney. Finding someone to take the lead vocal duties in Farm had proved problematical.

But before Pete joined, and even before Rob joined, there

were Jim and Bear. They met at a regular neighbourhood jam session in Turramurra in late 1970 and were among guys of mixed ability fighting for the opportunity to plug into one of the three inputs on the only amplifier. According to Bear, 'Initially Jim didn't own a "proper" instrument, he brought some sort of organ with him, but he soon got a $35 electric guitar, which served him for the next few years.' It wasn't long before they played their first gig at a local scout hall. 'We didn't have a name, or a list of songs, and didn't even know who was in the "group". We were introduced as the Purple Link, and from memory played some Beatles songs. I'm not sure who sang – we may have had a girl singer – but the drummer couldn't keep time, blaming the strobe light for interfering with his timing. The older people in the audience were not impressed and put their fingers in their ears. I believe Jim may have played his keyboard.'

Jim and Bear were both fifteen and relatively typical of teenagers anywhere learning to play musical instruments: they were attempting to recreate their favourite songs of the day in regular jams with their friends. Rob Hirst joined the Turramurra jam about a year later after being seen walking down the street playing 'air drums'. Rob was a pretty experienced drummer even then. He was drumming regularly with a jazz band and had a spot in the school military band as well. He first played with Jim and Bear at Jim's house. Jim: 'I had a little room upstairs in the attic and he lugged his drums up. We set up and he was warming up, you know, just playing a bit of time. I was looking really approvingly at Bear. I was getting a high, and suddenly it hit me – this was a *drummer*, it wasn't just some guy who had a drum kit.'

When the jam sessions got too cumbersome the group split into two bands. Half the group became Topaz, the other half, comprising Rob on drums, Jim on guitar and Bear on bass, plus Chris Hodgkinson on guitar and John Royle on flute, formed Schwampy Moose. Their first gig was at Jim's school, as a lunchtime event, at the end of 1971. They didn't play any original compositions. Bear: 'I was so shy I couldn't raise my head to look at the audience. I started to look up but someone threw an apple core, which hit my bass, and I kept looking at my feet for the rest of the concert. Rob was the only singer at that stage. One of the songs was "I'm a Loser" by the Beatles. Rob had trouble starting this in the right key – it starts without any guitar introduction. He started it in the wrong key, but once the guitar came in he adjusted to the correct pitch. A teacher came in from the staff room next door and told us to turn down, so we had to start the song again – of all the songs to have to restart! Once again Rob started in the wrong pitch. Chris had to have a music stand for music – not a very rock'n'roll look.'

At Rob's school, but in a different circle of friends, was another future Midnight Oil member. Martin Rotsey had a loose and unfussy band called Gunja. During 1972 Schwampy Moose played at a couple of shows with Gunja, and on one occasion they shared a gig on a ferry on Sydney Harbour and the combined band members jammed together. According to Bear, 'Martin played in a "Hendrixy", bluesy, Stratocaster style, quite different to Jim, who by this time was listening to some fairly challenging music – Yes, Focus, Emerson Lake and Palmer, etc. – while still retaining a love of the Beatles and interesting pop like Todd Rundgren.'

Martin didn't play again with Jim and Rob and Bear until Rob's twenty-first birthday party four years later. Before then Schwampy Moose briefly changed their name to Sparta, then settled on Farm. They had various other players come and go, including some singers, but the core of the band remained Jim, Rob and Bear. Bear: 'We could all play each other's instruments. At one stage we had a song in our set where Jim played bass, Rob played guitar and I played drums. We all sang. Rob sang lead, I would sing the higher harmonies and Jim would sing the lower harmonies. We were a three-piece band, and not very disciplined. By this time we were known as Farm, with the subtitle "Collective Ego". Rob was Keith Moon, I was Jack Bruce, and Jim was anyone as long as they were loud. A million notes, and not always in the same key.'

However, all of them recognised the need for a dedicated lead singer. Jim: 'It was Rob's band in those days. He sang, he did the bookings, he was "up", he got the business card made, and he put an ad in the *Sydney Morning Herald* for a singer to do this south coast holiday tour.'

One of the applicants for the St Cecilia's Day audition, and the only one anybody can remember, was Pete. Jim: 'Pete walked in the door, he looked really intimidating, he really looked so tall, that big brow of his was sort of "What's going on? Who are these wankers?" kind of thing. We did a twelve-bar, I think, but he started improvising, and it was just that what he did was – well, it was really unique. It didn't sound like anybody else. And I remember going behind a curtain – I don't know whether Bear was there for this conversation, but my recollection is that Rob and I spoke. And Rob said,

"What do you think?" and I said, "Well, I don't know, but he's really interesting. I don't know what else to say. It's not your normal thing, is it?" And he said, "No, it isn't really." And it was like "Well, he'll do!" So we went out said, "Okay, you've got the job."'

Bear remembers Pete's impact, too. 'He was instantly imposing, and I thought a little unsure of what he was getting himself in for. He sat at the edge of the room we were practising in nonchalantly whistling a Yes tune — our ad had expressed an interest in Yes and at the time I thought that was a bit calculated. He had experience as a front man, he had a presence, particularly with his height, he had a strikingly individual voice, and last and probably not least, he had a PA! His mum lived in Sydney but he was at uni in Canberra and was looking for something to do over the Christmas break. Bingo.'

The band thus formed did two tours of the south coast, the second exactly a year after the first. They only managed a few shows in between the two tours because they all had full-time university studies to attend to. When required, Pete would drive from Canberra to join them for a gig, often without much rehearsal. Bear: 'I can recall a song originally called "Section 5 Clause B". Peter heard the song for the first time a few hours before he sang it for the first time. Luckily he had a knack of making a song his own, as his lyrics and melody bore no resemblance to Rob's lyrics or melody. The words to this song were later replaced by Peter and the song became "Bus to Bondi".'

They did a handful of memorable shows, one of which was a poorly publicised triple bill at the Ryde Youth Centre. Local hard-rock outfit Finch were on first, followed by Farm. Bear:

'I had high-heeled boots and wore a fur vest with a black felt hat. I don't know if we were experimenting with "theatrical" makeup yet, but that would follow in the next few years. We were drastically out of tune and sounded terrible.' The third band on was AC/DC. 'Wow – they were just a revelation. The guitars, the vocals, Bon Scott – this was one of the best concerts I have been to, ever! Malcolm Young is the core of that band.'

Jim: 'They'd been on *Countdown* and all that stuff. It was loud! It was Bon. It was the whole thing. They played "Long Way to the Top" – it was that phase. There weren't a lot of people there – whether the advertising was bad I can't remember – but they came on and just stormed it. Angus was doing everything to get the crowd interested but they were skating round on boards not giving a shit. But they just blitzed them. Whether there were thirty people there or ten people or 100 000 didn't matter. And it sounded so great! It was such a good thing to get your attitude in line – seeing that kind of performance where there was hardly anyone there and they just gave it their all. I've never forgotten it. It was committed.'

In the year between the south coast tours the band did continue to look for another singer through more advertisements in the papers. But the search was a little half-hearted, as Bear recalls: 'After playing with Peter, with that certain special presence and individual style, we couldn't bring ourselves to take on someone who sounded like he was trying to copy someone else.'

Pete: 'Those tours were a lot of fun because I could surf during the day and the boys would be fiddling with their gear – they did that for the rest of their lives – and jamming or listening to songs or what have you. It was a very jammy band – it wasn't as tightly structured as what the Oils became.'

The coastal tours were full of unexpected occurrences. One of the memorable moments for Bear was after a gig at Port Macquarie. 'We had played the previous night and were sleeping in the hall as we usually did, with all the gear still set up. An elderly lady came in ready to set up for "housie" or some other pensioner-style activity. She got the shock of her life when she saw the mess the hall was in and the bodies still asleep in their sleeping bags, with only an hour or so before her event was to start, and got quite irate. As his opening sentence, Peter calmly responded to her tirade with "Listen here, sweetheart—", and proceeded to settle her down with reasons why it would all be OK. And it was. We could pack up quite quickly when we had to.'

The tiny little venues limited Pete's movements, but he wasn't so active in the very early days anyway. 'The stages weren't that big but I think I just sort of started to move around and do stuff, just enjoy the singing. I had to learn a lot of songs, so I was probably concentrating a bit on remembering them. I don't think I was charging around as much as I did towards the end, I was just doing my thing, not thinking too much about it.'

Meanwhile, back in Canberra, Pete continued to perform in his other band, Rock Island Line. His performances with them didn't provide much of a glimpse of his future stagecraft either. He did always seem connected to the music in a very physical way, and his size already gave him an advantage in stage presence. His basic action was a stomp in the style of the sixties mini-dance craze from the Sydney surf culture. He would lift one leg and then the other, shifting his weight – stomping. His head was down a lot of the time between verses, but it was always moving. He moved when sufficiently 'moved', but never strayed too far from the microphone. Pete: 'I'm sure I was a bit nervous and trying to feel my way, but it's never felt as though it's something I had to try too hard to do – although I tried very hard doing it. The being up on stage and doing it was just a case of finding a groove. When you find your groove you can settle into it and go with it.'

Pete's fine, almost white-blond, shoulder-length hair and tanned skin clearly marked him as a surfie. He looked like a person who was committed to being in the surf as often as he could. He wasn't overly muscular, quite lean and athletic, but instantly imposing because of his height. Pete was a product of the sixties – part hippy, part surfie, part angry student. We shared a love of the Beatles, and Dylan, and the Who, but Pete introduced me to the blues – to John Mayall and Muddy Waters. While we listened to these classic sounds from around the world, including the music of the US west coast like Jefferson Airplane and Crosby Stills Nash and Young, we discussed the broader implications of the times and indulged in other rituals of the counterculture. Apart from our shared classes in Political Science we also shared part-time jobs, like driving a St Vincent de Paul van – taking from the rich and giving to the poor! – and toilet cleaning in Burgmann College. Pete also did some bar work. We played Aussie Rules together – he was a novice ruckman and I was an equally novice rover – but we were really rugby victims from Sydney. We were also both volunteer announcers on the newly fought for and won campus radio station. We filled our application forms in without consulting each other and as a result Pete was a 'rock' announcer and I found myself a 'pop' announcer. We debate to this day the difference in the two musical genres.

When Pete went to finish his Law degree in Sydney I remained in Canberra, and although we stayed in touch it was a huge surprise to me when he crashed through the studio door during my radio program on 2XX one afternoon with a freshly shaved scalp and wearing a pair of blue working overalls with 'Death to Disco' scrawled across them. Pete's holiday band mates were getting serious. And so was he! While the records were playing he was telling me about the great songs Rob and Jim were writing, and a new guitarist called Martin who was really hot.

In the next few months quite a few significant things happened. The band finally solidified their line-up by telling Murray Cook – a keyboard and bass player who went on to play with many notable bands, including Mental As Anything – that he was surplus to requirements. Bear rejoined on bass after illness. Martin moved to full-time guitar to allow Jim to play keyboards as well as guitar, and the band made the acquaintance of Gary Morris. Pete also finished his Law degree and prepared to go headlong into rock'n'roll. And his mother died.

Pete's father had died a couple of years earlier from an asthma-related condition, so his mother was sharing their old wooden two-storey house with just her three sons, Pete, Andrew and Matt. Pete was asleep at the other end of the house when he smelt smoke. His mother's room was upstairs and by the time he got there it was engulfed in flames. A couple of times he tried unsuccessfully to fight his way up the staircase through the smoke and falling embers. He could hear his mother crying out for help. Rob received a phone call from one of Pete's neighbours with the news that the house was alight. He immediately jumped in his car and drove the ten-minute trip. When he arrived Pete had been forced out of the burning house and it was a blazing mass of beams, and obviously lost. Pete was pacing up and down among the flying ash and cinders on the front lawn just howling. Rob consoled him as much as he could but left him after an hour or so. Pete continued outside the house until dawn. It was obvious that no one could have survived the blaze, but unbeknownst to Pete both his brothers had been sleeping elsewhere for the night. First Andrew, and then a few hours later Matt, arrived home. Who knows the mixed emotions involved in the joy of seeing them and the pain of the news that Pete had to impart. When Jim arrived at Rob's house later in the day, Pete was sitting on the floor, his head in his hands, still with signs of ash and soot on him. Despite, or perhaps because of, the shock, the band actually played French's Tavern in the city the next night. People remember Pete having burnt ears.

This was in 1976, the year after the end of the Whitlam experience – that whirlwind of political reform that jumpstarted modern Australia after a quarter of a century of conservative government. Pete's mum had been involved in Labor fundraising and Gough Whitlam remembers her fondly. Pete helped to hand out how-to-vote cards prior to the 'revolution' happening.

Due to the severe financial strain his mum's and dad's deaths put on the family, Pete and his brothers had to find enough work to keep him at uni and the two younger boys at school. They washed taxis and squash courts at night, and lived simply in a flat in Neutral Bay. Andrew worked as one of the band's roadies for a while. Soon uni was finished and the inevitable career choice for Pete became reality – but it was no contest. He was never going to become a lawyer, and although he will say he's glad to have the knowledge that came with his degree, he was always more ready to try rock'n'roll.

But the death of his parents did change him. He gave rock'n'roll a major slice of his life but initially never counted on it for a lifetime career. Gary Morris joined as manager soon after Pete's mum died. 'I think the temporary mentality that Pete started to apply to everything was largely because of the loss of his family, and the way that loss took place. All his possessions had basically been taken away. It was a very deep pain that he was having to deal with. I remember for many years Pete just had a duffel bag with a couple of pairs of underpants, a few clothes, and that was his property. He'd throw it into a corner by a mattress on the floor somewhere and I think he vacated premises when the *Sydney Morning Herald*s piled up and pushed him out of the room. That was the way Pete lived. So the whole Midnight Oil thing to Pete was "OK, when its use-by date is up you just trash it: you don't hold any personal love of it".'

This attitude changed considerably over time, but in the years immediately following his mother's death Pete did seem to live life with a constant urgency yet disposability; on stage that attitude seemed even more in evidence. When he screamed, those of us who were close to him could hear more than punk punctuation. When he crashed around we saw more than a performance. He had lots of energy, but the direction of the future was not in the picture. Pete didn't make long-term plans. He didn't become a big-picture player until much later.

The band's songwriting started to get serious. Alienation, anger and frustration were central themes, but so too were determination and independence and integrity. Jim was the master musician; he'd had a childhood full of escape through music to draw on. Rob was a skilled wordsmith who also had a natural flair for melody and beat. They both wrote tunes and lyrics separately, but brought their work together relatively free of ego and the process of creating 'Midnight Oil' songs began. It was often a long and torturous road, with songs constantly being reworked, rejected and revisited until they fell into place. But the band threw nothing away. From those early years came a song called 'Drought', which eventually became the starting point for 'Blue Sky Mine' in 1990, and 'Blot', which didn't make it onto an album until 1998, almost twenty years later. Although Jim and Rob were musically the most prolific, the band established an arrangement – eventually codified in the details of their publishing company, Sprint – that provided income for all members in recognition of the essentially collective effort of bringing songs to fruition. This largely eliminated money from ever being a real bone of contention in the band.

Jim, Bear, Rob and Martin were typical of most musicians, in my experience. They were essentially artistic and sensitive and quiet, not the types to be impressed by contact sports, and somewhat different from their combined image with the band. Their shared passions were writing songs and playing instruments. Pete was quite different. He liked singing and dancing on stage but was not one to enjoy hanging around in studios or at rehearsals. And he did enjoy sport – especially surfing.

So far, with Farm, Pete had been relatively content to turn up and do his thing, but his decision to go full-time also coincided with Martin's joining, and the subject of a name change became a priority. They were determined not to be Farm any more, so after an indecisive session trying to choose a new name they selected four options and put them in a hat. The names were Television, Sparta, Southern Cross and Midnight Oil.

The first performance of 'Midnight Oil' is not officially noted anywhere. It seems it was so long ago that memories have faded, and no one in the band seems particularly fussed by that. It also turns out not to be nearly as straightforward as merely researching days and dates. There is also a problem with definitions, and as a result there are three contenders for their first official gig as Midnight Oil. If we are looking for the first time the eventual line-up of Jim, Bear, Rob, Martin and Pete took to the stage with no others, as Midnight Oil, then it is 23 April 1977, at French's Tavern. If, however, it's the first time the five were together, *plus others*, performing as Midnight Oil, then 11 November 1976 at Avalon RSL is the date. Despite the sympathetic historical connections – the anniversary of Ned Kelly's hanging, the First World War Armistice Day and of the Whitlam sacking – there is a third, probably stronger contender.

The first time the band introduced itself on stage as Midnight Oil was during a run of Saturday night residencies at the Regent Hotel in Kingsford in July 1976. A little black box with a blue light inside illuminating the band's new name, cut out in flame-like writing, was constructed, and a few days later it was placed on top of a smallish speaker box. A single globe hung from the ceiling above the band and Midnight Oil took to the stage for the first time. The date of that show at the Regent was 19 July 1976, with Martin on bass, Peter Watson (who had contributed the Midnight Oil name) on keyboard, Jim on guitar, Rob on drums and Pete singing. But no Bear, he was unwell. The band was paid $60.

This date suits the convention that says members come and go but once the band is named, that's their first gig. I am quite persuaded by that, however the first option, at French's in 1977 nine months after the naming, when the line-up is confirmed, has a certain natural 'birth of the band' feel about it. Your choice.

I first saw them at the end of 1976 at a French's gig, having at last moved up to Sydney from Canberra. Apart from being astounded at the tightness and volume of the band, I was amazed at Pete's progress as a performer. He was absolutely riveting, and with this powerhouse band that had so much light and shade – I just couldn't believe my eyes. My gut feeling was that what I was seeing was solid gold. They were a winning act, without any doubt. I remember thinking that if I had had any money then this would have been the surest bet I'd ever seen.

Up on stage Pete looked like someone I didn't know. He was ferocious and intimidating. He looked out of control. But Pete was always in control. It wasn't an act, more a free-form expression of the wilder side of him. I had seen that side on occasions, but this was sustained and intense and totally convincing. Pete always looked like a guy who meant business, on stage and off. He was not a very compromising person and had plenty of strong ideas about everything. He also had a strong 'Let's give it a go' element running through him. But when it came to the band's most serious business, contact with the music industry, another of Pete's assets proved useful. He had enough legal knowledge, and bluff, to know just how far the band could go.

However, Rob was still essentially the leader of the group and looked after the band's affairs. He had advertised for a lead singer, not necessarily someone to take over the show. Sure, the best lead singers have charisma and Pete undoubtedly had plenty of that, but he was also two years older and more experienced with the ways of the world than the others. Power shifted subtly within the band. Pete's role as front man entrenched his role as the spokesman and public leader of the band. Each member was essentially content in his role, but there was always concern that public utterances should be band utterances rather than just Pete's opinion. It was always 'we', not 'I'.

Martin fitted in, too. Apart from looking the right sort of relaxed and cool that the rest of the band may have secretly aspired to, he brilliantly facilitated the start of the guitar interplay with Jim that became a central element of the band's sound. He also freed Jim to play more keyboards.

The organisational part of Rob's responsibilities was proving more demanding and he was working flat out looking after the band's affairs from Albert Avenue in Chatswood. This was also the band's chief rehearsal spot, in either the garage or the living room. The crowds were building and the band were getting return invitations to the handful of pubs along the Northern Beaches where they played, particularly the Royal

Antler. The Sydney surfside suburb of Narrabeen became the band's home turf, and the Royal Antler became their regular gig.

Narrabeen remains one of only a handful of middle- and working-class beachside suburbs in Sydney. It is the only Australian beach featured in the Beach Boys' classic 'Surfin' USA'. It's a legendary spot for reasons beyond its being the birthplace of Midnight Oil, but Midnight Oil is very much part of Narrabeen folklore now. An early Antler story has it that one night, during an extended wig-out by the band, Pete disappeared from the stage. He reappeared some four or five minutes later, out of breath, with a big grin on his face and noticeably wetter than when he left. He had, according to legend, made a dash out the side door and across the street onto the sand dunes and down to the beach for a quick swim. Body surfing is one of Pete's more elemental passions, but as to the question of whether the story is true he will only say, 'It may be.'

Yes, it happened.

Another uncertain story concerns the arrival on the scene of manager Gary Morris Vasicek. Gary ran with a wild bunch of Narrabeen surfers and potheads called 'The Pack' that frequented the stretch between 'the Alley' and the Antler – a few hundred metres of beach. He was a regular at the Royal Antler on Friday and Saturday nights to drink with his friends and catch the live music. The first time he saw the band he was impressed; by the second he was convinced. Between the two shows Pete had shaved his head and the band must have suddenly looked as intimidating and unique as their music.

Going to the bald look was a radical move in 1976. At the time there was only Yul Brynner and grandfathers, although a mutual friend of ours had done it at university as a way of freaking his father out. It worked a treat, but none of his friends recognised him without his hair. Pete's hair was always so light that he really didn't look *that* different. He went to get his hair cut as a way of keeping it out of his eyes while surfing, but the result was too conservative looking – 'like a bank teller', I remember him telling me. So he went back and got it all off. The band first saw him bald when he arrived looking a little sheepish for a gig at the Leumeah Inn. They all laughed and ribbed him, like mates do, until Martin arrived. 'Cool,' he declared. (Some years later there was a suggestion from one of the record companies wooing them that they all shave their heads. That wouldn't have been cool.)

The Antler arrangement in those early days was for the band to play from 8 p.m. to midnight, comprising four half-hour sets with half-hour breaks between. This allowed some of them to read or complete uni assignments backstage. Rob remembers Gary coming in surrounded by beautiful women and a pack of tanned and confident boys who were his brothers. He was enthusiastic and confident and immediately engaging, so when he asked whether the band would like to do more gigs it resulted in the swapping of telephone numbers.

Gary became involved despite some hesitation from Rob and the others. Rob recalls: 'He was a really charismatic, blue-eyed, handsome young man who could have sold sand to the Arabs. He'd been a real estate agent and a professional golfer, spent time growing up in New Guinea; we got the sense that he was someone who had done a lot in the early part of his life.

He was very independent, confident, strong. He and Pete, I think, had an instant rapport. The rest of us probably weren't quite so sure. I'd never met anyone like Gary before. But his gift of the gab and charisma were undeniable.'

Gary: 'I used to go and visit them up at Chatswood at Rob's house where they were rehearsing in the garage and in his lounge room. I was fairly esoteric with a lot of my concepts, and we'd speak in terms of physical exuberance in the surf and the Oils' music sort of accompanying it, and ideas about doing various shows on the Northern Beaches, for my friends basically. I had no motivation to get involved professionally or otherwise, but it sort of took off from there.'

Gary claims to be the band's first fan. As a fan he wanted to make things come together for the band – for them to realise their potential. 'I could taste what it was – that's Oil,' he says of his qualifications to be the band's manager. Far from being a svengali figure in the classic and dismal tradition of band managers, or a limelight seeker, he was a catalyst in a very real and extremely productive sense. He prodded and he protected and he pushed and he promoted. He was a very rare blend – a dreamer, and a hard worker.

Gary was a handful almost from the beginning, but he got things done. He was a big talker, but when it came to the crunch he made sure the detail was right, too. Together he and the band started to strategise. At the end of 1977 they made a move into the city with a gig at the notorious Bondi Lifesaver, but their regular city haunts became the Rex Hotel, the Civic Hotel and, most of all, French's Tavern.

French's was a tiny place on Oxford Street in Darlinghurst, barely capable of holding a couple of hundred punters shoulder to shoulder. Before long that was the standard environment for an Oils show there. The band had a residency every Tuesday night for nearly a year, which really started to kick things off and change their profile from being purely a Northern Beaches surf band. The performances started to become impossibly packed no matter where they played, so gigs were independently organised at the big old town halls around Sydney's inner suburbs, such as Balmain and Paddington.

A lot of the record companies and industry people were starting to sniff around. This was 1977. One major night in early 1978 was 'Sex and Drugs and Rock'n'roll' at Paddington Town Hall, featuring Jimmy and the Boys and Midnight Oil, $2.50 admission. Two security guards were hired to keep the outside of the premises peaceful from 8.30 p.m. to 1 a.m., but inside the place was crazy with a couple of thousand of Sydney's most esoteric music fans. The whole affair was awash with amyl nitrate and clouds of local grass and charged with kegs full of beer.

For a couple of unsigned bands to fill the Paddington Town Hall was a substantial achievement and the record companies became *very* interested. Up until then Gary had been negotiating and organising each gig, but now he decided to approach the major booking agency of the time, Solo Premier. 'We just couldn't get into half these venues because we were independent. So I went and tried to introduce the band to Solo Premier and have them come down and see the band, and they didn't. They treated me like I was a peon. I took a bit of umbrage at their attitude, and I thought they were just jerks, pretty hardened agents who had obviously been at their level of the music business for some time making a quid. And here was this young know-nothing coming in and trying to be nice and introduce photographs of his band and get them to listen to tapes of their live songs – it didn't really impress them.

'I thought, "Well, that's too hard; I'm not going to wait around for these guys to come and see us." So I just started canvassing venues to try and put the band on myself and promote them with street publicity. I can remember that Midnight Oil were the first act to actually use photos on a poster in the streets. We'd go and put our own posters up around gigs, like at the White Horse Tavern out at Hurstville. I had the idea of picking the four points of the compass and working the inner city out to the suburbs on these four points of the compass. Gradually we got all these residencies. I had fairly free rein on promoting and production, I used to do the lights and pick the venues. The band were just pleased to have someone running around doing stuff for them.'

In April 1978 Double Jay radio featured the band in the station's first live-to-air broadcast from their studios. An hour before broadcast time the doors were opened and Studio 221 was instantly packed; several hundred fans were turned away. In May the band performed as a co-headliner in front of a crowd of 10 000 at a Double Jay event at St Leonard's Park in North Sydney. At both these events they were impressed by the work of sound engineer Keith Walker. Two other fast-rising local acts of the day, Cold Chisel and the Angels, also played at St Leonard's Park. On the sliding scale of new rock Cold Chisel had captured the looser, but still ballsy, blues and boogie end, while the Angels were dramatic, tight and punk-styled at the other. Along with Midnight Oil those two bands rose to dominate the live music scene in Australia known as pub rock. They all played the big suburban pubs, gradually eclipsing the disco rooms from the seventies. Many a disco ball was destroyed in those days by punters and bands alike. They were a red rag to a bull for the new rock.

In May Midnight Oil made their first interstate trip. After a straight fourteen-hour drive sharing the same vehicle, they arrived in Melbourne in the early hours of the morning. As they pulled into the parking area of a St Kilda hotel often frequented by local musicians, Martin thought it was raining. But it was one of the members of Ol'55 pissing onto the windscreen from a room on the first floor. Welcome to rock'n'roll.

During the year the band had record deals offered to them by seven different labels. Gary took the 'Magna Carta of Oil demands' into the meetings after extensive consultation with the band. 'When it came to sitting down and working out what we wanted, you had the full focus of Pete and Rob, with the occasional jolt from Martin, wanting to work out their control. Rob was especially looking at it from a historical point of view, especially the management issues behind the Who and the Beatles and these sorts of things. Rob was really up on a lot of that. Pete, having a legal background, was really aware of personal rights and legal issues, and I was basically a bit of a gringo. I'd put them all down on paper: all our rights, what we wanted to do in terms of the manager getting budgets and things like that – and to not let record companies take over.

'I went to see all these people and basically they all laughed at me. It was like "Where are you coming from?" So first the promoters rejected us and now the record companies. They all wanted to sign the band, but this list of demands was just unrealistic. We were fairly downcast about that but we thought, "Oh well, so what? We'll try and work it out. We might try and make our own label", and all these dreams started coming up. The music business at a very early stage was holding us out. If we were to be allowed in we'd have to surrender all our rights, we'd have to be owned, and we couldn't do that. So here we were gradually forming independence, and I think, realistically, we were the first independent Australian band – by default, basically.'

Chris Neale was an independent studio owner who came along to a show. He had been doing a lot of work with Ken Harding, the manager of a record pressing plant for Seven Records, the music arm of Channel Seven TV. Chris invited the band to his Airborne Studios in Brookvale, and they were enthusiastic about the studio. Over time they started having discussions with him, their intention being to make their first record at Airborne Studios with Chris producing. The recordings would be pressed at Ken's plant and Gary would negotiate a distribution deal through Seven Records. That was the grand plan.

Gary remembers Chris was working with Air Supply and the Little River Band at the time and told him about the Little River Band getting $20 000 for a gig. 'I just thought, "Woah, what a massive amount of money to get for one show." And here we were, happy with 200 bucks. Basically this looming gigantum of the music business was coming into our focus – we felt that we could actually get involved and maintain our integrity and our sovereignty in the process.'

So they went in and met with Ken, who had by then bought the record pressing plant. He was trying to set up independent labels to operate through Seven Records and said that although he wouldn't let the band own their own label, they'd be able to control everything about it. They could name it and design it, and would be given a budget they would control. For the band this seemed ideal: they would be able to manage their career *and* have major distribution because Seven Records was distributed by RCA. Everybody liked 'Powderworks Records' as the label name – it was the name of the street where Gary lived in Narrabeen and became the name of the first song on their debut album.

Gary: 'We had a logo designed and we basically controlled all the creativity. We then had to make a hard decision. I've seen the band, and myself, have to make these decisions over time where there is loyalty to people who become great friends of the band, but whose ability to keep ahead of the curve of the band's needs in terms of their professional skills or their talent isn't there. The first serious decision of this sort had to be about Chris Neale.'

The band had become close to Chris but had also got to know Keith Walker because of the shows they had done with him for Double Jay. They were playing as often as they could, usually three or four shows a week, and by year's end had performed almost 200 gigs. They really wanted to capture their live sound for the first record. The dilemma confronting the band about whether to do it with Chris or with Keith, who was experienced in capturing their live sound, was soon settled. They didn't really like the stuff Chris had been working on in his studios with bands such as Air Supply; it was too produced and too soft. Gary: 'They ended up going with Keith Walker, and Chris basically took it pretty badly. He felt he'd been betrayed, because he'd introduced the band to Ken Harding, and he felt like he had some kind of right to do the first record. So that's how things took off and Powderworks Records was formed.'

They had decided on a producer, and once they learned that the legendary Albert's studio was available the decision about where to record was made, too. Bear remembers actually seeing his heroes from the Easybeats. 'When we first looked over Albert's, where AC/DC did some of their most famous early recordings, Harry (Vanda) and George (Young) were in there, with George behind the mixing desk and Harry being made to hit a woodblock for several minutes.' And outside through the King Street window they could see the partially built Sydney Tower at Centrepoint.

Like most bands facing their first record they were bursting with enthusiasm, even though for financial reasons the recording had to be done after gigs, in the midnight-to-dawn hours. At least they were warmed up. They were tired but they knew the songs backwards, so they approached the sessions well prepared. Jim remembers it with the affection you might expect for a first effort. 'It was the most prepared we ever were, because we'd been playing things live for so long and didn't even have to think when we did it. It was just an outpouring. The playing and everything was great; I really enjoyed it.'

The album was recorded very quickly – the basic tracks in four sessions, and some guitar overdubs on day five. With the eventual release of their self-titled debut LP – sometimes known as 'The Blue Meanie', or *Powderworks* – in November

1978, Bear recalls that people started to sing along with the songs at gigs. The band were also able to pay each other a little more, due to a small record advance and a higher fee per gig.

Having a record out also meant they got asked to play on ABC TV's popular music show, *Countdown*, which was recorded on Saturdays in Melbourne. The band played on the Friday night at the Bondi Lifesaver with Rose Tattoo as support. It was a late night, with most of the guys not getting home until around 3 a.m. They had to be at the airport at 7 a.m. to catch the 8.30 flight to Melbourne. They arrived at their regular hotel, the Majestic, in Melbourne's St Kilda and went straight to sleep. Gary went off to *Countdown* to see if everything was OK. According to Bear: '*Countdown* had arranged for a blue set for us to perform one of the singles from our first album; however, they expected us on the set at 8 a.m. and we were sleeping instead. Gary was a cocky young buck who thought he could talk anyone round given the chance. My recollection is that words followed between Gary and the *Countdown* staff, with the result that another band was pulled in to take our place that day.'

The later story that Midnight Oil refused to play on *Countdown* added to the band's reputation for thumbing their nose at convention, but they had gone pretty close. They certainly knocked back all future offers to appear, arguing that they didn't want to mime their songs as required by the format of the day. The band did offer to provide video clips – just like all the international acts – but *Countdown* demanded exclusive first play or no play at all when it came to videos, and Midnight Oil were not prepared to accept that condition. As a result the band's videos failed to be seen on *Countdown* either. There were quite a few new TV rivals to *Countdown* who treated them much more generously, but *Countdown* was regarded as the make-or-break program by the music industry and the decision by the band not to appear was widely regarded as commercial suicide.

But they were increasingly finding new, non-industry ways of operating. 'The first year I think we sold 5000 records,' remembers Gary. 'Radio didn't touch it, and I think for the next one only Double Jay and 3RRR in Melbourne were playing us. So that was our exposure. We were putting on great shows, great concerts, and part of that was developing a new ability to create shows in various places, especially town halls. I found myself approaching a lot of the unis and they had the Movement Against Uranium Mining, Greenpeace, Save the Whales, a lot of these grass-roots entities were already forming in the universities. They had great art facilities. They'd be screen-printing all their artwork and had great postering and great propaganda going out. It really dovetailed into the psyche of the band, especially Peter's, of having some kind of social purpose behind making music. It was sort of going back to that Dylan, Baez, sixties kind of influence. So the university activist areas really started to fit in with what we were doing. We worked together and put on shows and that's how that part of it started.'

A band press release from April 1978 has a certain 'Gary-ness' about it: 'Anyone new to the band is at once struck by the lead singer's desperate, almost demented, appearance – always moving, he jolts, falls, twists about, singing fiercely, and is never less than a startling on-stage presence. But long-time fans also notice his quick sense of humour, and the band's acute involvement with the atmosphere of the music they are creating. Their songs are tough mood-setting powerbursts; they use tension created between machine-gunning rhythm guitar, exceptionally expressive bass, and fast intense drumming to lend impact to the high vibrating vocals and searing lead guitar. It is this, and the lyrics simmering with images of social unrest, hostility and searches for escape, that have evoked strong audience reaction everywhere they play.'

Bear: 'We played with many other bands at this time, initially supporting them and later them supporting us. We played with Dragon (a great band when they were firing, but often they weren't), Mi-Sex, Mondo Rock, Split Enz, Skyhooks (after Shirley and Red left) and the Sherbs. Another band who started supporting us was the Farriss Brothers. They were a good band but their lead singer, Michael Hutchence, had no charisma or presence – and he didn't, back then. Gary was soon to take them under his wing and assist with management. He chose their new name – INXS, inspired by a TV commercial he saw for IXL jam.'

Gary: 'I had INXS as a support act to keep the production flowing. When Midnight Oil went off the road INXS could continue to use the production and crew and keep the juices flowing in terms of economics.'

Soon it was time for a second album, and this time the band chose a producer who was a musician. Les Karski had arrived in Australia as a member of British band Supercharge and decided to stay. He made extensive notes after listening to the band's demo tape. His recommendations included: 'Not quite so much waffle in solos for "Stand in Line" and intro too long.' He saw 'Don't Wanna Be the One' as a possibility for the single – ironically it didn't make it onto the album at all.

Of 'Profiteers' he said the intro was too long and the direction 'a bit too jazzy/clever/old hippy solo waffly'! The intro was also far too long for 'Eye Contact' and 'lyrics totally unintelligible'. In general: 'Some effects could achieve better separation. Not quite so much soloing, suggest trying certain effects, phasing, delays, doubling with synthesiser, more dynamics could be achieved with bass parts. Some effects would greatly enhance vocal impact, simple back-up vocals help during choruses.'

The band did six weeks' pre-production before entering Trafalgar Studios in June for five weeks of recording before emerging with the *Head Injuries* album. Again the recordings were done in the midnight-to-dawn shift. Bear: 'The last overdub recorded was harmony vocals for "Koala Sprint". They were recorded after a gig at the Stagedoor and finished close to nine in the morning.'

That evening the band commenced another intense schedule of events. They took the 5.30 flight to Canberra for a gig that night and the next morning flew to Melbourne for a full week of gigs, then were booked to leave for their first New Zealand tour from Melbourne. It was a busy time for the band, almost too busy. Pressures on Gary were growing and the band were having a hard time keeping exact tabs on what he was doing and how he was doing it. Bear: 'Often the band and Gary were pulling in different directions. Once Gary had made up his mind what had to be done, even if the band categorically forbade him to do it, it was hard to prevent it from happening. The fact that we didn't have the money didn't stop Gary – many were the cheques that bounced in those early days.'

Gary was a law unto himself, and the extreme workload was starting to spin him out. 'I was getting to a point where

I was working about eighty hours a week; the band were becoming very demanding, they were getting used to their own way, they were getting a lot of things done the way they wanted it. And there was only me. I didn't even have an office apart from Rob Hirst's hallway with his phone. I was paying rent to Rob for using his front room as my bedroom and office. So doing that in the morning, running around during the day, and then setting up lights and doing the light show at night for five or six nights a week, because they really wanted to work, wanted to play. And we were sort of on a roll; audiences were paying the money to come along. I was promoting the shows, finding new venues, and it all took its toll.'

In the midst of the preparation for the New Zealand tour Gary was invited to a Billy Graham Crusade. Bear: 'I never really understood what Gary was on about at the best of times. He was always an extroverted evangelist for some cause, moving way into your personal space and staring at you with glazed eyes. Now he was talking about God, using a mix of new age/spiritual/druggie language, and I didn't have a clue what he was talking about. Having God in the picture really turned Gary's world upside down. He lost his drive and passion for the things he loved formerly, and one of these was Midnight Oil.'

Gary: 'At that point, when I walked away, rock'n'roll had no meaning for me. I lost all interest in the New Zealand tour. I lost interest in the gig that was being put on at Parramatta Park. I introduced Midnight Oil to Zev Eizik and introduced INXS to Chris Murphy, and basically stepped out of the music business.'

But the New Zealand tour had to go ahead, with or without Gary. It was their first overseas tour, and the first time any

Australian band had attempted a tour of NZ without record company support. Bear remembers problems with New Zealand customs when they had to pay some sort of security to prevent them selling all their equipment while visiting. Jim remembers a different customs incident. 'Bear tried to smuggle Velveeta cheese into New Zealand! He thought he couldn't get it over there. Now, NZ is a country of great cheeses, but he had to have his Velveeta, which is the most bland – it tastes like non-cheese, like all the life has been extinguished from it. And the customs officials pulled him over for it. It was impounded. That was typical of Bear.'

New Zealand was pretty quiet that first time through. Pete does remember an incident where he and one of the road crew, Colin, were confronted by notorious Maori bikie gang the Mongrel Mob in a small cafe somewhere on the North Island. After finding out they were from Australia *and* a rock band, the next question was immaterial. 'What's that you're eating?' said the front guy, pointing at Colin's burger. There was a pause before Colin said, 'Why? You want some?', then another pause. Then he shoved it in the guy's face. In the moment or two of delayed shock Colin leapt the counter and dashed out a back door. Pete says there was a nanosecond before he did the same. They shamelessly hid, not even daring to look out the window of their motel room.

The size of the band's gear and the volume of their shows did attract some attention. There was a picture of their sound-mixing desk featured on page one of a local newspaper.

On tour at the same time, in local band the Swingers, was future Oils bass player Bones Hillman. 'I met them in about '79, in a motel in Wellington where the Swingers were staying and the Oils checked in as well. We were kicking a soccer ball around. They were the first Australian band we'd ever met and I remember hearing Rob and that accent and we went, "Wow, get a load of that shit!" And then we went and saw them play at the Rock Theatre and they were the loudest thing I'd ever heard in my life. Some guy called Pig was doing the sound. They parted the audience. It was incredibly loud.'

Bear: 'The final gigs in Christchurch were much better. We had five nights in a row at the venue, and word got around the city that we were worth catching. By the final night the place was full. At the finale, Martin took a container of talcum powder, took off the top and exploded it into the air. The effect was spectacular with the coloured lights. This was a change from our usual finale, when Rob would stand on his drums with his legs apart, and a roadie would discharge a CO_2 fire extinguisher into the audience from between his thighs.'

Back in Sydney they recommenced touring with the ongoing help of Chris Plimmer and his Nucleus Agency. They would do two or three months at a time of nightly playing, constantly gigging. And they had to press on without Gary. Chris was an independent booking agent who had helped the band when Gary's overtures to the major agencies had been rejected. He was a constant figure at their shows during the next few years, working very closely with them in setting up special gigs and coordinating the tours. He also fought shoulder to shoulder in defence of them – literally. Pete remembers one night on Caves Beach, near Newcastle, at a big open-air show when things turned nasty. 'Obviously there were occasions when the crowd had a malevolent edge to it – Caves Beach is a good example. A gig where everybody clearly had too much to drink, a lot of younger people, under age, drinking heavily. It was very crowded and there were probably a lot of people there because it was an open-air show with other bands on too. They weren't specifically Midnight Oil fans – just there for the night. And that was very, very wild. Kids all around on the cliffs, Chris Plimmer and half a dozen security guys in hand-to-hand combat with about 1500 thugs who were trying to break the gates open. It did look like World War Three.'

Meanwhile, the cost of putting on professional shows and creating special events continued to be greater than the money earned from the gigs. Financially they were going backwards. Eventually the band entrusted at least some of their affairs to Zev Eizik. Zev ran the ACE agency in Melbourne and was a promoter and venue owner. He was pretty feisty, and was later involved in a notorious series of punch-ups with Elvis Costello's manager, Jake Riviera, stretching over two Costello tours.

From Zev's stable of tour managers came one who fitted no one's idea of a rock'n'roll tour manager, Constance Adolph. She was five foot nothing in her high heels, but had a pile-up hairdo that more than compensated. She had been in the entertainment business for most of her life, first in the USA with a childhood TV career as 'little' Connie in Disney's Mouseketeer Club, then in London working with record companies. She had been working at Virgin Records when Sex Pistols manager Malcolm McLaren came in. 'He said, "I've got a band for you." He had hot-pink plastic pants on, with a see-through vinyl shirt, and in the pocket was a little cassette,

Midnight Oil makes you dance; Exxon Oil makes us sick: the band's protest performance on a truck top in front of Exxon's New York headquarters in 1990 *(Chuck Pulin/CBS Records)*

Pete at a press conference with fellow NDP Senate candidate Jean Meltzer during 1984's Australian federal election campaign

Almost seeing eye to eye with a John Howard postcard in 1998 — but not with the prime minister's policies *(Dean Sewell)*

Pete's not *that* big, and Bob Hawke isn't *that* small, but at the opening of a new Australian Conservation Foundation building in December 1989 they celebrated the then PM's changed Jervis Bay policy *(Sebastian Costanzo/ Fairfaxphotos)*

Pete in Rock Island Line in Canberra, 1973, with Damien Street on bass. The 'rock'n'roll, rockabilly and new wave electronica' band (as described in their one and only review) was a diversion from Pete's legal studies

Pete lets his hair down in Farm at a Sydney University gig in 1975

Jim also had more hair in Farm days, and a rather groovy silk jacket

In the back bar of the Antler Hotel in 1978, prior to going through to the main performing room (from left: Pete, Martin, Bear, Rob, Jim) *(Phillip Morris)*

On stage in 1979 at Flicks in Manly, with Bear (right) on bass, before the physical demands and stress became too much for him

Pete on the move at Rosehill Speedway in 1979, as the band started to get used to larger outdoor shows *(Bob King)*

Pete often did the first few songs with a T-shirt wrapped around his head, a look much imitated by young male fans *(Adrienne Overall)*

Left to right, Jim, Martin and Rob singing the 'Antarctica' chorus at the Sydney Entertainment Centre in 1993 *(Bob King)*

Rob's 'Keith Moon trick' of putting water on his drums added a little something to his already stunning display *(Kevin Fewster)*

Sometimes Pete's hands seemed almost as big as his head. His left hand became the band's logo

Michael Lippold watches for trouble from side stage during the band's first US tour in 1984, with a set list nearby so he can keep track of the show. Giffo is on bass *(Adrienne Overall)*

and that was the demos for *Never Mind the Bollocks*. I'll never forget saying to Simon Draper and Richard Branson, "This is the next big thing" and them saying, "No, it'll never happen!"'

After short and expensive spells at A&M, then EMI, the Pistols did sign with Virgin and Connie had plenty to do with them. However, one of the first major tours she did was with Led Zeppelin. 'I was in Europe with them for eight months. That was fabulous, absolutely phenomenal. I was their production manager. That's what made me decide if I ever found another great band, I would go back on the road – and it just so happened it was the Oils.'

After a vacation in Australia Connie had decided to stay, and was soon working for a local record label. 'Gary rang me up at Wizard and said, "I know you were involved with the Sex Pistols and I'd like you to come and see my band at the Bondi Lifesaver." And to be perfectly honest, the first time I saw them I'd just come out of England where all the punk things were happening and the Oils were kind of old style compared to what I'd been working with. This was '77, I think. Gary introduced me to the band afterwards and they were really nice guys – I thought they were sweet boys. A year later Peter called me, by then I was with ACE as a road manager and we were bringing in international bands, and he said, "Gary said if we ever had any problems you'd give us a hand", and I said, "Sure, what's the problem?" Peter goes, "We need a manager."'

ACE were international concert promoters who didn't manage bands, but Connie managed to convince Zev to check them out. 'So Zev comes up to Sydney and we were touring Ry Cooder. Once Ry Cooder was on stage at the Regent, we knew he'd be there for about three hours. We walked down the street and went into the Stagedoor to see the Oils, and I've never seen anything like it. It was packed – the walls were sweating because it was so packed. There were so many people in there that we were offered a spot behind the bar so we didn't get crushed. When the band hit the stage my mouth fell open. I could not believe that in one year this band had – well, they blew my socks away, absolutely blew me away. And Zev, he was blown away too. We went backstage after the show, and you know what the Oils are like after a show – they are absolutely knackered – and they're really sweet. They can hardly talk, they can hardly breathe coz the place was so full. The place is supposed to hold four or five hundred and there were like 1300 people hanging off the rafters. Zev and I were walking back to Ry Cooder and Zev says, "We've got to do it, let's do it." We had lunch with the band the next day and of course they are very intelligent guys – they weren't like the Pistols, trust me! That blew Zev away, too, that these guys really had their act together; they were intelligent, and talented. And Zev said to me, "If we take this on, you'll go on the road with them." I was only touring international acts in Australia and I was like, "What – do pubs? I don't do pubs, I do concerts!" But I said, "OK, I'll give it a go."'

Connie became part of the family. She was tough, but she was like a mother hen. She also had the band wrapped around her little finger. One evening before a show she sent Jim out to try and find her some replacement fingernails! She was tailor-made for the Oils: she was a talker and she was sharp, and she could go icy cold or scream with laughter at the flick of an eyelash. Connie was ruthlessly efficient and extremely entertaining at the same time – and a great dancer. The band called her the Boogie Queen, or 'Boog' for short. They didn't quite find that combination in a tour manager again until Willie MacInnes many years later.

Connie: 'We took a band that was only playing Sydney and basically broke them in Australia. And that was Zev's doing. Zev's attitude was "They are not just an Australian band, they will be treated like an international band." That's why all the promo stuff was like what we did for international bands. Local bands didn't do street posters like that. I remember the first tour, we plastered every city we were going to play in and people didn't realise Midnight Oil was from Sydney. They thought it was an international band coming in.'

The band's gigs were by now becoming legendary for their extraordinary impact. First they would make the crowd wait until everything was as technically perfect and reliable as possible, which often seemed much longer than you waited for any other band. Then, when the show finally started, it never let up until they were gone. It was a journey interrupted only occasionally by technical problems and bad behaviour, but nothing stopped the energy once the band were on stage. It was partly Pete's incredible magnetism as a performer and partly the band's devastating combination of guitars and drums. They would build momentum by plunging into their next song before the applause from the song before had begun to fade. Every night these incredible performances – and then they were gone from the stage.

The Oils chant began in this environment, with punters calling for the return of the band – 'Oy-YERLS, Oy-YERLS' – but they never came back out, not in the really early days.

Pete: 'We didn't do any encores for the first three years of our career. I always had a strong view that you had to get as much out of a performance as you could. If you thought you might be going back for an encore, you wouldn't finish at a maximum point. But we got to the stage where we did start to do them. If you're sensitive towards the audience, then you've got a choice of either denying them what they really feel they deserve or giving it to them. Also, occasionally, if we hadn't done them the joint would have got wrecked! That "free" period of just five people up on the stage, one set of instruments in their hands, and fifteen songs – "Let's play eight from top to bottom, then we'll fall over, throw water all over ourselves, suck some air in and play the other seven, then see ya later!" – we probably couldn't have done it for thirty years, but it was great fun when we were doing it.'

After the New Zealand tour Bear was increasingly unwell. He had a nervous disposition and a sensitive stomach, and suffered from life on the road. 'I was going a little crazy. I had developed a duodenal ulcer, and was unable to perform on stage without prescription medication for my nerves. My mother and father and I holidayed in New Zealand for two weeks when I was on a band break, and although I thought the holiday would get my health back on track, I went a bit unhinged. I had got to the stage where I couldn't escape the stress and the ill health even when I wasn't on tour.'

It was also apparent to all that he was not suited to the life the band had planned. Jim: 'I really liked Bear, I used to travel around with him, he used to drive this Hillman Hunter. He was my friend and we used to hang around together. We had some great conversations about music and other things, but I soon realised as my world was starting to grow he was still staying with his parents and still worrying about petrol receipts and driving all over Sydney to find the cheapest petrol. It was intensely annoying. It was like he was on a different trajectory. The worst part, though, was that his bass playing wasn't as aggressive for the pubs as was needed. He was like a folk musician – very gifted, very self-taught, could sing, a really good ear for harmony, things like that, but we wanted an animal. We were turning into animals and he chose not to. He was really happy to point out that we were and he wasn't.'

Bear: 'My time with Midnight Oil was drawing to a close. I had not been well for some time. I was hoping to hang out until we achieved our goal of playing in England, but my ill health was affecting the band's performances, and it didn't give them confidence to be organising overseas tours. Each way I turned there was stress. The last few weeks of my stay with the band were hard. I had lost my energy, my appetite and my emotional sense of well-being. I was a wreck in all senses of the word. The day after my last gig with the band, in March 1980, was the day they were shooting a film clip for "Back on the Borderline". It would have been nice for me to have been in it, but I couldn't make it. I could only get out of bed for about fifteen minutes at a time before I started feeling very sick.

'Midnight Oil had two weeks off after filming the clip. In the middle there was an opportunity for a gig in Canberra. Zev phoned me up to persuade me to do the gig. He said, "Other people have ulcers and do gigs. Why can't you?" But I knew I couldn't get out of bed, let alone play a gig in Canberra. After about a month of recuperation I still felt sick a lot of the time. I went to the local shops, but felt really weird – disconnected, like I was watching someone else going to the shops on TV. I really thought I was going crazy. Meanwhile Midnight Oil had auditioned lots of bass players, and had settled on Peter Gifford, not only because he had all the right musical qualities and was a nice guy, but also because he pulled a good sound out of his equipment. He was made of tougher stuff than I was, and yet even he would not last the distance.'

three

instant relief

Yoin is a Japanese expression for the reverberation that continues after a stimulus has ceased. It is often applied to the after-effect that accompanies a great performance, and in rock terms it's more than the buzzing in your ears or your soaking-wet T-shirt. *Yoin* is an awareness of an additional impact after something great has been experienced.

Awesome is a faddish English word like fabulous, or fantastic, or hot, or cool, or sick, that comes in and out of vogue and often has little to do with its real meaning. But awesome is the word most used to describe Midnight Oil's live performances over these last twenty-six years by fans and journalists alike.

Music journalism has been described as being 'People who can't write, describing something that can't be explained, for people who can't read'. Only the second phrase is worth responding to. It is hard to describe music. Music is magic. In the creole of northern Australia music is *mujik*. Music is ethereal, and its effect is unpredictable. What works and why and for whom is the result of intensely personal reactions. On a CD or the radio we take the music on our own terms, in our context, and are freer to resist its wily charms. Live, when you have direct contact with the musicians and their music, you are much more vulnerable. In their space, with lights and volume on their side, a skilled musician can cast a spell over you. Sometimes it doesn't last that long – just until the end of the song, maybe – but sometimes it follows you out into the street. And sometimes it follows you home and becomes part of your life.

Most people do not walk away from a live Midnight Oil show unaffected. There is a resounding *yoin* to every performance. Reviews of Midnight Oil shows are always extraordinary – most writers struggle with the twin demands of suitably extreme descriptions and retaining journalistic distance. Most aficionados will coolly tell you of the band's prowess in many facets of the music business but declare them virtually peerless in the live department. And fans will tell you the records are brilliant and the political thing is either inspirational or immaterial, but the live shows are universally . . . awesome.

Here in Australia you could guarantee that most people would be convinced after witnessing just one show – introducing your friends to their first Midnight Oil performance was one of the most satisfying things you could do. However, some critics speculated that it may be just an Australian thing, a thing peculiar to Australian pubs and the Australian personality. In 1983 American *Rolling Stone* music editor David Fricke was working for *Musician* magazine and visiting London when he saw the band for the first time. 'They had this amazing show on this tiny stage with these huge white lights – airport runway lights blazing in your face. And they just totally rocked the place! I didn't know that much about the material apart from what I'd heard on *10,9,8*, and it's like, "Wow! This is it." And that was it – I was on! I was onboard.

'Subsequent to that, it may have been the same year, I went to Australia for the first time to write about everybody I could. As part of the trip I went to Adelaide and the Oils were touring Australia. They played at the Adelaide Town Hall and again it was unreal, because in England what I had seen was this amazing band, but in Australia, in Adelaide, I saw an amazing *culture*, because I saw the audience. I saw the way the audience glommed onto them with such jubilant ferocity. You know, I've seen people drink, but I've never seen people that drunk and that ecstatic at the same time – absolutely focused on everything happening on stage, and especially on Peter. You look at him and he's so big and almost overwhelming physically. But at the same time the intensity of his act, there is so much *giving* in it. It's coming from his voice, it's coming through his body movements, and the way the audience would react to that and then send it back to the stage was like these tidal waves of excitement. And then Rob's thing on the drums with the sticks going in the air, and the guitars just firing all over the room! I wish I had a tape of that show – it was one of the most amazing live experiences I've ever had, because it was one of those rare times when not only were you amazed by what you saw on stage, but you were amazed by what was around you on the floor. The way people were just so *inside*, not just the songs and the performance, but they were inside what the band wanted to give them. It was an astonishing experience and really a rare example of the genuine electricity of live performance. And its reciprocal electricity. This was a peak experience for me.'

In the early days the band didn't want to play concerts.

They were wedded to the intimacy of the small gig. They moved reluctantly into larger venues when their popularity meant conditions became impossibly uncomfortable for all concerned in the small clubs and bars. After a while Pete and the band took to the larger concert venues and quickly learned to translate their performance to the bigger rooms and stages. Soon even massive outdoor events were attempted and the band learned that even there a similar intensity could be achieved.

The person at Sony in the USA appointed to look after Midnight Oil was Mason Munoz. His first view of the band in a big arena was an eye-opener. 'It was at a place called the Meriwether Post. They call them "sheds" here in America. It's an outdoor venue, the stage is covered and part of the audience is covered, and the hillside is there and it's covered with people. I couldn't get out of New York in time and took the late train to just outside of Washington DC and walked onto the site. They were probably half an hour, forty minutes into the set and it was the first time I had ever seen 10 000 people at a rock show dancing. It just didn't happen. You usually had a few hundred people dancing but I walked in and there was just this sea of humanity going *crazy*, dancing along with Peter up on stage.'

Pete's performance was obviously central to the band's live appeal, but he fed directly off the band and they fed off him. And as the show progressed he fed off the crowd, too. The atmosphere on and off stage was focused yet free-wheeling as band and audience just locked in and let go. There was always the sense that the whole experience had been as intensely felt and shared by everyone.

•

In 1980, when Bear was unable to continue, the bass-playing job went to Peter Gifford. Giffo heard of the vacancy crossing the Harbour Bridge listening to Double Jay while on his way to a casual night of roadie work. A few hours later he was auditioning with one of the biggest live bands in the country in a small rehearsal room at Rhinoceros Studios. 'When I went to do the audition there was just Rob and Jim and Martin. Rob was very friendly – as he is – and made me feel at ease. We just had a bit of a play, but struggled a bit to come up with a song we all knew. We played a few things. They said, "Do you know 'Run by Night'?" and I said I'd heard it on the radio, so they showed me how it went and we played that and started to get along all right. Then Pete turned up, and he was a sort of fearful-looking character to the uninitiated, and he says, "Can you sing?" and I said, "Yeah, a bit", so we sang the backing vocals in "Run by Night".

'Then they said, "Can you get a copy of *Head Injuries*?" and I said, "Yeah, I can get that, no problems." I didn't want to make anything too difficult for anyone so I actually went out and bought the album – which was a pretty mean feat because I didn't have any money. I was broke, on the dole, lugging some gear around here and there. So I put it on my Walkman and was listening to it and I thought, "Fuck, I never knew this existed!" I was so impressed with it. I think it's a phenomenal album, one of the greatest pieces of work to date from the band. When I went back we played through the songs a couple of times and then they said it's time to go to the pub now. I went, "Oh yeah!", because I liked that language. The vibe at the pub was "We like what's going down here", and Pete said, "We'd like to give you a go. We'll give you three months' trial and in three months if we don't like you or you don't like us, well, that's fair." I thought that was pretty good and I said, "When would you like to start?" and they said, "Well, that's the bad news – we start touring in eight days!"'

When Giffo joined, the band were really ready to do some serious playing. They played hard and they played a lot, and Giffo added grunt and a bedrock bottom end to the sound. That is not to say he was without finesse; his inventiveness and skill quickly became integral to the band's playing and recording. But grunt was what was needed, and he delivered that in spades. In the engine room he and Rob propelled the show, and Giffo was usually leading the way, shovelling coals on the fire at breakneck speed. Rob: 'His bass playing through those eighties albums was for the band the definition of power and energy, and as the other half of the rhythm section he was a joy to play with. Giffo was much imitated. He redefined the look of the band – that really tough, ripped-sleeve "just got out from under the car" look. His real job was a carpenter, a tradesman, that's what all the Gifford brothers were sent off to do. Music was just something you did as a hobby. But he also had a great musical sense and a talent that was undeniable.'

Giffo remembers some challenging shows in his first few weeks of being in the band. 'We did the first show at Wollongong and it all came together, it just kicked arse, went bang, and everyone was happy. The boys were grinning and I was pretty pleased myself. There were about 600 people if I remember rightly, which was pretty big-time for me. We had roadies and a Ranger truck and all the good stuff. So it was pretty exciting. I think the third gig was a live-to-air at the Royal Antler – which freaked the living daylights out of me!

It was a positively frightening event. The place was chocka, the energy was like— there was condensation dripping off the ceiling. Those were the days when you could shove as many people as you could fit into the room and no one really bothered much. It was like standing room, elbow to elbow, just sardines. And what I remember was I got on stage and was emotionally overwhelmed and nearly came to tears, because I stood on the stage and the audience were just so— Oil! The hands were up, they were screaming and shouting out and we hadn't played anything yet! And I've gone, "Fuck, I'm part of this?" And I could feel that welling-up of emotion – you feel happy and overwhelmed with pride or happiness or something. You think, "Wow. I'm here. Crikey, what's happening?" That was the Antler, and that was a fabulous show. Peter got a feather pillow, and we had the industrial fans going on the side of the stage, and he ripped the pillow open and punched it and I didn't see him doing it but I knew he was going to do something, and then all these feathers came out and I was blinded by this snowstorm!'

Also in Giffo's first couple of weeks was the last-ever night of the legendary Stagedoor Tavern, a dingy venue beneath a tall office block adjacent to Sydney's Central railway station. Pete was without his driver's licence and I drove him to and from that gig. On the way he told me how the whole 'Midnight Oil will destroy the Stagedoor' campaign by the venue's management had escalated to the point where he had been interviewed by the police that afternoon and asked about what he actually planned to do and say that night. There had been an injunction against the event sought by the police, which Justice Helsham rejected. He said he knew Peter

Garrett, and his parents, and was confident that the words 'Destroy the Stagedoor' on leaflets meant they were only going to lay waste to the place in rock'n'roll terms, not literally. We were chuckling at the ridiculousness of it all when we realised that the couple of blocks surrounding the venue had been cordoned off. A lucky parking spot didn't leave us too far to walk, but there were police everywhere – even on the surrounding rooftops. Then we saw a squad with shields and helmets.

Getting in was a story in itself, not that the police were any problem as they knew who Pete was, but getting through the crowd to the dressing room was the most difficult 30 metres I think I have ever travelled on foot. Trying to keep Pete moving by clearing a path of sorts through wall-to-wall people is always hard, but considering that they couldn't actually move they were not at all keen to feel someone trying to push through. When they noticed that I had Pete in tow, it didn't make things any easier. Pete kept his head down and his hat on and didn't do more than nod in acknowledgement of the greetings and friendly pats on the back. We kept moving, Pete pushing my back determinedly. Thankfully the atmosphere was so noisy and it was so dark and crowded that we made it through to the band's room, just past the toilets near the stage.

The atmosphere was tense and electric, and airless. The air conditioning had broken down and the police were refusing to allow fire escape doors to be opened because of the security risk. And it is true that the security situation was extreme – in addition to almost 2000 crammed into a room licensed for 300, there were at least a further 1000 outside. For a while the band considered cancelling the show, but the ramifications of doing so in this sort of circumstance seemed even more dangerous.

Giffo: 'That was like frightening shit, you know. Being young blokes we were sort of fearless, but getting older you wouldn't put yourself in that situation. I didn't realise how serious it all was until we got there and there were about 200 riot police around the block. The whole thing was lit up with spotlights. The police were out in significant numbers – hundreds. I remember they wouldn't open the back door, it was positively dangerous.'

When the band appeared on stage they were accompanied by a roar that must easily have been heard by the assembled militia, and fans, on the outside. Almost immediately the equipment started to break down under the abnormal conditions. Halfway through the first song the band members were all dripping with sweat – even Jim. As the gig progressed, Rob was having to blink his way through a positive cascade while Giffo and Martin were moving as little as possible, resulting in little puddles forming where each of them was standing. Pete was famous for the amount of liquid that could pass through his system during a show, but tonight he kept the front few rows permanently soaked from the sweat that poured off him as he charged about the small stage. I remember thinking he was like a wrestler that night – he was bouncing off the ropes, looking for that bit of extra something from somewhere. Occasionally he clung to the mike stand and tried to suck in some air, the torn remnants of his white T-shirt stuck to his upper torso.

As the gig got more and more manic, with each song treated by band and crowd as if it were the last, Pete felt it timely to say a few words. He could barely talk at all but managed to advise 'caution when dealing with animals' and wished everyone a safe trip home. With that the band launched into the final song, which ended with Pete and the band stumbling off stage, and the crowd – if they'd had room to stumble – would have done the same. Everyone was in almost as bad a state. We all needed oxygen.

Giffo: 'Pete was in a shocking state after that show, we all were, but he was very bad. I remember in the back room he was lying on the floor after putting in an hour and a half of solid slog, 1500 people or whatever, with no air in the place whatsoever. He's lying on the floor in the changing room after putting in a monumental performance, and we're all completely stuffed, and he's blue – blue and white, with goose bumps, shivering, almost dead. He looked like he was dead, everything had gone from him. He had the oxygen mask on. At first he was trying to get air from the crack at the bottom of the back door. We were so angry that the police wouldn't let the back door of the Tavern open. We were locked in, in a room right at the back where there was no air. It was potentially a very dangerous situation for everybody there.'

Some punters ended up in paddy wagons and some copped a bit of a bashing that night as they exited through a row of police who channelled them into a park across the road.

This was yet another extreme performance from the band and Pete, and an unforgettable night for the audience. It is the stuff of Midnight Oil's legend. They gave it their all every night, night after night. It certainly seems a very extreme way to make a living. So why does someone put themselves through that? For the sake of entertainment? Pete: 'It's not entertainment, it's honouring the moment. It's all about honouring the moment and being as fully into the moment as you can be. And some of those moments in some of those places were very extreme, there's no doubt about that. But you just do it. That is the business of performance and being on the road and being a band, and making that night as though it would be the last night – some of those gigs did occasionally feel a little bit like that *would* be the last night, with armed police surrounding the place, the plumbing works failing, the air conditioning being off and so on.'

Just after the final Stagedoor show the band welcomed on board a roadie who would stay with them for thirteen years and eventually become their production manager. Michael Lippold had worked for four or five years as a docker on the notoriously violent Melbourne waterfront. His brother was a roadie and Michael went to work with him and learned the ropes with various Melbourne bands. When he was asked to work a night for the Oils, he didn't really know of the band. 'The first thing I noticed was a mike stand, and that the guy tuning the monitors was standing on a box to reach it. I said, "What the fuck's going on?" and all anyone would say was, "You'll see." They weren't just putting sandbags in the drum kit, they were fucking nailing it to the stage! But no one would say anything. So the set-up was finished, and when I came back for the gig it was packed, which was pretty amazing. So I started to think they were a big band. Then they came on. Halfway through the first song I shit myself! "What the fuck is going on here? They're destroying everything!" I didn't know who was worse: the audience or the band. I was on the side of the stage and it was like warfare. I was trying to fix things, trying to stop things falling over – I'd never seen anything like it in my life.

The band had a crew of four guys – one each for lighting, stage monitors, front-of-house sound and on stage. Michael was the stage guy. He had done lighting and stage previously, but nothing like that first gig with the Oils. 'People weren't trying to tear down stuff that I'd spent all day putting up!'

'After the gig they asked whether I'd like to do some more shows with the band, and I said, "I'll need some time to think about it – I'm still not sure what happened!" Because it was frightening. OK, perhaps I should have worked it out from the nails in the drum kit, and maybe I could have worked something out from the ten-foot microphone stand, but still. Nothing prepares you for it. If you've never seen them or know nothing about them, nothing would ever prepare you. So anyway, I got in the truck and off we went – I didn't get back for six weeks. Constance said, "The band want to offer you a retainer." They would give me a hundred bucks a week if I promised to come back and work for them. They had first option on my services.'

Zev Eizik was managing the band at that stage and paying the bills. Michael remembers an early lesson from him. 'Zev was awesome. I've got nothing but good things to say about Zev. I remember once being in his office and he shafted me – financially. But while he was shafting me he was explaining to me how he was doing it, how I'd left myself open to it, and how in this business it would continue to happen to me if I didn't watch out. But unapologetically he shafted me! I walked out shafted, so it cost me money, but I really felt like I'd learnt something – I felt really good about it. Zev was a master.'

The band regularly did huge national tours, such as Advance Australia Where in 1980 and the Scorching of the Earth in 1981, each one trying to reach as much of the country as possible. Connie: 'We went to South Australia, we did the Top End, we went to Cairns and Darwin, and we *drove* to all those places! I saw Australia this way. The boys wanted to drive to Perth, but I said, "No way I'm driving across a desert, three days in a car, with you guys. I love you, but – no!" We ended up flying. I made them fly coz I said they'd be totally stuffed when they got there if they drove and we had six nights booked in a row.'

The band also drove around Australia as a way of saving money, but after two tyre blowouts in one week in hire cars at about 140 kilometres an hour – first on the Hume Highway between Melbourne and Sydney and then on the Pacific Highway on the way to Brisbane – they were forced to reconsider the wisdom of this policy. Pete was also accumulating several hundred dollars' worth of speeding fines, and eventually lost his driver's licence. It was an occupational hazard of Australian rock'n'roll at the time: all the members of Cold Chisel had lost their licences in the space of one trip to and from Melbourne; they subsequently bought a Range Rover and had it fitted out with airline seats to be driven around by their tour manager. But Pete doesn't like to be a passenger. He loves to drive almost as much as he loves to surf, and does both with the same sort of energy and enthusiasm. He always drove when the Oils travelled and was generally extremely safe. He would drive to Sydney overnight after a show in Brisbane or Melbourne, with the rest of the band sound asleep all the way. He has had no serious accidents in around three decades of driving, and even when he had to deal with the high-speed blowouts – which woke the band up very quickly – he successfully brought the vehicle to a standstill.

As a result of Pete not having a driver's licence I was asked to drive him and Martin the three-and-a-half-hour trip south-west to a gig in Canberra, leaving Sydney on a Friday afternoon. We were running late and hadn't even made it through inner-city Newtown when I had a minor brush with another vehicle. Fortunately it was unoccupied and stationary at the time. I wanted to own up to what I'd done, but after plenty of encouragement/insistence from my passengers I drove on. Getting at last through the outer Sydney suburbs and onto the relatively open road I pushed my dull-metallic-green HK Holden as much as I dared. Alas, the speed was too much for the Goulburn police a couple of hours later. Their siren made me think immediately of the crime scene in Newtown as they pulled me over and made me get out of the car. While they checked my details on their radio they questioned me about my companions. 'In a band' turned out not to help the situation, and I was made to sit in the back seat of the police car while they drove all the way back to Goulburn. Pete – despite not having a licence – was forced to follow driving my car, because Martin didn't know how to drive. Precious time was ticking away as Pete and Martin and I sat in a holding area at the police station while further enquiries about my past were made. Eventually they produced a list of unpaid parking fines that came to almost $200. As luck would have it Martin had exactly 200 in his pocket – apparently an unspent clothing allowance from Gary – and we were able to be on our way, slowly – well, quite slowly. I got them to the gig, but they missed the sound check by two hours and went virtually straight on stage.

There were plenty of shows in Zev's hometown of Melbourne, where healthy support from the small but influential community radio station 3RRR ensured the band had a growing cult profile. They had virtually no airplay on commercial radio from the first two albums, and it was not until they did their first recording session with Giffo for the 1980 *Bird Noises* EP that their music was heard by the wider community. Ironically it was the most atypical of their songs, the gentle instrumental 'Wedding Cake Island', that first made it onto the major radio stations.

The government-owned but independently minded Double Jay (2JJ) had been the band's sole source of regular airplay in Sydney, and they were about to start the move towards a larger audience with better coverage by moving to the FM band. In celebration of the end of Double Jay and the start of Triple Jay (2JJJ-FM), a big concert was staged at Parramatta Park. It was a stinking-hot January day. There were big crowds around the harbour for a ferry-boat race, and several thousand turned up at the Sydney Cricket Ground to see New South Wales play Victoria, but out in the city's west there were over 40 000 at the Last 2JJ Concert Circus. There was a big line-up of mainly 'm' bands, it turned out – Machinations, Matt Finish, Mondo Rock, the Radiators and Moving Pictures – and Midnight Oil. There were special rail concessions; sixty cents could get you a return ticket to Parramatta from anywhere in the Sydney suburban area.

By the time the Oils came on most people had been in and out of the Parramatta River a couple of times and it was like a huge hippy festival. There were assorted stalls for food and fashions and various amusements to do with the circus. There was a high-wire act with a motorbike – the Globe of Death – and the whole show was quite an extravaganza, in an amazing setting. Michael: 'I remember standing on that stage and I swear there must be a little hill there, because it looked like the crowd went back to the horizon and actually dipped over the horizon. They had this steel ball with a motorbike in it, right in front of the stage, and that fucking crowd was just awesome! That was a great show, the biggest one I'd ever done.'

Soon after the last Double Jay concert the band did what turned out to be a significant gig at Selinas in Coogee, one of the biggest of the beer barns on the south side of the harbour. In the audience of almost 3000 was Glyn Johns, famous producer of the Rolling Stones, the Beatles and the Who. The gig almost didn't happen due to a last-minute imposition by the venue of a 'no T-shirts' rule – every patron had to be wearing a collared shirt. When the band found out, their first thought was to cancel the show, but then someone suggested getting some shirts and giving them away at the door. So that's what they did. Michael: 'They were only Kmart or Target shirts with a bad stencil on them, because it had to be done really quickly, but the band were like that – generous to the fans.'

Glyn probably didn't need a giveaway collared shirt to get in, but he was impressed enough by the show to ask whether

INSTANT RELIEF

the band would go to London and record their next album with him. Rob: 'He saw us as a combination of old and new, as he told us in the Sebel Townhouse later. I think he could hear the energy of other bands like the Stones and the Who and people he'd worked with over the years, but also hear all this new "punky stuff". He was aware of what was happening but he hadn't, up until then, been part of it. He wanted to be part of it.'

Before Michael arrived the band had struggled with security – people were forever jumping up on stage from the crowd. It was easy to understand their excitement, and Pete dealt with them patiently, sometimes enthusiastically. Usually they had a bit of a dance, sang a shared chorus if they were lucky, and then were lowered back into the throng below or ushered to side stage. When the band played at venues that included stage security as part of the deal, the invaders were occasionally treated very roughly, sometimes being thrown headlong into the dancing bodies a couple of metres below. One incident, captured for posterity on the *Best of Both Worlds* live DVD, sees a bouncer do just that during 'Power and the Passion' at the Capitol Theatre. Maybe it was because he'd just sung 'Sometimes you've got to take the hardest line', but Pete grabbed the bouncer by the scruff of the neck and yanked him nice and close so he could be heard. The chewing-out lasted quite a while, but Pete only admits to saying, 'Don't treat our fans like that.' The humbled bouncer left the spotlight and was seen only fleetingly again. Bad behaviour by security staff at the established venues was one of the reasons that led to the band banning twenty-two of those venues during a three-year period and one of the reasons they started to favour one-off events.

These big one-off events had their own problems, like the night at Caves Beach, but usually Michael or Pete was able to nip potential incidents in the bud. Each was on the lookout for bad behaviour that impinged on other people's enjoyment. Pete was well known for going into the crowd to investigate. 'I think in the first five years I went in a fair bit just to sort people out and remind everybody we were trying to do something different. We were trying to have people come into the performance experience with the band, to be as physical as they wanted to be, but also to think about the other people who were there – smaller people, women, whatever. And we were also trying to train security guards as well not to be violent towards people. I've always had a concern about the welfare of the crowd.

'I've always felt it was partly our responsibility – it's partly theirs, of course – but partly our responsibility to try and shape the whole way people rub shoulders with one another in that environment. And certainly it's obvious that there was a tradition, particularly in the early days, it's kind of a male tradition, to come to a place, jump up and down, step on people if necessary, and if someone disagreed with you then punch them or whatever. And they would want to take on security, or security would want to take them on, and an Oils show was never meant to be a gladiatorial spectacle. In order to show that, I spent a few years down there just whispering in people's ears, convincing them, and whispering in security guys' ears as well.'

Sometimes he had to get a little physical. 'Well, I can

remember some instances. I never flattened anybody, I don't think. But I think I frogmarched a few, and twisted a few little ears and marched them out. But it's a funny thing, up to about 5000 people, if there was someone in that crowd who was a malevolent force for some reason, I was like a heat-seeking missile – I could spot them straight away. They were so tightly packed in. I used to jump in, but not launch, and as I was going to jump or step down a little bit of room would be made.'

Jim: 'Pete would always get into crowd control, doing his own security, putting the lights on someone who was creating a problem. We always had a pretty good line on that – Pete would always do it! He'd wade into the crowd to try and sort things out. There were so many gigs we did where the conditions were just abominable – people pressed up against the barrier, fainting – we were passing out water and stuff.'

When Michael arrived he was often involved in defusing violent situations, but Pete would still go into the crowd if he had to. Michael: 'A lot of times he'd go in just because he saw it and I couldn't. And he'd see it, and if it was getting hot and he didn't have time to tell me he'd just jump in. Any time I was in there the crew were always watching me, I knew that, but he was always watching me too. And he'd come in a couple of times to help me. I don't know if he could fight, but he was frightening. I remember we took these guys on in New Zealand. We didn't want to fight them, but we were standing watching this brawl go on and after a while he said, "You're right, Michael, let's go." And off we went. It was outside after a gig, and we grabbed these guys. I grabbed mine, he was giving this guy a savage kicking, and I fucking stopped him. And then Garrett grabbed this other guy who was giving the father of this young bloke a kicking in the front yard of this house. And the guy that Garrett stopped turned round to throw a punch and just looked at him and shit himself! He'd never seen anything like it. But yeah, he would go in, he had no fear, he was pretty courageous.'

'There was a night at Cronulla Workers, they had a high stage. Garrett would send me off, he would spot trouble and he'd send me in there: "Michael!" "What? You want me to die?" So I'd jump in off the stage, and they were about ten foot out, so I had to take quite a leap off the stage so I could land right in the middle of them. With the Oils' crowd you couldn't fight your way through so you had to try and land right in the middle of the trouble. That was really effective coz you'd come from nowhere and you'd just land in the middle and "Waaah!" and then you'd disappear. But I knew I was in trouble when I passed these guys, surfies, and they weren't wearing shirts, and I passed their chests, their jutting chests, and my feet still hadn't hit the ground – I was still travelling. And I'm thinking, "Fuck, I'm in trouble!" I hit the floor and I'm looking at all these chests, and they're big fuckin' healthy surfies and I'm right in the middle of about half a dozen of them. So I just went "Waaah!" into this guy's chest, "If ya want to fuckin' fight then don't come back!" and then I was gone. I couldn't get out of there quick enough. I was a fucking leprechaun talking to the giants, trying to frighten them. They behaved themselves then, but only because I don't think they knew what had happened.

'I learned to be a roadie in the pubs of Melbourne, and we fought every fuckin' day. So I had no fear either. I'd jump in so fuckin' hard, lay the rave about peace – "The band's into peace, so get cool or get the fuck out of here" – and they'd behave themselves. If I had to go back a second time I'd take them out. I mean, take them out— outside.'

Another memorable night was when the power went off at the Manly Vale Hotel. Michael: 'It used to hold about 2000 people, a big barn. They were selling the beer in six-pack coolers, which is a bad idea. Cans, really bad – but that's how you bought beer at the bar. I remember the power went, not just the gig, but the whole fucking suburb. That was us. Apparently we blew the sub board off the wall in the hotel. I don't know why. It was dangerous – 2000 drunken surfies, in the dark. The Manly Vale manager said, "We've got to make some kind of announcement to calm them all down." So I said all right and went out with a torch and the two of us walked into centre stage – bad idea! The torch was the only light and there were 2000 punters drinking six-packs of cans, OK? You know where this is going, don't you? They only had one thing to aim for – my torch. I remember standing next to the manager, he's on my right in the dark. I grabbed his arm. "Here you go. I'm off. See ya later!" I gave him the torch and I'm gone. The microphone didn't work coz the PA was out, so fuck that! I knew my way round the stage in the dark – and he didn't. So he had to cop the cans even as he went off. That was a great gig, that one. They eventually got it going again, but it took a long time, a good forty-five minutes. It was a fuckin' long time, but no one went. They got bored throwing things, though.'

After a while people got to know Michael, and together with Pete he ensured that most gigs were trouble free. The band *were* into peace despite the physicality of it all, and so for the most part was their crowd. Generally the Midnight Oil crowd was a huge, friendly, surging mass and into whatever the band delivered. Pete: 'That's probably why I stayed performing as long as I did, because I respected them, I was exhilarated by them. We were in the company of a bunch of other people I didn't really know, yet we were able to make a connection. I think it was very loyal, basically friendly – although not necessarily to our support bands! It was out of the realms of everyday experience, in that environment.'

As the eighties got under way the band shifted up a gear. They had Zev, they had Connie, they had Michael, they had Chris Plimmer, and they had Giffo. In May 1981, after another quick tour of New Zealand, the band headed for the UK. They managed two sell-out nights at the prestigious but small Marquee Club despite having no record company support and very little promotion. They did their own handbills and postering.

Mostly they were in England to take up Glyn Johns's offer to produce the next album. *Place Without a Postcard* was a celebration of their live playing. There was a minimum of studio effects and a concentration on capturing the first takes as Glyn attempted to catch that Selinas magic. Songs like 'Don't Wanna Be the One', 'Armistice Day', 'Written in the Heart' and 'Lucky Country' immediately became live favourites back in Australia.

A particularly memorable rendition of 'Written in the Heart' occurred a month prior to the album release during the band's headlining performance (with Split Enz) at a big two-day festival at Tanelorn, a hamlet a couple of hours north of Sydney. It was a sea of tents and humanity and there was a cloud of dust in front of the biggest canvas, the roof of the stage. As the band walked into the backstage area the Sunnyboys were playing 'Happy Man' and the crowd seemed in full tribal mode. A few hours later, well past sunset, and the temperature had dropped. It had become a cold night and many of the several thousand people had blankets and several open fires had been lit for warmth. When the band took to the stage Pete was wearing a lumber jacket and a beanie. The beanie remained on for quite a few songs, but eventually the heat or the mood moved him and he pulled it off. The crowd seemed to take a collective deep breath: there was steam absolutely pouring off his head. As he moved he left thick wispy streams of steam behind – he was smoking. When he stood still it just looked— primordial.

In early 1982 Midnight Oil, in association with Triple Jay, organised the Wanda Beach Youth Refuge gig. Twenty thousand fans attended and again it was a magnificent outdoor setting. Behind the stage were the sands of Wanda Beach and the ocean. The sky was putting on a show as well, with some lightning, and there had been quite a bit of rain during the support bands. By the time Midnight Oil were meant to play, the canvas roof was sagging with water in a couple of places and equipment was under threat of being soaked. There was a problem actually getting the band plugged into the PA system. Michael: 'The electrical distribution box on the stage for all the power was full of water. I got the stage manager who worked for Jands [the production company] and I said, "Here, plug that in" and he said, "You plug it in", and I said, "Nah, it's your power, you're the one who's saying it's safe, you part the water and plug that fuckin' thing in there. Coz that's what you're going to have to do – that's gonna have to go underwater to get plugged in – and I ain't touchin' it! And all those other plugs in there, what are they powering? Coz I ain't touchin' them either." And he said, "It shouldn't be like that." And I said, "That's exactly my point." Somewhere along the line I think I did advise the band that it wasn't safe. And I think I may have used as evidence the fact that the distro box was full of water, and there were things turned on in there, and they were connected to it. And that ain't good! So yeah, I think they were warned. Yeah, Wanda Beach probably was dangerous.' That night the band flew to New Zealand to play the legendary Sweetwater Festival.

Soon they were thinking of a new record and again looking to England as the place to record it. Gary had reappeared and this had led to friction with Zev. There was much discussion about tactics regarding living and working overseas, and Gary's view seemed to be more in line with the band's. Zev offered his resignation and it was accepted. Connie stayed with Zev at ACE but she had become a much-loved part of the band, so when ACE was winding down after a hugely successful U2 tour a year or so later she returned to work with Midnight Oil. 'Both Gary and Zev were very good managers, but Zev and I were more like partners when we were working with the Oils in the early days – Gary is Gary, he manages the band. I was just the road manager then.'

The band weren't keen to jump straight back into Gary's arms, though, and for quite a while Pete and Rob were effectively managing the band. At this stage they had no record company deal and no official management, but were pushing forward with their plans to at least move the band to London and see what they could organise about a new record once they got there. In May 1982 Pete wrote to promoter John Jackson in the UK, saying that the clubs being considered for the proposed London dates weren't quite right – the Zig Zag Club may be too large and Dingwalls too small. 'Our intention is to concentrate on a small scale in one place as a residency.' Also, 'in the absence of Zev Eizik please direct enquiries through Chris Plimmer, our Sydney agent. We will bring another non-playing band member with us when we come. He has previously worked with the band in a management capacity prior to Eizik and will act as representative for all business. His name is Gary Morris.'

Finding a producer wasn't hard in the UK once aspiring young Town House studios engineer/producer Nick Launay saw the band. He'd heard the *Postcard* album thanks to his Australian girlfriend and future manager and wife Nadya Anderson, who was an ex-3RRR announcer living in London and a big fan of the band. Nick had admired the Oils' musicianship but was involved in a whole different scene of punk and post-punk music. His most recent jobs had included albums for John Lydon, Gang of Four and Killing Joke. He had been working at Town House studios during the golden year of the Jam, XTC and Simple Minds, and was not really into Australian pub rock.

Gary had to spend quite a bit of energy creating interest in the band's forthcoming gigs (which ended up being at the larger Zig Zag Club), and Nick got caught up in it. 'I remember being at the Town House and there was all this talk about Midnight Oil. Hugh Padgham had been asked to produce them because he'd just done the Police album. He was going to the gig and Nadya was going too coz she loved the band, so we all went and saw them play at . . . an old theatre, it shut down after a while, might have been the Zig Zag Club, quite a big venue. All these record producers were there, all these people I knew were there. So obviously Midnight Oil had done a really good job in getting the word out that they were about to make an album, and there was a bit of a vibe. I watched them and I thought they were amazing. I remember thinking, "This isn't my kind of music, but . . . !" I was just blown away by the performance. It had all this guts and stuff and I thought, "How come their album *Place Without a Postcard* was so straight and professional?" when here's this band as raw as guts, the singer is going off, and it's all mayhem. They were kinda punk, in their own way. They didn't have punky hairstyles and clothes, but what they were putting out was totally punk. It was in your face and all the songs were really fast and noisy and great guitar sounds and they were loud and the audience was going crazy. So I was like, "Wow. This is good. I like this."'

Nick ended up producing the extraordinary *10,9,8,7,6,5,4, 3,2,1* album, which changed the profile of the band back in Australia forever. It stayed in the Australian charts for over two years but was largely unavailable in other countries at the time.

Before leaving the UK the band, through Glyn Johns, accepted the offer of a spot supporting the Who in Birmingham on the opening night of their world tour. Midnight Oil played in front of 11 000 initially wary Who fans but eventually won them over. The Who were impressed, too, and offered the band the support spot on their fifty-six-date tour of the USA. After several days' debate they turned down the offer. This was the first of the band's so-called missed opportunities. Their discussion involved considering whether touring without a record available was a good idea, especially since they would have to delay schedules for their Australian tour and the release of the newly recorded LP. The band loved the Who, and the high-level exposure to the huge Who audiences could have been significant, but they had been away from home for almost six months.

Jim, in particular, was determined not to. 'I really wanted to go home. We'd been away for months in England, living there and then changing our plan from living there and playing there to recording there. Then the plan to go straight to the States and do this huge Who tour. But we had no record company over there, and there wouldn't have been any tour support as far as I know. We would've been chasing around after the Who in their Lear jets with our little band and I didn't fancy it, I just wanted to go back to Australia. And I really pulled it big, I really spat the dummy and said, "Look I'm not doing it. I'm going home." And I fucked it for everybody.'

On the other hand, Rob was in favour. 'At the time I thought we should have done it, but I was acutely aware that I was the big Who fan in the band and that maybe I was letting that interfere with my judgement as to whether it was the right time to do it. The match of those two bands, Midnight Oil and the Who, was certainly a lot closer than some of the other tours we did later on.'

Of course, the band didn't realise they were on the verge of releasing their first hit record at home. When they returned from England they staged the remarkable Capitol Theatre shows, which grew from the proposed three nights to five and became one of the legendary stands of the band. The upper balcony had to be propped up between the first and second nights because of fears that the crowd's dancing would bring it down. Dancing on the balcony had to be forbidden for the rest of the run. That didn't stop the ground floor going crazy, as the film footage that survives ably illustrates.

When *10–1* was being recorded the band were in dire financial straits, but by the time they came to play the songs live back in Australia 'US Forces' was being played on commercial radio, the album had gone straight to the number one spot, and some of the financial pressures were off at last.

Gary was back on the scene but only in a relatively unofficial capacity, mostly just advising or giving his opinion. The band had felt dissatisfied by how things had gone with Zev. They felt they had lost a certain amount of control and Zev had been taking the band into an area that had more to do with top-heavy industry than building it up from the street – the way Gary and the band had done previously. Gary's input for the Zig Zag shows had been appreciated and things had gone pretty well for the Capitol shows – Gary had coordinated the event plus two film crews. 'Pete invited me down to the Moomba Festival in Melbourne and on the side the band said, "Do what you want to do. If you want to give a hand, give a hand." So I walked on the stage during the set-up and saw a lot of stuff going down which was pretty sort of loose and untogether and I just started stepping in and giving my opinion – and got everybody off side. Michael Lippold and the road crew were off side. I think that was the first time I met him. He wanted to work out a way to break my legs!'

Michael: 'I was voted to neck him. The crew got together and said, "He's got to go." He just turned up at the Myer Music Bowl Stop the Drop and tipped everything upside down. No one had said boo or "We've got a new manager". I said, "Listen, Gary, the crew think you're fuckin' insane, you're terrorising everyone, and basically . . . I've been told to neck you. So we've got to work things out. You're obviously the manager of the band or something, apparently – it was someone else yesterday, but anyway . . ."'

Gary: 'At that time I had no intention of getting involved with the band again. It was like, "Just one for old times' sake, do your thing". So I did my thing.'

Gary had a couple of ideas. According to Michael it was Gary who suggested the exploding dummy. 'He said, "During 'Read About It' Garrett's going to sneak off stage and you're going to run out with this life-size mannequin of Garrett wired with explosives. And this guy hiding behind the amp line – an explosives expert – is going to blow it up."

'So the plan is when the lights go out in "Read About It" and it goes all black, Garrett sneaks off the stage, I race out with the dummy, race back off, Rob hits the drums, lights go on, and bang! Garrett explodes. And I said, "Well, there's a problem" and he said, "What?" and I said, "Well, it's fucking daylight out there." "It'll be dusk," said Gary. "Dusk ain't dark, Gary. It's still broad daylight, we're outside – we can't make it dark. OK, it's broad *dusk*light, but it's still not dark! These people are going to see me with the mannequin, you know that, don't you? And how's the six-foot-ten guy gonna sneak off stage? They're gonna notice. He does all this jumping around to attract their attention and then he's just going to disappear, in the dusklight? Gary – you're fucking insane!"

'So I went to the band, and I said, "Look, this guy is fucking out there! I don't know who he is, or what he's got organised, but do something about him." "Oh well," they said, "you've got to understand Gary's different." "Different!" I said, "He's fucking insane, and he won't listen to anyone!" So that went on all afternoon, discussions about this. So we do the show. It comes up to "Read About It", near the end of the set, and it's fucking daylight, mate! So I'm standing side stage with the dummy all dressed up like Garrett and it's got all these wires trailing off behind it. So "Read About It" gets to that spot where the music stops, and Garrett walks off – because there's no point in sneaking, is there? It's daylight! And I say, "Do I have to do this?" "Yeah, yeah," says Gary. So I go out and put the fucking thing leaning up against the microphone. I'm not down low or anything, what's the point – I'm not invisible. These people can see me, and I've got family out there and they're watching me embarrass myself! I go to walk away and the thing falls over. So I catch it, and try again, go to walk away again, and it falls again. So I grab it for the third time and I turn around to the guy behind the amps – all I can see are Kilroy eyes – and I go, "Blow it!" And the guy is going, "Oh nooo" and shaking his head. And I go, "Blow the fucking thing!" "No!" "Blow it – trust me, I'll get away. Just blow it!" So I'm standing there having this argument with him, screaming, all in front of thousands of people, yelling, "Blow it up! Now!" So he blows it. I go to move and it goes "Phssst!" and this little bit of smoke comes out from under one armpit. The whole thing is supposed to blow apart! So I just push the thing over and walk off in a huff, shaking my head and going, "I don't fucking believe it."

'Now, for the encore, it was Gary's idea to bring Garrett down on a rope playing the guitar for "Wedding Cake Island". Well, he got fucking stuck up there, didn't he! High enough to make it an interesting jump down with a guitar, but low enough that you couldn't hide him. Perfect, neither here nor there, and me underneath going, "Throw me the guitar and jump down." And he's starting to spin! Gary Morris's first day on the job. Yeah, I worked for that man. And nothing ever changed from that day on. That's the way it was with Gary – every day, always something. You'd be forever walking into a gig, anywhere in the world, and saying, "I'm really sorry about the people I work for." Coz you'd see their eyes roll and they'd say, "This guy just rang and . . ." I'd say, "Don't tell me – Gary? Look, I apologise, for whatever it was. Let's work it out."'

By the time of the Melbourne Stop the Drop show *10–1* had been on top of the charts for two months and 'US Forces' had become the band's first radio hit. But rather than cashing in, they used their huge profile to stage yet another big outdoor benefit gig. This time it was Sydney's turn, where the band organised and headlined a show called Jobs – Every Home Should Have One, at Penrith Park in the western suburbs. Like the Melbourne show it raised about $45 000, this time for youth centres and refuges for the unemployed.

Then there was the unannounced New Year's Eve gig at Mulawa women's gaol. They were doing almost anything, it seemed, except conventional gigging. The Mulawa gig was almost called off. There had been trouble during the day and one wing of the prison was being denied the opportunity to see the band. One woman had apparently attempted suicide;

the sirens had gone off. The crew set up the band's equipment on a small concrete loading bay. There was a 10-metre stretch between the 'stage' and a 2.5-metre wire fence. Behind the fence the girls were separated into three groups by more wire fencing – the bad girls, the really bad girls and the girls so bad that you weren't allowed to talk to them. Through the fencing one of the women told me Chrissie Amphlett from the Divinyls had been there a few months back – as an inmate. 'Paying off parking fines. I got a lot of good writing done in there,' Chrissie told me some years later. I was the only person between the band and the wire fence, alone on the dance floor, but closest to the bad girls. One of them asked me to dance when the first song started, and I soon found myself dancing with a whole cage full of gyrating women. My sweaty T-shirt could have bought me anything, but no offer would convince me to part with it – I definitely wasn't going bare-chested in that environment! The crew all went home shirtless, but refused payment. Michael in particular found the whole exercise depressing. It was a full-tilt gig, but weird, and not the wild knees-up that 'New Year's Eve at a women's gaol' might imply.

It was during the latter part of 1982 that Gary was formally accepted back on board and became the band's official sixth member. 'When I came back we ignited a relationship with Sony and basically *10–1* was the first release out of that.'

Jim: 'As soon as Gary got back we got our mojo back, in a way. We made *10–1* and all lived together in St John's Wood as a group of people. He and Pete were trying to get the deal with Sony together.'

Back in Australia, band headquarters was established at Kangaroo Street, Manly, and for a time Gary shared the place with Giffo and Pete. When Pete moved out his spot was taken by Michael. With a view of the Pacific Ocean and a pet wallaby called Ruth it could have been idyllic, but there was never any food and most of the cupboards were filled with empty beer bottles. Michael remembers it fondly. 'We didn't do cooking or anything in the house – well, *I* never cooked anything there, ever. I saw Gary cook six chops once, on the griller, and I don't think he ever washed it! In the middle of the day, in the office, he just put six chops on a plate and ate 'em. That's the kind of house it was. No food in the fridge – none. It was a fun house, that.'

In the end the messiness of the place led to the cleaning lady throwing out several years' worth of press clippings that Gary had been keeping in a garbage bag. When Gary hired Stephanie Lewis as his assistant it was to try and re-source as many clippings as possible (not many) in an attempted cover-up. The band never found out. Gary needed a fulltime assistant as the band's affairs were becoming more complex. Stephanie kept things humming while attempting to satisfy Gary's various expectations, a job she managed to do extremely ably for the next couple of years.

Kangaroo Street was a hive of activity twenty-four hours a day: international stuff would come clicking through on the telex during the night to the sound of Michael and Giffo's drunken drum and piano lessons. Michael: 'We had the wallaby there – Ruth. I can remember a Telecom technician who came to try and fix the telex machine. It was about eleven o'clock and we'd just got up. He said, "Have you guys got a cat?" And we said, "Nah, nah, we don't have a cat, mate." The only time he'd seen the particular problem before was in an office that had a cat. Then the wallaby came out of the kitchen through Gary's office – boing, boing, boing, boing. "What was that!" he said. "Was that a kangaroo?" "Aaahh . . . yeah." Ruth had been pissing in the telex machine and had caused identical problems to the cat!

'We'd go down to the Manly Pacific Hotel and Giffo used to sew these bags and he'd have the wallaby down his jumper in a bag. We'd be leaning on the bar and all of a sudden this head would pop out. And wallabies look like rats when they're little and they've got no hair. This rat head popping out of Giffo's jumper! We had a lot of fun with that wallaby.'

Giffo: 'Gary picked Ruth up on the road somewhere – her mother had been killed. She was an orphaned black wallaby or swamp wallaby. I raised her on a teat. The girl who lived next door in Kangaroo Street worked at the zoo so she gave me information, and I raised Ruth to a fair size. It was a pretty good project. Once you've had one of those you wouldn't ever bother with a cat. They're quite unique, interesting things.'

Around that time the band flew to London for a big CND show at the Lyceum, and then home to the news that they would be the first local band to play at the newly completed Sydney Entertainment Centre. Their three-night stand there would complete an extensive national tour that included Darwin and Alice Springs for the first time. While up in the north, the band took a sidetrack to visit a friend. From Darwin they headed to south-east Arnhem Land to play at a tiny Aboriginal settlement called Numbulwar. The gig was arranged by Richard Geeves, Pete's friend and ex-bandmate from Rock Island Line who had driven the band's van on their first tour of New Zealand, who was teaching there. It was the band's first experience of remote Aboriginal communities. They loved Numbulwar and came back for another show three years later.

Shows generally were becoming further and further apart. In 1984 the *10–1* album, with virtually no record company support, went into the top 100 in the USA, so the band did a small exploratory tour before landing in Japan for the three months it took to record LP number five, *Red Sails in the Sunset*. The rest of that year was taken up by an extensive tour of Australia, mixed with Pete's exhaustive commitments as an aspiring NDP senator for the federal election. There were big shows all around the country, ending with the epic nights at the Hordern.

In early 1985 a show on Goat Island – an extraordinary and unique venue for a performance – was filmed and broadcast in honour of Double Jay/Triple Jay's tenth birthday. With the Sydney Harbour Bridge standing like a giant proscenium arch behind them and the afternoon sun reflected off the sails of the Opera House in the background, the band delivered a stunning show in a stunning setting. Several hundred lucky Triple Jay competition winners were on the island, and around half a million Australians experienced the event via televison and radio. Scores of young people literally risked life and limb by swimming across from Balmain Wharf through the shark-infested harbour waters to see the gig. The show is included on the *Best of Both Worlds* DVD.

Not long afterwards the band headed to France for their first European dates, the first of which was an outdoor event in Brittany with the Clash. They also headlined a gig at the Hammersmith Odeon.

From there it was on to the USA for a tour with UB40, who proved a contrast in not just musical style but also in how to approach live performance. Giffo: 'That tour really highlighted exactly how spot on and accurate and the same every show was that UB40 did. We used to write different set lists every night and we'd sort of taken it for granted that that's how you did it. But other bands are highly choreographed, highly organised and so polished that it's the same night after night. We wouldn't know what we were playing until Pete finished the set list five seconds before we went on stage! "Where's my set list?" The Boogie Queen is trying to get them all written out coz this is before the days of the photocopier or the printer; it was all textacolour and half a dozen sheets of A4 paper. Then you knew what you were playing. It had a sort of a formula – it started with a song and we did a few in a row, then a little bit where Pete waffled. It was never the same, but it had a structure to it. That kept everybody on their toes, including the audience. To me, that's the right way to do a show.'

They were home again briefly before heading back to the UK for some warm-up shows at the King's Head and then on to the famously muddy Glastonbury Festival – it didn't disappoint. On the local front they were hardly seen, apart from hit-and-run anonymous appearances like a night at the Antler as Ebb Tide and the Shorebreakers.

The band were always open to new stimuli and opportunities to do things differently, and as 1986 dawned, an idea to tour some even more remote parts of Australia took shape. The proposal was to travel into Central Australia and tour remote Aboriginal settlements. By July it was all organised, with the Warumpi Band from Papunya coming along as well. The Black

Fella White Fella tour took the Toyotas from Alice Springs and hit the road first at Mutitjulu near Uluru, then Docker River (official population 275), then Warakurna, Kintore, Papunya and Yuendumu – a journey of about 1000 kilometres over the roughest roads in the country. Then they drove back to Alice Springs before heading to the Top End for shows in Maningrida, Galiwinku, Yirrkala, Umbakumba, Numbulwar, Barunga, Wadeye (Port Keats) and Nguiu (on Bathurst Island, population 909). Unhappily it was the last major tour for the Warumpis, but for Midnight Oil it was to prove one of the most significant tours the band ever did.

Giffo managed to complete the tour and contribute to the recording of the desert-inspired *Diesel and Dust* album a few months later, but his health was suffering and the outback trip was virtually his last tour with the band. Giffo reflects on what he thought Midnight Oil's musical appeal was: 'There's some great playing goes on from some people in there, but we weren't highly polished musicians, we were just passionate guys kicking some arse. I think it was greater than the sum of its parts – there was just sort of a magical formula, and I think the live dynamic shifted a little bit when I joined. It became a bit tougher and a bit more driven along, and I think that helped the band to become more popular. But it also became a little simpler and not as quirky as when the Bear was playing. I don't think it was really obvious to any of us until after I left the band. I think then it was a bit clearer what my role was in it. There was sort of a dynamic that we all took for granted. When I went my own way I went to see a show at the Hordern Pavilion and Bonesy was playing and it was only then that I realised how good the band was. Once you're inside something you don't see it. I remember thinking, "Now I know why all these people come and see this band! I can see why it's so popular now."'

Pete: 'The early pub era was the most physically punishing because we were doing it really hard and they were really hot rooms. So by the time [you took into account] the condensation, the sweat, the beer and the foul air, and you'd driven from Brisbane the night before, and you had 1500 surfers in the Antler and the joint was like a little cartoon coz it was bulging at the sides – by about four o'clock the next afternoon I used to feel roughly human. We used to play at eleven or twelve at night in those days, so I'd have eight hours to sort of reconstitute my DNA, get all the molecules circulating in the right direction, and off we'd go again.'

But Giffo was right to leave. He was unwell with symptoms uncannily similar to Bear's. Many of the gigs in his last year he can barely remember, even the desert trip. 'I don't remember much about that, I was quite ill then. I was quite stressed out. It wasn't a very happy time for me. One thing I do remember about it was we were in swags out at Maningrida listening to the Warumpi lads playing a set. I was lying in my swag and the music was drifting across. We were quite a way away, a couple of hundred yards, maybe further, but it was just enough to hear it but not enough for it to be loud, and it was just so – suitable, and pleasant.'

Giffo badly needed the quiet life. Rob: 'It was bad for his physical and mental health. It seemed to me that Giffo was disappointed with almost everything he'd done. He had a very English, self-deprecating manner, not helped by his drinking, which probably made him more melancholy than usual. I think deep inside Giffo there's a real pride – and there absolutely should be. But in the end it was his decision that he couldn't tour, and I think that was partly because it looked like *Diesel* was really going to go through the roof and all Giffo could see, quite rightly as it turned out, was months and months of being by himself in hotel rooms, and I think perhaps he was instinctively afraid of what that might lead to. He was having "episodes". I think it was a survival reflex.'

When Nick Launay heard Giffo was leaving he was devastated. 'Apart from the rest he was a great person. My first thought was "What an idiot – they've just got there!" They'd just recorded this hit record. Now they were going to be flying around in luxury, life was going to be easy, tours were going to be easy. I heard he left because he didn't want to tour America; that was the big thing. He left this rock band at their peak who, for all intents and purposes, were going to get bigger and bigger, to go to Byron Bay and start a bikini shop? "What? What?!" But when you look back on it, he was there for absolutely the best years of Midnight Oil, before all the pressure started, and then went to hang with near-naked women and, from what I hear, has made a pretty good living out of it! And also, he's a rock star. He retired as a rock star – young! Who's the idiot?'

It was a tough job being in Midnight Oil, and once the new album was recorded it was going to get tougher. In some ways the psychological demands are more than the physical – or musical. Rob comments with typical modesty and erudition: 'There are hundreds of thousands of musicians around the world who are better players, better writers, than we are, all of us, but that's only one part of this . . . You actually have to somehow drag from deep within yourself the determination and savoir faire to do it every night, in the public gaze, in front of extremely demanding crowds.'

Pete: 'I think the primary thing was to feed off what was happening musically and to give the songs as much physical and emotional presence as you could summon up. And additionally, and over time this obviously became a bigger part of it, to establish a bridge for the people you were in front of and bring them into your world of performance, by going out to them and expressing yourself a little more fully than you would at a dinner party!'

David Fricke saw many shows over the years. 'The Oils could do slow material, they could do soft material, they could speak in whispered tongue, but you didn't go to see the Oils live for that – you wanted them to just pin you to the wall. If you knew enough about them, then that's what you wanted; if you didn't know anything about them, that's what blew your mind. So even though there were arcs within the show, you wanted to have your mind blown, and sweat. You wanted to sweat as much as Peter did, and that's really a traditional thing. In a sense they were a very traditional rock band. I always thought it was funny when the initial reviewers here in the US started referring to them as the Australian Clash and Australian political punks. I'm thinking, "These guys are the fucking Who – except there's more of them, and the singer doesn't look like Roger Daltrey!" There was nothing really normal about Peter's stage presence: he was extremely big, really bald and extremely physical, but in a way that was not at all sexy. And it wasn't meant to be. It was a very basic expression of how his body reacted to the music.

And, as abnormal as it was, it was also an expression of real sincerity because it wasn't an act: there was no pose to it.

'He was such an unusual front man that he became a truly *amazing* front guy. He broke a lot of rules just in terms of the way singers are supposed to pose, the way they're supposed to be sexy, the fact that they shouldn't be taller than everybody else in the band! It was not important to broadcast the meaning of a song with a particular physical gesture. That works for Springsteen, it works for Sting, and for Jagger, but Peter didn't need that, because there was so much literacy and so much content in the songs already. That quality really added so much to the band, because if they had had a more conventional singer, conventional-looking singer, never mind the voice, then they would have been an amazing rock band; with Peter it became transcendent, but in a very earthy way. Peter, physically and visually, was the focus of that because he wasn't planned. Jim and Martin are kind of low-key guys, you know, speak big with the instruments, Rob is singing in the back and he's one of the great physically visual drummers in the business, but still, they were around Peter; they were bringing the noise for him and he was sending it further out.'

Like David Fricke, Mason Munoz had been around a while and seen the best the world had to offer. 'Jimi Hendrix was my first concert. I think of all the bands I saw throughout the years – Robert Plant, he just stood there; Roger Daltrey swung the microphone but basically just stood there. When you go through the pantheon of rock and think about all the great front men, nobody moved like Peter. Mick Jagger dances, but then on the other hand he has a teleprompter on both sides of the stage to remind him what his moves are supposed to be.

Peter's performance was something that was totally spontaneous, totally uninhibited, just the coolest thing to see, and the coolest thing to experience. I think it was something that really drew people in. You should probably talk to David Fricke from *Rolling Stone*, but I think David's comment to me after we had dinner last year was "Without question one of the all-time great front men. Without question." Unique. It's just totally uninhibited and free form, and hypnotic, mesmerising – it's unforgettable. But would he have been that dynamic had he not been backed by that ferocious band? I don't know. I've got to believe that all those elements fed off each other.'

Rhonda Markowitz was also a seasoned rock'n'roll observer. 'For as many people as he frightened – and he does frighten people – that many and more were turned on and amused and thrilled and pleasantly freaked out by his stage presence. I'm trying to think of antecedents, but basically the first time I saw him it was like, "What the hell was that?" I think that was my general response and it made me laugh out loud – but with delight. I really thought of Pete as a one-off. I didn't see him like anyone who had gone before. In terms of other people who had that same kind of "thing", I can't think of anyone. There were a lot of people who gave their performance their all, kind of ripped their throats out and so on, but I don't see him as part of a continuum.'

When Pete was on stage it was hard to think of him as my friend: he was such a different character up there. It was still Pete, but such a focused yet wild version of him that it wasn't a side I ever saw anywhere else. While he was performing he was totally a creature of the stage. He commanded that area and did his thing to the maximum, and heaven help anyone who got in his way. Not that he was out of control, he was just big and moving fast. Rhonda: 'Basically there was always this tension where they were waiting to see him knock Jim or Martin into the audience – you were waiting for him to collide with them.'

David: 'You kinda worried that someone would accidentally crown him with a guitar head, because he was doing that Frankenstein hyperdance back and forth like in "Only the Strong" or any of the mad rockers, and he would go into that crazy sprint back and forth and circular things with the hands out.'

Michael: 'I only ran into him a couple of times, but fuck, you knew it! Knocked the shit out of me. I remember I went to his wedding and he got up on the fuckin' dance floor and when he got off I said, "You actually dance like that!" It's not a stage act. He nearly killed everyone on the dance floor! No wonder he wanted to be on stage – there would be no room for him on dance floors. Garrett on stage, yeah, he was fucking awesome.'

Pete: 'I always loved the time on stage, probably more than anything else. I felt that it was partly a privilege and partly a real – calling, to be able to make music and keep it real. I certainly felt that what Midnight Oil stood for was not compromising on its performance, as well as its views.'

Finding a precedent for the way Pete performs on stage is difficult and most people struggle to make comparisons – even Pete. 'I never had any real musical performing heroes at all. I liked music a lot, but there wasn't anyone that I – I think it just kind of happened partially on its own. I could *appreciate* some people and what they did. Obviously I appreciate people like James Brown, and Prince, they come to mind in particular. It's a natural feeling for me in where it wants to go. It certainly is heading towards as far as it can take itself – or it certainly did at times – as a performance. Performers who do that, who might include people like Henry Rollins, maybe Rob Younger, Iggy Pop, and maybe Jello Biafra as well, had that same physicality and engagement in the way they performed. But I think what we were on about was very different to those people.'

Pete was undoubtedly very active and unpredictable on stage, but he was usually pretty calm and serene at other times, especially just beforehand. He could prepare for a show lying flat out on the floor with plastic chairs piled high and precariously around him, surrounded by guitars being tuned and Rob doing nervous drum rolls on a rubber mat. It didn't seem an ideal place to relax before a show. There was an inevitable growth in the excitement and noise level around him, but Pete was committed to the time with his eyes shut. He was miles away. He says he was 'trying to dive down into the clear line between the music and the singing and the stage experience, and shutting out all the other things that might be distracting. I didn't prepare myself for performance by doing scales or any of that stuff that people do. I was more interested in just trying to make the vessel I inhabited only be afloat on the sea of music and movement and word – not having anything else as an obstacle in its path.'

Midnight Oil didn't often play with bigger acts, certainly not in Australia, where it seemed to them that everyone fawned over visiting bands no matter what their quality or status. A show in Brisbane with the Ramones was the only exception. Overseas, apart from supporting the Who, it was a similar story. But the Oils did accept an invitation to co-headline a WOMAD tour of the USA with Peter Gabriel. *Diesel and Dust* producer Warne Livesey, despite loving the band, expected them to be overshadowed by Peter Gabriel's state-of-the-art production and performance. 'I'm a big fan of Peter Gabriel, so we watched his set and it was really awesome. He has great musicians playing with him and all this stuff going on, all these videos happening and great lights, back projection, and hidden cameras attached to his head, all the things that Peter Gabriel can have. He did really well and got an amazing reaction out of the crowd, but when the Oils came on it was a different level entirely – they absolutely slayed the place. They just blew the place away. And I thought, "That sums it up: these five guys can come on and do a pub rock show to 15 000 people and blow away one of the most expensive productions from one of the most talented people in the music business." That to me is the Oils: they don't need any gimmicks. There's just something about them, and they're not like any other band of that nature. Five people locking together in a live performance. They are one of the best live acts that has ever been around.'

The period when Giffo was in the band is generally regarded as the powerhouse years, but there was never a time when Midnight Oil weren't an absolutely full-tilt act dedicated to delivering the sum total of everything they had. When Bones took over the bass playing role he didn't shirk the task either. 'People ask what a Midnight Oil gig is like and I say get a pair of Doc Martens and tip the water out of the fuckers after a show. That's what it's like. It's not just being moist under the armpits, you know; you work your arse off – every night. We don't go up there and just go through the motions; otherwise we would have stopped doing it. The band lashed out and did its stuff night after night – for years and years and years.'

four

crossing the bridge

The band had already been led through a couple of levels of security in getting from their dressing room to the stage marshalling area. They were still in the concrete bunker under the stadium, but were now within sight of the passage that would take them up onto the stage. A global audience of almost four billion awaited them, plus 120 000 in the stadium and perhaps hundreds of thousands more at giant video screens around the city and the harbour. It was the closing ceremony of the 2000 Olympic Games.

The band were gathered with brass players Glad Reed and Kathy Wemyss to play 'Beds Are Burning', although the deal was, as is usual at events like this, that apart from Pete it was essentially a mime job – but at least the live brass would be heard by those close to the stage. There was only one live radio microphone and Pete had been issued with it in the dressing room. It was only a few minutes before show time and the band had yet to remove their black overalls to reveal the SORRY messages emblazoned on their shirts and trousers.

In fact, there was still debate about whether they were

going to go ahead with the SORRY statement. When the original offer to play had been made, they considered long and hard about whether to even accept the invitation, and as the band and Gary sat by a dry creek bed in central Australia discussing the offer they were seriously divided on the issue. Rob was the keenest and identified the key to convincing the others. 'If we could transcend just playing "a song" and pick "*the* song" that meant something, and put it in the right context. Gary got really excited about that idea, I think it might have been Gary who suggested, "Do a land rights song." Was it going to be "Dead Heart"? Was it going to be "Beds"? Once Gary was excited then Pete began to be swayed by it and got less positive that we *shouldn't* do it. Gary, I think, suggested the sorry-suits idea and it all snowballed from there. Having said that, it was only minutes before we actually went on and people were still debating it – in the bowels of the Olympic stadium.'

The band had had some sadness in the days and weeks before the show: Bones' father had been dying. 'It was a strange release for me – my father had died a few days before. I'd been overseas for the whole of the Olympic thing, my dad had a brain tumour and he couldn't recognise me. Giffo was on standby to do it; I didn't think I'd be back. It ran right down to the wire and I ended up turning up and doing it. We had rehearsals out in western Sydney in some industrial park on a thirty-eight degree afternoon. Pete wasn't there, actually, a roadie stood in for him for the camera shots and so on. I just sort of hung around Kylie Minogue. She was a babe – I just needed some comfort. She's a good person.

'On the actual day we went out at seven in the morning and were held in this large bain-marie area where the celebrities of

Australia were hanging around. It was a non-alcohol environment in case anyone went on the turps and screwed up their part. If you wanted to go to the toilet there was an usher who escorted you. They didn't want you to get lost in the elevator system or lose your pass or anything. It was the Olympics, man, it can't go wrong. All the extras, dancers, fly suits, birds, whatever they were. Like a really big Easter Show. We were just about to go to the stage to do our bit when Pete realised he'd left his radio-controlled mike in the dressing room – miles away! Classic Pete, actually. We still had the hard yakka dungarees on over the sorry suits so we didn't blow the SORRY concept. Walking out on stage it felt like a real family thing, it had an incredible warmth, an incredible vibe about it. And I'm really glad I was there to do it. Once you went out there, it was electric. Mega scale of things. We probably looked like ants on a pile of sugar. After the song I jumped off the stage and I think I molested a guy in a *Bananas in Pyjamas* suit and ended up among the Canadian athletes with a bottle of red wine – which I probably wasn't meant to do.'

Sitting in a little cave on Balls Head looking west down Sydney Harbour towards the setting sun it could easily be 1770, or 1492, or maybe 40 000 BC. All buildings and signs of 'civilisation' have been removed by the fast-failing light. People with white skin are unseen. The harbour and its bays and estuaries are alive with fish and the surrounding land is home to thousands of kangaroos and wallabies and several large family groups of Indigenous people.

Many visitors see modern-day Sydney as a paradise of sorts,

but in days past it was a very different paradise. To be born in the Sydney region meant a life not quite as difficult or harsh as further out in the bush or the desert. Food and resources were plentiful and, like Aboriginal society all over this huge island, life was rich with culture and ceremony. There were special places and special events – and special responsibilities to each other, and to the creatures, and to the incredible landscape. The men were especially responsible for the care and maintenance of the land, but with the arrival of white people came the beginning of the erosion of those responsibilities and the breakdown of traditional culture. The local people were driven out of the area and so began the 'sorry' times and a pattern of European expansion in Australia that mirrored the same insensitivities Europeans had visited on Indigenous cultures everywhere they went.

The members of Midnight Oil grew up in Sydney and had very little contact with Aboriginal people. Unless you lived in the inner-city Aboriginal enclave of Redfern, this was not unusual. Government policies were for the most part designed to sweep any remaining Aboriginal problems away, and certainly the media were not interested in Indigenous people unless it was their corroborees, or drunken brawls in outback towns. One of the first songs the band wrote about the situation was 'If Ned Kelly Was King', one of Jim and Pete's from the *Place Without a Postcard* album.

Three black boys sit in the corner
White woman waiting to talk
Lots of intention but no understanding

Ignorance was rampant, not just in the general community but in government at every level. Even the experts were ignorant. Partly this was due to lack of communication by Indigenous people about their culture; some of them even spread disinformation. To share things as precious and valuable as their ancient secrets and customs with people who, in their relatively short stay in this land, had done so much to earn the distrust of the locals must have seemed most unwise.

Aboriginal people made individual engagements with white society through relationships – business, sporting, personal and otherwise – with various degrees of success. On the *Red Sails in the Sunset* album Rob and Jim contributed 'Jimmy Sharman's Boxers', Rob's recollection of seeing the famous troupe of Aboriginal boxers that used to visit Sydney each year as part of the Royal Easter Show.

> *Fighting in the spotlight*
> *Eyes turn blacker than their skin*
> *For Jimmy Sharman's boxers*
> *It's no better if you win*

Another song of Rob and Jim's on that record, 'Kosciuszko', is concerned with the issue of misappropriation of Indigenous lands.

> *Older than Kosciuszko*
> *Driven back to Alice Springs*
> *Endless storm and struggle*
> *Marks the spirit of the age*

Gough Whitlam's government had reawakened our responsibilities to the country's original inhabitants. Some land had been symbolically handed back with the pouring of a handful of dirt from the prime minister's hand into that of an Aboriginal elder. The country now knew the right thing to do, but several years had passed since Whitlam and the process that had been started had stalled appallingly.

Midnight Oil played several Rock Against Racism gigs in the early days, often with Adelaide's groundbreaking Aboriginal band No Fixed Address. However, without direct contact with communities, it was only their heads that were aware, not yet their hearts. In 1983 they played at Numbulwar in southeast Arnhem Land and, despite its being one of the most isolated, protected and environmentally rich Indigenous settlements, it was still a shocking eye-opener for the band. The conditions were Third World at best, and the people's dependence on white society for food and shelter and medicine and law left them with a culture of divided loyalties and very little cohesiveness. The landscape was full of food wherever you looked. There were big crocodile prints on the river banks every morning, the mangroves were full of mud crabs and shellfish, the trees were overflowing with exotic birds and berries, and yet the place was also a mess of discarded western paraphernalia, from motor vehicles to disposable nappies. It was a nightmare nestled in paradise.

That same year a band from the central Australian desert settlement of Papunya recorded a groundbreaking song called 'Jailangaru Pakarnu' ('Out from Gaol'). The Warumpi Band were a bunch of shy local blokes who had joined with a young white teacher to play for fun and relaxation. Their mixture of country and rock with Indigenous words and locally relevant lyrics made them instantly popular and in demand in their local community. They started playing further afield and eventually made it to Sydney, where their culture shock matched that of the Oils' in Numbulwar. Like the Oils there was a mixture of awe and alienation that sowed the seeds of a larger quest. They wanted to communicate their message and tell their story, not only to the white communities who they could see did not understand, but also to other Aboriginal people in an act of solidarity.

Lead singer George (Djilaynga) was an energetic and flamboyant performer who was actually from the Top End but living in the centre when he teamed up with the others – Sammy Butcher on guitar and Gordon Butcher on drums, a floating population of bass players, and Neil Murray, the young white guy keener on his guitar than on his teaching duties. It fell to Neil to coordinate the rehearsals and the songwriting sessions, and keep the show on the road. Neil's book, *Sing for Me, Countryman*, chronicles many of the challenges and joys of this band's unique and distinguished career. Unfortunately, although they still manage to this day to occasionally get together and play, they stopped touring in July 1986. That was the date of the Black Fella White Fella tour with Midnight Oil through their home country and across the Top End of Australia.

Several months before embarking on that tour Midnight Oil had been asked by the traditional owners of Uluru (Ayers Rock on the old maps) to write a song for a film that was being made about the handing back of the rock to the local people. Bob Hawke's Labor government had facilitated slow but badly needed progress in several areas of Aboriginal wellbeing, and the documentary called *Uluru: An Anangu Story* was being funded by Film Australia. The Oils came in and saw the footage of the handing-back ceremony and basically went away and wrote the song 'The Dead Heart'. Heading again into Aboriginal land at Uluru to do a film clip for the song with Ray Argall re-stimulated the band's interest in more Indigenous contact, and before long the business of organising a tour of central and northern Australia began.

It was proposed that the Warumpi Band accompany them, and Gary thought the government minister responsible for Aboriginal affairs might help with the Warumpis' expenses. 'I had a meeting with Gary Foley, a leading Aboriginal land rights activist at the time, and put the idea to him. He said, "Look, here's Clyde Holding's contact, go and talk to him and tell him if he doesn't agree we're going to come banging on his door and give him a hard time. Here's Pat Dodson's number out at the Central Lands Council, give him a call, tell him I said blah blah blah." So I rang up Pat Dodson and said, "This is the idea, what do you reckon?" I spoke to the Warumpi Band guys and they were up for it. Then Pete and I went down to Canberra to meet with Clyde Holding and we nutted it out. Pete was really interested in the whole Aboriginal issue and wanted to know the political processes Clyde was going through at the time – that was very interesting. We came back to Sydney and followed it up. Clyde agreed to sponsor the Warumpi Band, ABC agreed to pay for the documentary and Midnight Oil funded its own costs. And we went out and did the Black Fella White Fella tour.'

The events of the tour are covered in a book called *Strict Rules* by Andrew McMillan, a journalist who accompanied them for the duration. Andrew's interest in Aboriginal culture and his appreciation of Midnight Oil's music makes for absorbing reading on many levels. His first-hand account of the local people's startled response to the frontal rock attack of the Oils, and how the band quickly learned to turn things down a little and listen to what was going on around them, is part of a wider picture of cultures gently clashing and coming together. His observations of Gary Morris in the wild are startling. Gary's acts of bravado and eccentricity often left members of both cultures open-mouthed – wading into crocodile-infested waters, wrestling with pythons and crashing insensitively through sensitive situations.

Charlie McMahon is a didjeridu player who has a metal hook replacing the arm he lost in an explosives accident as a teenager. He first jumped up and played his didj to 'Stand in Line' with the Oils one night at French's Tavern in 1978 and subsequently did so whenever the opportunity arose. In 1984 Charlie had joined the band for their very first dates in the USA, when they played eleven shows in a brief tour designed to meet the people in the major cities. Later in the year Charlie found himself on the spot when the nomadic Pintubi tribe was discovered in the Northern Territory. The first western music they heard was a cassette of Midnight Oil in Charlie's vehicle as he drove them into town. His regular job was in Central Australia working with Aboriginal communities building bores, so when the time came for the nuts-and-bolts aspects of the tour Charlie was the obvious choice. He coordinated the tour group's camping and guiding requirements and contributed plenty of common sense and a touch of sanity as well.

Trombonist Glad Reed was on the tour as a temporary member of the band, and she and Gary's assistant, Stephanie

Lewis, and Charlie contributed to the family feeling of the touring group. Glad and Charlie were among the very few musicians ever to augment the band's basic five-piece line-up. There was a brass player from New Zealand, Mike Russell (always known as 'Garfield' because of the cartoon image on the front of a pullover he wore constantly), who did a couple of American and European tours, and later there was keyboard player Chris Abrahams, but very few others. Jim: 'Glad was really good, and she could play some keyboards too. A really good presence, on stage and off.'

Glad was part of inner-city band Just A Drummer when I slipped a note under her Woolloomooloo door some time in 1986 saying the Oils needed a brass player. A few years later, when she and her partner, Dave Claringbold, were living in Normandy, France, with their new band, Red Ochre, she joined Midnight Oil on stage for two nights at the Zenith Theatre in Paris and also played in Red Ochre as the support act. She played and recorded with the band on several occasions, most notably on the 'Beds Are Burning' single, and in the performance at the 2000 Olympics, but her outback trip was as significant for her as it was for them all.

During the trip the band were invited to view sacred items and sites, and knowledge and views were exchanged. The two bands performed together every night and on one occasion changed places on stage mid-song by segueing from the Warumpis' 'Blackfella/Whitefella' into the Oils' 'Dead Heart'. When Giffo came on stage and plugged in and then Rob and Gordon Butcher swapped the drum-stool spot the song shifted seamlessly and broad grins broke out on the faces of the crowd seated in the dust in front of the stage.

Jim: 'When we were with the Warumpi Band we were all together travelling around as a bunch of people. I thought they were *really* good. Hearing them play out in the desert at Docker River for the first time, it just made so much sense what they were doing. They had a song called "Island Home", and I remember seeing George and Neil write it in Maningrida. I was on the veranda and they were sitting on the lawn playing with the sun setting over them; it was just gorgeous. Then they asked me to play a bit of organ on it, so for the last few shows, Yuendumu and then most of the nights on the Top End part of the tour as well, I would get up and play. Then they came down to Sydney to record it and it was the first time I'd been in the studio with anyone else. I was a bit nervous, you know, brought my little Emulator keyboard, threw it down on the console and just did it. I did it coz I really liked the people – I thought, "This is really good". From then on I always did stuff with Neil, helped him out with his various projects, produced one of his albums and always had some sort of hand in what he was doing. But something did go down in the desert between us all, and my relationship with Neil comes directly from that.' Giffo also contributed to the Warumpis' *Go Bush* album by playing bass on 'Island Home'. Jim was credited as Tjapanangka and Giffo as Bulangi.

Giffo had reservations about going into Aboriginal land. 'It's tough for the Aboriginal people, it's a terrible situation – they're living in tough conditions. You can't even offer a solution because it's one of those things that's already suffered from too much interference. In some ways I didn't feel we really belonged there, and I did say that I didn't feel comfortable being in their space. But it turned out well for everybody in the long run. The Oils became the champions of their cause. And we got a great album out of it. But in some ways I almost feel a bit guilty, it was almost like rape and pillage yet again. We get inspired to write a great album and it goes right up the charts, and what do they get out of it? Well, I guess firstly they got entertained and had a good time. They also got some serious support for Aboriginal issues. But we did get shit-canned by the *Sydney Morning Herald* and some others and I tended to think that was a tough one, you know. Should we have been there or should we not?'

Pete, however, was very sure that the band should have been there. 'I always felt that it was something that was very natural for us to do. That it was consistent with our own values, and that if we did it in a way that was genuine, then, notwithstanding the fact that Indigenous affairs and politics in Australia are pretty vexed at the best of times so there's always going to be choppy water, that we'd be able to bring something to the exchange, not just simply take something away. I had travelled up there before the other guys did, and had seen and felt that we would be welcome in these places – and we'd been invited. Half the thing was going back to Numbulwar for the second time. I went to Numbulwar four times in nine years, so it wasn't a case of it being a flavour-of-the-month thing from my point of view. I knew it was something that was embedded in our consciousness. It felt to me like if we weren't your classic stereotypical, flashy, narcissistic, shooting-to-the-top-of-the-pops, wine-women-and-song rock band – or parody of that – then what was our preoccupation likely to be? To go into the heart of the continent we had to go into our history, because it was so fresh and so recent that the worlds were very real for people, and inhabit that space for a while. Slim Dusty had been out there to play; he probably didn't carry it as far as we did in terms of rhetoric and albums, but what we were doing, to me, seemed to be consistent with what we were as a band and certainly how I felt about things.'

Rob was also sure the visit was done the right way. 'I remember at the time there was some lurking criticism by the cynics that there was a sense of exploitation by us going out and breezing through these communities and using what we saw and heard in a commercial way with the album that followed – that in some way we'd made a killing from our time out there. But our introduction to the desert was through an invitation by the folks out around the Rock to write a song about the handing-back of Uluru. The desert tour was conceived as a joint project between ourselves and the Warumpi Band. It included the people who really knew the desert, like Charlie McMahon and the members of the Swamp Jockeys, who later became Yothu Yindi. We actually went about it the only way that white people from the big cities could do it, and that was to try and represent as accurately as possible the sights and sounds and smells of a place we'd never been before.'

Michael Lippold was part of the two-man crew for the tour. 'It nearly killed us, that tour, but it was a great experience. I'd do it again. Pat Pickett and I worked our rings off on that tour. I did get a bad back out of it, which I'll have to live with for the rest of my life. I was doing lights, stage and monitors, Pat was doing front of house. We had no other crew, disgusting conditions to work under, but that's all right, that's where we were. We were the first to meet the blackfellas everywhere – we'd get into a place, get out of the car, get the football out and start kicking it and slowly kids would appear. We'd been up to Numbulwar before. On that tour I met blackfellas who had never met whitefellas before. It was a really good experience; it was really good for me. The Aboriginal people were really shy. I used to put the lights up, literally – I'd hang them from trees – and the blackfellas would stand where the lights finished. If the lights finished fifty feet from the stage they'd stand there. Very shy, but they loved the band. I got a much better knowledge of blackfellas. I did use racist language, I understand that now, and I've tried to tone it down, but I wasn't a racist. I'd just never had anything to do with blackfellas. It was a good experience.'

By the time they came back from the tour, 'The Dead Heart' was attracting considerable airplay and was at number four on the charts. This was great news for the people around Uluru who were to receive all the royalties from the record's sales. However, rather than cash in themselves with a few big shows or a tour of the capital cities, the band went straight to work writing songs inspired by their heart-opening few weeks away.

Nick Launay helped produce 'The Dead Heart' for the band before they went on the tour. 'They were doing "Dead Heart" as a charity record and I happened to be in Sydney at the time. I went into the studio and mixed it for them. They were struggling. They'd recorded it all themselves at Studio 301, but they couldn't get it to sound right. I didn't get paid anything because it was a charity thing, but they paid me later when they put it on the album – you know, the big hit album!'

Another person who heard the song in the studio in Sydney was David Fricke, on another of his treks down under. '"Dead

Heart" is basically an acoustic song with some French horn in it towards the end, but it's got this incredible locomotive drive. I thought, "Man, this sounds really weird and different, but boy, is it cool. This really rocks." It doesn't have blazing electric guitars in it, but the power! It doesn't just knock you over; it gets into your skin, and *then* it knocks you over. It's very loud and intimate at the same time.'

'The Dead Heart' was people's first taste of the themes on the new record, but there was more to *Diesel and Dust* than the desert songs, as Pete points out. '*Diesel* is partly about our whole take on Aboriginal culture and the desert, but it's also our take on political activism and what's going on, plus other whacky things about world domination and American presidents and things. It's a multifaceted album, and some of those songs were written or partly written before we did the trip. A lot of people think all the stuff came out of the desert trip, but "The Dead Heart" and some of those songs were there already. We came back from the desert and then songs like "Dreamworld", "Sometimes", "Gunbarrel", "Whoah" and others came along.'

Rob's copy of the tour schedule has his rough notes of the first lyrics for 'Bullroarer' (*In the desert in the dry I've seen the wild horses*) and 'Gunbarrel Highway' (*Nothing could be longer than a corrugated road*). 'We had a bunch of great songs, born of an interesting tour and coming from a very different place than the cities we'd been lurking in. We'd actually managed on songs like "The Dead Heart", "Bullroarer", "Beds", "Warakurna" to capture the rhythms and the moods and colours of the desert of our country in a way that hadn't been done before. That's not to say that other people hadn't attempted it, and succeeded brilliantly, but I feel sure that our contribution is as valid. The result was an album with songs and their attendant film clips that could not have come from any other place in the world. It redefined the band's sound to something else, which involved campfire guitars and simple rhythms. I remember at the time thinking I'd like rhythms that never changed, that sounded like a Toyota four-wheel drive banging across the Gunbarrel Highway, that kind of thing – quite the opposite of what we'd done, where there were gear changes every chorus and massive fills full of guitar riffs. It was all to do with songs and space and rhythm. I remember the band being quite calculating about its songwriting process. We sat around one time in Giffo's little shed in Seaforth and said, "OK, we've got all these songs, which are the hooks? Let's get rid of everything else." That was a calculated way of going about writing songs, but what it actually meant was the songs became simpler, with fewer parts and gear changes, more space, fewer instruments, less production, and they certainly didn't suffer from that.'

At the helm for production of the album was Englishman Warne Livesey, who was largely unaware of the subject matter. 'I think I'm always sensitive to what an artist is trying to say, not in an intellectual way but a fairly natural, more like a feeling or vibe kind of way. Trying to get into what an artist is about and go with that and to gear what I do to enhance that. Obviously as you're working with somebody like that you pick up more and more – you get into their world. There were a lot of conversations going on and obviously the guys were very knowledgeable, particularly Peter, who has done so much work and has so much knowledge in that sort of area. And that would just be part of the vibe and the atmosphere of the whole process of making the record. It was definitely in there.'

Songs like 'Beds Are Burning' and 'Dreamworld' were standing out already from the demos Warne had heard. But some, like 'Bullroarer', were pieced together in the studio, and there were several others that weren't quite complete but were interesting ideas as a basis for other tracks. During the recording process quite a deal of rewriting occurred. Warne: 'The writing and rewriting goes on all the time anyway, with them. Things tend to shift a little, not like completely rewriting something but there is certainly a process of maybe working on lyrics or changing bits of melody and just always trying to improve what's actually there. I seem to remember with "Beds Are Burning", for instance, that we re-recorded the vocal about three times on that song with slight changes in the performance and the delivery, and maybe a few lyrics and a few different melody approaches, particularly in the verses. I think the chorus we had pretty much set, but the verses went through a few transformations. That process continues all the way through the recording, really. Obviously the strength of the lyrics was always there anyway, but I think we concentrated a lot more on melody on that record. Having Pete project that melody, and then also with all of the other guys in the band and their singing abilities enhancing that, to strengthen that melody even more.

'Of course the other thing that goes with that is the guitars. It was very much more a record of vocals and guitars than perhaps the previous couple of albums. But it's just a shift of emphasis. The guitars and the vocals came up maybe 10–15 per cent, and the bass and drums dropped down 10–15 per cent, but they're still very much a part of the whole thing. I think also that Rob's contribution to the album probably was much more diversified: it wasn't just about "Well, he's a great, pounding, energetic rock drummer", but also, I think, from a songwriting point of view he was much more involved and did much more singing on that record than he had done before. Rob has reminded me on several occasions since then, although I don't quite remember it specifically, that I said to them the first time I heard "Beds Are Burning", "That song's going to be a massive hit". And that was obviously the key, although they set the record up really well with "Dead Heart", which came out prior to the album coming out. "Beds Are Burning" was obviously the track – it was a top ten hit in quite a lot of countries, and number one in a few countries, and really got the album selling. Like with a lot of these things, it comes down to one song. If you've got that one song that people connect with on radio, you can really sell a lot of records off the back of that. And because they're such a strong touring band as well, they just backed it up so well.'

Gary had done a lot of groundwork in America. He had tapped into the highest levels of management production and promotion, but neither *10–1* nor *Red Sails in the Sunset* managed to sell enough to be able to take full advantage of it. The USA is a big place, and with a market that size, whether you like it or not, you have to have a powerful machine alongside and some luck. Gary had the big machine ready and 'Beds', with a bit of luck, was the song that could do it. Sony was a little slow to realise what was happening when the single and the album started to sell, even though sales and airplay for 'The Dead Heart' had been significant.

Chris Moss watched from Sony's Sydney office as 'Beds Are Burning' started to grow and grow. 'This was over a long period of time – nine or twelve months. So it was like, "There's something in this. What do we do? We need to get the band over there." Mitch Rose from CAA [Creative Artists Agency] worked to get them over with definite dates, and we worked out the costs. Everybody felt it was a critical component to get the band into America because that was going to be the kerosene on the fire and away it would go. But Jack Rovenor [at Sony] procrastinated and wouldn't make the decision, took weeks and weeks of back and forth with tour forecasting on what they were going to sell, what they'd sold previously, what they would have to sell, and realistically it was only twenty or thirty thousand dollars needed for the tour – which they were going to recoup from record sales anyway, so there was no risk involved here. Everyone believed in the act, but Jack wouldn't make the call in regard to the money. We got down to the wire, with twenty-four hours before we would have to call off the tour, and we didn't know when there would be another opportunity – that window was going to go. And of course I had the dragon over my shoulder going, "Mossy, what the fuck are you doing? Get this thing happening!" – that was Gary. But it was Jeff Jones who finally just said, "Fuck it. Do it . . . we're on!" He approved the money without the authority of his superior.'

Gary had a call some time later. 'I remember Jeff Jones ringing me up and saying "Gary, *Diesel and Dust* has sold 250 000 records and we're getting some really good action on 'Beds Are Burning'." I went, "Oh, that's really good. What are you saying to me?" "Well, we're gonna spend some money now." Up until then they'd spent about 300 grand and I thought that was pretty good, and now they were going to spend some money! "We're gonna roll this one out," he said. He wanted me to talk about it and go through it all and that's when I saw the next level, when a record company is serious about an artist – how they "roll it out". He said, "We've got this situation where everybody's running for cover because of the payola/pay for play inquiry. What's happened is – and we didn't pay for this and it's happened as a bit of a freak of circumstance – but while we've got all these investigations into the independence of radio promotion no one is plugging music, so everyone's picking music on its own merit." So what happened was the radio stations all decided to pick "Beds Are Burning" by "this Aussie band Midnight Oil" just to prove that they were not under the influence of payola. So they all started playing "Beds" right across America. And as a result it started to convert to record sales, and "Beds Are Burning" became a hit in America. And as a result of being a top ten hit in America it converted to Europe and then went around the planet.'

Gary felt there was a sense of providential intervention regarding the success of 'Beds Are Burning': 'Somehow, as a result of bringing the spirit, the energy and the cry for justice out of the western deserts of Australia, that cry parted the waters of American radio and *Diesel and Dust* was given passage. It's as if it managed itself and I was simply going through the process of saying yes or no.'

If it wasn't a reward for purity of intent, maybe it was the fluky coincidence of the professional radio pluggers all going to ground while the payola scandal was being investigated. If not a god-sent opportunity, then definitely a classic 'right time, right place' situation. Or was it just a great song? 'You could tour for ten years on the strength of that song,' Bob Dylan commented side stage one night, and he was right, especially when people went and discovered the album was full of similarly potent songs. Then, if the new fans discovered the band performing in a town near them, a whole new unforgettable side of the band was revealed.

It also helped that the song's title rolled off everyone's lips and was susceptible to superficial radio jock innuendo – and some really did think 'Beds Are Burning' was a song about hot sex. It was undoubtedly helped, too, by a great video clip that attracted high rotation on MTV. David Fricke recalls, 'You would see the video for "Beds Are Burning", which at the end shows the band dancing with the Aboriginal kids and the families. And these are not the beautiful people that you would usually see in a Michael Jackson video or a David Coverdale with his hair flying in the wind with some woman in a leopard-skin bikini in some phoney hard-rock erotica malarky. It was a really basic song about something very true and starring people who were very poor, were not beautiful in a conventional "Hollywood music video" sense. And yet people cottoned onto it. And let's face it, most Americans would not know what Aboriginal culture is. But you didn't have to know it was about the way Aboriginal tribes had been treated the same way Native American Indians had been treated. All you had to know was that it was a very committed song played by a very committed band. There's something in "Beds Are Burning" and "The Dead Heart" and all those songs on *Diesel and Dust* – it's true, it's bona fide rock'n'roll poetry, and a purpose beyond talking about me, myself and I.'

There was certainly something coherent and complete about the album. The shared genesis of much of the material gives the whole album an unmistakable cohesion. For the first time the band held back some of the extremities of their sound so that the difference between the more ambient/acoustic-oriented songs and the rockier ones isn't as much in evidence. David Fricke: 'It's one of the great "road" records of all time and it's not about staying at Holiday Inns, bad food and groupies. It's about getting your own tucker out there under the stars, it's about sleeping next to the jeep, it's about the *real* road. And it's all in those songs, even though the songs are about different things. But that experience binds them all together.'

Diesel and Dust was recorded in the first few months of 1987 and released in the middle of the year. Between its recording and release Giffo departed from the band and Bones Hillman became the new bass player. 'I flew into Sydney for an audition and there were posters advertising the *Diesel and Dust* tour at the Hordern Pavilion as I was leaving the airport, and I remember thinking, "Man, Giffo really left them in the lurch." They were really on the spot – it was only a month before the first shows.'

Bones had been combining some house-painting work with playing part-time in a covers band and was living in Melbourne with Neil Finn. It was Neil who told him Rob Hirst had telephoned about Bones possibly joining the band. Bones thought he was joking and went out to the pub and never phoned back. Luckily, a couple of days later Rob phoned again. 'The one thing I was really impressed about from the start was that they weren't attempting to poach anybody, and I admired that. They could have gone and snapped anyone from any Australian band and that person probably would have thrown their hat in and joined Midnight Oil, but they were looking for someone who had been around and wasn't necessarily playing in a band at that time. I flew up to Sydney on three occasions. I'd had a pre-release copy of *Diesel and Dust* and had to learn a couple of things off *10–1* and a couple off *Red Sails*, and then we played a couple of Beatles covers. It went on for quite a while. It was an incredible time.' Bones beat a handful of contenders but was contracted only to play for dates in Australia and Canada. 'Gary Morris was blunt and made it quite clear that after that it would be reviewed.'

Several months later, when the tour finished up at Festival Hall in Melbourne, the band all went back to Bones' place. 'We had a few beers and a bit of a hug and it was sort of like, "Thanks, guys, see you later". I didn't really know what was going to happen after that point. I'd made a fair bit of money for the first time, and I went and bought an EH Holden and cruised around Melbourne like King Shit for a little while. It was just like wait and see. And either way it was a good credential to have on my resume if I had to find another gig. Anyway, they called about three months later, early the next year, and said we're going to America, and we then toured *Diesel* for about nine months.'

The band did two trips to the USA with a tour of Europe and the UK in between. They were the first of the really big tours, where dates were often added faster than they could play them. Whole countries were added as the single and album took off on charts around the world. The band had a hit single in several countries and they were playing big venues with lots of promotional support from Sony operations everywhere. There were plenty of records in the shops in every centre they went, professional advance promotion for the tours and enthusiastic publicity. There were also full houses and over-the-top shows. In America the band had chosen to take as their support band a group only a few months old from Yirrkala in north-east Arnhem Land. Yothu Yindi became part of the Diesel and Dust to Big Mountain tour and had dancers and didjeridus and rhythms that set the stage perfectly for the new Midnight Oil material.

The bill also included an American Indian band, Grafitti Man, and the tour adopted the Navaho land claim for Big Mountain in Oregon as a central issue for the concerts. Grafitti Man was led by John Trudell, a Santee Sioux Indian who was a Vietnam veteran, former leader of AIM (the American Indian Movement) and spokesperson on Native American affairs. 'Grafitti music' was described as poetry rock and was a mixture of Trudell's spoken-word material on the 'real' workings of American politics with a rock and blues style backing. The other major presence on stage was Quiltman, a Navaho spiritual leader, who sat quietly and played an Indigenous tambourine, imbuing the whole proceedings with cultural gravitas and a certain air of portentousness.

It was just before they all left for the tour in early 1988 that the head of Sony Australia, Denis Handlin, received the call from his counterpart in the USA about the band being invited to play at the Grammys. Despite the fact that an appearance on the annual television spectacular was seen as immeasurably valuable in the promotion of 'Beds Are Burning', the offer was refused so Pete could fulfil his prior obligation as MC with Gary Foley of the Long March for Justice, Freedom and Hope at Bondi Beach, where 4000 people from Indigenous communities converged.

While overseas, the desert trip and the Australian Indigenous cause were central to the press coverage. Even though on radio the subject matter may have escaped some listeners, the video clips for 'The Dead Heart' and 'Beds Are Burning' were graphic and relatively unambiguous. In interviews the subject was inevitably raised and the band became de facto advocates for the Aboriginal cause. Pete: 'It was important to be able to give a meaningful answer if a question was asked, but I was always at pains to point out that these were our own impressions, views and beliefs – that we weren't speaking for other people. We had been there at other people's invitation and we were entitled and had been invited to tell the story, which we clearly had by the Warlpiri elders, by Johnny Scobie. They very clearly said to us, "We want you to tell other people what's going on out here and what you've seen, we really hope you'll do that." And I think we did do that faithfully, but I've never felt that we were spokespeople or anything else of the sort, we just had to do it as true to our own experiences as we could.

'I remember the audiences themselves, particularly in Europe, getting onto the band's wavelength for six months or so, when "Beds" was getting played – being genuinely interested and intrigued with what we had to say. And I think that was quite a remarkable place for us to be in at that stage, given where we'd come from and the kind of people we were and our attitude towards the industry and so forth. We weren't fish out of water; we were strange creatures from a different universe. But we were playing guitar and drums and singing songs and people were moving to it and singing along with us.'

The band may have sold more records in Germany, but in France the per capita sales were extraordinary. The French media and music buyers just loved what they saw and heard. Salomon Hazat was the promoter who first brought Midnight Oil to France, for the Brittany festival with the Clash in 1985, and watched their growing appeal turn into unbridled fascination with the release of 'Beds' and *Diesel*. 'We quite like Australia because it's a mystery. It's the hat, but not like an American cowboy with nothing under the hat. The members of Midnight Oil were not only musicians, not only artists, but human beings as well who could speak about something else. Midnight Oil are a band that don't need to speak too much about their music because there are more important things in life than music – people are dying, people are not feeding themselves well enough, there isn't enough water everywhere, things like this. The French media like it if a band can go a bit further than just rock'n'roll. With Midnight Oil it was very strange – "The guy is not speaking about himself, he's speaking about Aborigines, he's speaking about equality between people", and so on – and people said, "Why doesn't he speak about himself?" Anyway, with luck, and there is always luck, they had a very, very, very strong song and "Beds Are Burning" sold a million records. This was not often the case at the time – only Michael Jackson and one or two like that. Unfortunately, they did not capitalise in France. They should have come at the time and stayed and played, but they did what they wanted and hopefully they are happy. When they had this huge hit they were bigger than U2, but maybe not the Rolling Stones because they had already had twenty years of success before.'

Rob: 'When we arrived in Paris after *Diesel* had been released it was like we were huge fucking celebrities on the scale of Gérard Depardieu or Vanessa Paradis or someone. We were being stopped all over Paris, people recognising Pete of course first and then the band, it was huge. It caught us completely by surprise. The French have always been fascinated by exotica – people and places that are so far away from the French idea of countryside and personality. And here was this group of five what appeared to be bushmen, playing in the centre of this faraway continent *Australie*, and it was like a new frontier for them. It's like it really touched a chord. This music was entirely exotic and different-sounding and yet it was rhythmic and melodic, and of course all French music is melodic, it's in their language. It was almost as if we'd come out of the pages of Camus' *L'Etranger*, except replace the deserts of Algeria with the deserts of Australia, or as if the film clips had been beamed down from the surface of Mars or the moon!'

The band had no problem with their anti-nuke profile despite the fact that the French government was a target for criticism. Rob feels that their strong standpoint on political issues was appreciated by audiences. 'Well, the people who came to Midnight Oil shows were those who were horrified by what France was doing in Mururoa and they were the ones supporting "If it's not safe to do it in the Massif Central then it's not safe in the South Pacific". We had terrific support for the stance. One of the other reasons the band touched such a chord was because in France politics isn't just left to politicians. People of all ages and sexes discuss politics, in bars, in cafes, in unis, in schools. When the French strike it's a massive strike – it's *grève général*. When the French students have a *manifestation*, a demonstration, people get killed! There's tear gas and it's serious stuff. It's not a bunch of uni students from Sydney Uni or Uni of NSW out for a bit of a lark down George

Street. Politics in France inflames passions, so whatever the French thought about our stance it was still something they could relate to – the passionate point of view. And we put the music across passionately, and Pete put it across passionately in articles and from the lip of the stage. So even for those who were hardline about France's nuclear ambitions, they could understand that we had an opinion contrary to theirs.'

As they travelled, the band were inevitably drawn to other countries' Indigenous issues and found many similarities. Pete: 'The colonisation experience has a number of parallels, obviously the situations are different for different countries. They've got their own belief systems, cultures and languages, histories, but there is still a commonality of dispossession and a commonality of the experience of trying to assert rights for land, rights for fair and equal treatment under the law. And we had some really profound experiences in North America and Canada. We received an eagle feather from Indigenous people in Canada who we had relations with and did work with and did a press conference with on the steps of the Parliament – near Manitoba. We toured with Quiltman and John Trudell and we took Yothu Yindi to America. We didn't go to Hollywood, we went to Wounded Knee. That was the Midnight Oil journey.'

Over the following years the band continued to follow that journey with new songs and benefit concerts, and with strong support for many Indigenous initiatives such as the Building Bridges project – and there was the performance of 'Beds Are Burning' at the Olympics. It's hard to imagine a more high-profile event, but for the band it was not persuaded to do it for the purposes of self-aggrandisement or promotion. It was an opportunity to say something about the linkages between music and sport and politics and culture in general. Cathy Freeman had been simply inspiring and in some ways it honoured her, and her people's, quietly humble achievements. The decision to have SORRY on their clothes allowed them to simply sing the song without having to say anything else. Nevertheless, I'm sure some people were a little nervous that Pete had a live microphone to billions of people – or at least he thought he did!

The band were standing with their instruments at the ready and the moment had almost arrived when Pete realised that the microphone was back in the dressing room. Suddenly he turned tail and was gone, disappearing into the bowels of the building with security in pursuit, bouncing off the walls of the concrete cavern brushing aside the questions, the startled looks and the parade paraphernalia and regalia. Past a Mambo Jesus, then a Hills hoist, then some Bondi lifesavers, a lawn mower, the Shark, the Body, Hoges, Kylie – through a celebration of Australian achievements past, present and future, all mingling in various stages of preparation for the big event. Visions of a lifetime growing up in Australia were assembled as a celebration of what Australia thought it had become. Were there fresh doubts about being part of this? Were Midnight Oil laying claim to iconic status by playing here? It surely wasn't just another gig. It was art in action and it was aimed directly at the prime minister, John Howard, who was sitting somewhere in the stands. It was his refusal to apologise on behalf of past governments for the reprehensible treatment of Australia's Indigenous population that was the basis of the whole 'sorry' campaign.

When Pete arrived back, slightly breathless, with the radio microphone, Bones was white with fear. With only seconds to go, doubts or not, they all took the overalls off and climbed the steps to the stage with a united front. As usual when it came to divisions within the band, it was never the cause itself but the tactics and detail. Rob: 'As soon as we walked out into the stadium people started cheering, an enormous roar went up. And we knew that despite the John Howards and the shock jocks around the place, the majority opinion was with us.'

Around the harbour, thousands of people who had been sitting in parks enjoying the ceremony on the big video screens leapt to their feet. Suddenly there was a new electricity and the crowds were dancing. Mothers and babies, girls and boys, bikies and businessmen – and many were singing along.

The time has come
A fact's a fact
It belongs to them
Let's give it back

John Howard was unmoved, and we've still not heard the 'S' word. Pete and hundreds of thousands of others have crossed bridges all over Australia; so far, in vain, as other Sorry Days have come and gone. It seems Howard may well have decided to go to his grave, or into obscurity, before saying it. To many around the world, and even some in the stadium, the white words on the black clothes meant nothing. The gig was just a gig. The band played a great sing-along song that got the party started. But by wearing the sorry suits the band removed as much ambiguity about their inspiration and purpose as possible.

The band members all made small individual contributions over the years to Indigenous projects, too. Rob and Martin did a trip out to Utopia, north-east of Alice Springs, to conduct music workshops. Jim produced a record for Nature Nature featuring didj player Henry Phineasa and flute player Dave McBurney, and he continued the Warumpi connection through his work with Neil Murray. Pete contributed to Yothu Yindi's hit single 'Treaty', which was single of the year at the Australian Record Industry Awards in 1991. His name mysteriously appears and disappears as a co-writer, along with Paul Kelly and Yothu Yindi, on different pressings of the record.

'Mandawuy got in touch with me and said they'd been workshopping a song in the Northern Territory with Paul Kelly called "Treaty", and would I be prepared to work with them on it. I said, "Yeah, sure, I'd be happy to." They came down to Sydney, Mandawuy and Paul, and came to Glebe, and played pretty much the "Treaty" that you hear now, but vocally very different, and said, "What do you think?" I said, "It sounds to me like it's pretty much there as a song. I don't think I can help all that much with it." I had a few suggestions. And then they said, "Would you come to the recording session and sit in on it and give Mandawuy a hand?" And I said, "Yeah, I will." So I went to the Vault and had a listen to what they'd done, and the producer, who I knew, said, "What do you reckon?" and I said, "Well, I'll do a version of it, as a bit of a guide, then Mandawuy can pick up on those bits that he likes, bits of phrasing, whatever." So that's what I did, and that's what he did. And that's how it happened. Then they offered me a credit on it, and I said, "Well, I haven't done that much", so I said no. They put my name on it sometimes and they don't at other times.'

The Black Fella White Fella tour and the album it inspired changed the band's lives. The increase in business was exponential, but so was the band's workload. Once 'Beds Are Burning' became a hit the touring nearly killed them. It was a whole new ballpark, as they say, playing in the big league. The band had no plans, no expectations and no real way of knowing what they were in for and what was the best way of dealing with it. With Gary's help and advanced connections they made decisions on the run, in band meetings backstage and in hotel rooms all over the world. But how ready were they to tackle the task, and how hard was it to stay on top of things? Pete: 'I think we were ready up to a point. It was just which point you picked. Was it world domination and Madison Square Garden, or was it self-imploding homesickness and drudgery in the back of a bar in San Francisco? Was it just getting enough to last for the next six months, or moving to another country? I mean, there are so many different issues that raise their heads when a record starts to get away like that one did. And I frankly think that we were probably too busy playing to think about it that much, and I don't think it mattered to us *that* much. It certainly didn't matter to *me* that much. I think we considered things as best as we could at different times, but by that stage, when you're running around at that pace, you can't really be on top of everything, can't think everything through. Also, a lot of it is out of your hands at that stage. You've got a global audience, you've got record companies with all the record company industry stuff going on, you've got media, and you've got a number of hours in a day to do things. You've still got one another to get on with, you've got kids and wives at home, and somehow you try and make all the bits and pieces fit.'

Thankfully, the addition of Bones to the line-up contributed to the band's ability to deal with some of the tensions and demands. Not only was he a journeyman player capable of playing night after night, he was also psychologically suited to the essential camaraderie of a band. Rob: 'The venerable Bones "Wayne" Hillman was not only the perfect choice in terms of elevating the vocal side of the band to new heights and adding a very melodic attitude to bass, if not the heavy downbeat style that Giffo had perfected, but his irrepressible sense of humour and refusal to be dragged into the kind of abyss of seriousness the other members were prey to was for me the only reason the band lasted through the difficulties. He was exactly the shot in the arm we needed. In the nicest possible way he made fun of us. We needed to laugh at ourselves, because the whole thing, which had started as a band in a garage in Chatswood, had become this often quasi-religious proselytising juggernaut. And it was up to someone from the inner sanctum to take the piss. Bones had a way of making the band collapse in laughter about it without taking offence.'

But now there were new pressures, expectations for the follow-up album. Songs had to be written and decisions made about how to approach them. Pete: 'I was aware of that. I felt it to the extent of knowing that we had to have something that would stand up and wouldn't be completely flattened in the rush for the door as everyone said, "See ya later" – which would have happened.'

Writing new songs was never a problem for Midnight Oil, but the bar they had to jump, and the stakes the band were playing for, had been raised by the whole *Diesel and Dust* experience.

five

hear the time clock sing

Despite the excitement and air of anticipation around the recording of *Diesel and Dust,* it was a very relaxing album to make. It was the closest the band ever recorded to home – none of them lived more than twenty minutes away from the studio.

Since the band had recorded their debut album there, Albert's had moved from the inner city to Neutral Bay on Sydney Harbour's north shore. The old Albert's was famous as the birthplace of AC/DC and the spiritual home of many other bands Harry Vanda and George Young had an interest in, like the Angels and Rose Tattoo. But the new Albert's was very small and was set up more for making advertising jingles than rock albums. David Bowie was apparently shocked when he saw the size of it many years later. 'They did it here!' he said. The playing area was tiny, plus the band had to work very hard to get it sounding lively. First the road crew brought in sheets of plywood, and then Rob suggested getting some corrugated-iron roofing to line the studio to try and combat the dead sound.

'Not that Albert's was a bad studio,' says producer Warne Livesey, 'but it wasn't really the right place for us to be in to make that record. Paradoxically we got quite a good record out of it. I think it sounds good, but it was a very small studio. It had great gear and everything and at the time it was the best room in Sydney that was actually available. By the time we came to *Blue Sky Mining* Rhino had opened, and that was a big studio with big playing areas, with three isolation rooms and a big space to put the drums, so it was a lot easier from that point of view. We had a lot more space and it was easier to get sounds.'

Making a record is not a simple process. A studio is more than a room with a microphone and a tape machine. And a producer contributes much more than turning the machine on and off. The producer effectively joins the band and contributes to the creative kitty. Sometimes they even play. The band enter the studio with most if not all of the songs already written, and they have usually spent time in pre-production with the producer in a rehearsal room or cheap studio doing some preliminary arranging or recording of the songs or song ideas. Some of the songs may have already been performed live and the recording of them can be simply an attempt at capturing that live version or augmenting it in some way, depending on what occurs spontaneously in the studio. Some songs may have been already roughly recorded as demos by the band and are used as guidelines for the real thing. Occasionally some songs may only be ideas in the composer's head when the studio process starts but, despite this being an unreliable method, it can end up capturing the essence or mood of everything going on.

The studio environment is a combination of expectation and expertise, inside a rope of time and money. But it can be a fiddly process, and trying to estimate the time or the cost when so many elements may not go to plan, especially when a small brass or string section might be needed, is problematic. To go into a studio with too many half-formed songs can be a recipe for an expensive disaster, but it can also result in something inspired that makes a hitherto unanticipated connection with the public and becomes a big success. The inherent pressures in the studio situation can bring out the worst and best in people; it is a creative melting pot where the best results are usually achieved if egos are left at the door. That being said, strong feelings and instincts are important, even crucial – it's a delicate balance and every recording session is different.

From a musician's point of view, the success or otherwise of an album is unpredictable, if not a complete lottery. Nobody can really know the outcome of the process in advance, and certainly not the commercial results to follow. Albums are often grand visions made up of hundreds, probably thousands, of moving parts, put together by a variety of methods and in a variety of situations. The whole enterprise is a volatile coincidence of culture, economies, talent, inspiration and magic – an artistic gamble that is an unavoidable part of being a modern musician.

Recordings last forever, yet they are utterly contemporary – an audio snapshot that illustrates something of the signs and sounds of our times. Before *Diesel and Dust* there had been five Midnight Oil albums and two four-song EPs.

The most significant pre-*Diesel* album was *10,9,8,7,6,5,4, 3,2,1*, recorded in the prestigious Town House studios in London in 1982 by young English producer Nick Launay. (Some, including Nick, always refer to it as *10,9,8*, but others call it *10–1*.) Nick had a background as a studio engineer but, thanks to working with John Lydon on the *Flowers of Romance* LP, had a newfound reputation as a producer. With Lydon it was essentially a two-person effort, but with the Oils he found he was working in quite a different environment. 'They are very much a band. Every time there'd be a discussion everybody would be involved – should this go there, is that verse too long, do we need a pre-chorus or not, are we going to have a solo or not, do we need an instrumental? It was always everybody's decision. Everyone had equal rights. They were very equal in decision making. Lots of discussion, and rather than "I think it should go like this", it was more like "Let's try this".'

Nick also produced *Red Sails in the Sunset* in Tokyo in 1984 and the 1993 'comeback' album *Earth and Sun and Moon*, but neither was as pivotal as *10–1*. It was a groundbreaker for the band that stayed in the Australian charts for over two years, eclipsed longstanding records for sales and longevity and garnered impossibly laudatory reviews. 'Our own little *Dark Side of the Moon*,' says Pete.

The band's previous album, *Place Without a Postcard*, had also been recorded in England, but in less salubrious and very different circumstances, at Glyn Johns's farm in the south of England, far from anywhere. When Glyn invited them over, the band thought they would be working with him at Olympic Studios in London, where his work with the Who and the Stones had been done. But Glyn wanted to use a newly built studio at his farm in West Sussex. Jim remembers the little farmhouse where the band was accommodated. 'The walls were completely covered with all of his gold records and we'd be sitting there looking at Joan Armatrading, the Eagles, the Beatles, the Stones, the Small Faces, you name it. We'd be listening to the out-takes of *Let It Be* – Glyn actually did the version of *Let It Be* that was released in 2003, which is the tape that he basically ran off for us to listen to as what he thought our album should be like. He wanted a rough album and so we had that tape there sitting on a wee box in the living room. We listened to that – we never used to listen to our own stuff.'

The recording sessions were interrupted by Glyn's frequent trips to London, leaving the band to their own devices. Giffo would get involved in some carpentry, Rob was always happy to read and Jim and Martin were happy enough just to play their guitars – although Martin was sometimes so bored he took to riding around the country lanes on a bicycle. Pete found Glyn's Rolls Royce a temptation. 'Because Glyn had been such a successful producer the place was full of gold records and he had two or three cars in the garage – and we were completely stone broke. We were so broke we had to scrimp and save our money to go up to London on the train for a couple of days. Giffo and I decided one day to borrow the Rolls and see how good its brakes were. So we got some VBs, which some kind Aussie had brought to us, and set them up on the armrest between us and headed off towards Brighton. When we reached 100 mph we hit the brakes as hard as we could – and the beer didn't spill! We thought that was pretty good.'

Giffo: 'We were baling hay in our spare time! It was Glyn's hay season and he'd had the hay people around and they'd baled all the hay and the bales were sitting in the paddock and it started to rain, and we had to bring them in coz if they got wet they would rot. Glyn had this old tractor and a trailer and we kept putting the hay on it to bring it into the shed. We're supposed to be making an album and we're out hauling hay in the moonlight! And it was raining. Maybe some of the others would have rather been doing music. Glyn just wanted to be a farmer. He wanted a bit of a lifestyle thing. Anyway, the hay kept falling off the trailer because all the sides were buggered. So when Glyn was in doing some recording work, guitar overdubs or something, I went out and ripped all the boards off this trailer and got it back to a bare chassis and scraped all the steel and painted it, then scraped the wheels and painted them. But he's looked out the window and gone, "Oh my God! What's happened to my trailer?" To me it was an easy job but Glyn's not a very practical, handy sort of person. Anyway, I got it all fixed up.'

Giffo also made some kitchen cupboards for the cook. 'She had this pissy little kitchen with no bench space. So I got some old planks of wood that were lying around and made her a little thing. You can't cook for six blokes without places to put pots and pans. I made her a little cupboard, a little unit. It was a roughie, but it got her out of trouble. She thought that was the bee's knees. And then after that there was the duck house. The foxes were getting the ducks, so I made a house for them. We were there about three months, I think. It was quite a while. Pink Floyd were playing up in London and I never went to see them. I think I was still building the duck house. I regret not seeing Pink Floyd do *The Wall* at Earl's Court – that would have been fabulous.'

In the studio Glyn had a very definite way of doing things. Jim: 'He wouldn't really let you go and play guitar in the studio without him being there, because he'd want to get everything on the first take. Inevitably we'd sit down with him with the song, or whatever the idea was, and try and impress him with what we had, which we did for a while until we were sort of getting into the songs on the album that were a little bit unformed or incomplete. And in those situations he sometimes used to get up and just walk out. He'd say, "I'd rather be having fun on my tractor than listening to this crap." He was about to mix the trilogy – "Quinella", "Ned Kelly" and "Loves on Sale" – and I came up with the idea "Before we do that, can we put, like, a little synth line and a cow bell in the chorus?", and he looked at me and said, "Are you trying to ruin my life?" He did it really reluctantly, with very bad grace. I couldn't wait to get out of the place! Glyn seemed to thrive on conflict and what it produces, but sometimes he was really rude, really opinionated.

'At the time I thought, "I hate this guy, I really hate him." I'd never been out of Australia before, and here we were with this famous producer with a Rolls Royce and a whole lot of expensive cars in the garage, and stables and land, and he walked around taking pot shots at rabbits with his gun. He was an English eccentric, landed gentry.'

Most of the songs for the album were relatively recent compositions, but 'Don't Wanna Be the One' was written by Rob and Pete in 1978–79 and had been originally titled 'Head Injuries'. Apart from failing to make the cut for, but lending its name to, the band's second album, it didn't make the *Bird Noises* EP either. The song only appeared on *Postcard* after extra writing from Jim and Martin at Glyn's farm. It survived in the band's live set for the whole of their career, probably because the lines 'If I don't make it to the top, it will never bother me' and the rebellious spirit of the song seemed to be so fundamental to the band's attitude. Pete's scream to finish the song was never less than convincing.

A strong sense of Australia pervades much of the record, which is one of the reasons A&M in London passed on the option of releasing it. The poignant 'Burnie', about the pollution of the ocean off Tasmania by paper millers, was the band's first deeply green song because it was about commitment as well as the issue itself. 'If Ned Kelly Was King' links mining companies and injustices done to Aboriginal people, and 'Lucky Country' samples the Australian psyche and embraces the sights and smells and ways of home. Pete: 'I think we would have had those songs about Australia anyway, even if we'd recorded it in Australia. Quite often artists, writers, whatever, are in other countries and it gives them a better view of home and helps bring that view into full bloom. And certainly for me, it was an important record for us to do because it said some of the things about Australia and Australian culture that I felt we needed to say, and which we'd experienced because we'd been doing such a lot of touring.'

Once the songs were recorded and mixed, Jim still had reservations with the overall sound. 'There were a lot of problems with the speed of the record; it sounded slow to me when we got the test pressings. I got really antsy about it – it was like Glyn's tape machine recorded too fast so that when it played back it was slow on other machines. It wasn't an even pitch, the whole thing was flat and it sounded really slow and leaden. It got to the stage where I actually rang up the master engineer in LA, Doug Sacks, and said, "Look, here's a tuning fork. Can you tune up the tape to this tuning fork? Here's a song that's in A." And he did. And he said, "You're right, it's flat."

'When I look back on it now I think Glyn did a superb job, because he understood what the band sounded like, despite our best intentions and what we thought records should be like at that time. He loved what the band sounded like and didn't think it needed a lot of augmentation. And I look back on it now and see why he just wanted to use first takes.'

Pete: 'I enjoyed it, even though I thought Glyn was pretty difficult to work with and clearly was nursing some of his demons in the bottom of a brandy glass. He had a particular approach to recording, which I liked, and I felt we probably could have got a bit more out of it if he had put a bit more time into production. But I think it stands up pretty well.'

Apart from Pete's vocal contribution, the thing that made the band's records sound different from their contemporaries was undoubtedly the guitar interplay of Jim and Martin. On *Postcard* this musical relationship really gelled, but it was obvious from the band's very first record that they had two seriously good guitarists. All the songs on the self-titled debut record are full of inventive multitextured guitar, not quite intertwining as on albums to come, but synchronised and complementary. The two guitars, together with Rob's drumming, drove the band's live performances, but that first record didn't quite capture the live sound the band was after. Producer Keith Walker did his best, but something was lost in the mix, as they say. By most standards the recording sounds a little thin, but the effect of the guitars is still inescapable.

Many of the idiosyncrasies and hallmarks of Pete's vocal style are already in evidence – the pitched rave, the falsetto, the harsh whispers, and the heart-stopping screams. On some songs he's still finding his voice, but he's never tentative about it. In 'Dust' he has a little scream, and in 'Used and Abused' he delivers his first full-throated example, with grunts and growls to boot. But it was his committed delivery as much as his singing style that became such an important part of the band's appeal, on record as well as in the live context.

Their early music was not lyric-based, and often Pete's voice was used instrumentally and the songs didn't follow the standard verse/chorus pattern. Nor did that early music resemble the vocal thrash of the punk bands of the day. They may have been sharing stages and trading riffs with the all-black brigade, but there was always far more brightness among the darkness of the Oils. The bluster of the opening, 'Powderworks', contrasts with the slightly uncomfortable but beautiful 'Head Over Heels' and the bleakness and desperation of 'Dust', while rockers like 'Used and Abused' and 'Run by Night' are balanced by the quixotic, escapist 'Surfing with a Spoon' and Jim's highly personal album closer, the moody 'Nothing Lost, Nothing Gained'. There were plenty of ideas and much skilled playing and the record was highly praised as a debut rich with potential – but it didn't set the charts alight.

The band's second LP, *Head Injuries*, was produced in Sydney's Trafalgar Studios by newly arrived Englishman Les Karski. Most of the songs were already live favourites, or were soon to be – 'Cold Cold Change', 'Bus to Bondi', 'Back on the Borderline', 'Stand in Line' and 'No Reaction'. 'No Reaction', in particular, was absolute dynamite live, and for the first time their recording did the song justice: a killer rock'n'roll start, Pete in great vocal form and doing his first wild harmonica bit, slashing guitars, and the classic line 'You're almost (but not quite) more than we deserve'.

The band were much happier with the end result of this recording. The intense pre-production sessions with Les had paid off and they had gone into the studio well prepared. The album was recorded after gigs over five weeks in midnight-to-dawn shifts. Bear recalls the tactics Les and the band used to capture the songs. 'In general the method of attack we settled on was to play the track again and again. The first time we played it, it would have heaps of energy, and with each successive performance it would get tighter and tighter but tireder and tireder. We would then take a half-hour break or so, and come back and nail the track with a take that was both tight and energetic. This worked for most numbers. However, "Stand in Line" was a great song that we didn't do justice to on the album. After playing it so many times, my wrist was tired from muting the bass strings at the beginning of the guitar solo. To get the track recorded, Peter had to hold his index finger against the strings next to the bridge of my bass for the first few bars and then gradually release the pressure until he could remove his finger. The definitive version of "Stand in Line" was recorded live at Parramatta Park, with Peter Gifford on bass, and was included on the *Scream in Blue* album.'

Head Injuries was released in November 1979 along with the single 'Cold Cold Change'. But neither made any commercial impact, as only the new public radio stations 3RRR, 4ZZZ and 2XX, along with the ever-dependable Double Jay, played them regularly. The album was, however, a steady seller, and by the middle of 1980 it had achieved gold status. Pete: 'In some ways, if you never made another record after *Head Injuries* you didn't have to – because it really did sum us up. It summed up those three years or five years of having nothing in the world to equip you but everything in the world to aim for.'

After *Head Injuries* and prior to *Postcard* the band chose to do an EP, although the four songs were originally recorded as demos for a new album. Again Les Karski produced. Each of the band members essentially contributed one song, except for Giffo, who had only just joined the band. Pete: 'Rotsey's was "Wedding Cake Island", "Knife's Edge" was . . . well, I don't know which came first, my lyric or the lick from Jim, "No Time for Games" was certainly Rob's melody but some came from Jim, and "I'm the Cure" was Jim.'

Jim: 'We wrote in the studio quite a lot coz we were very unprepared for that record, but we had "Wedding Cake Island", and "I'm the Cure" was the thing I had on the demo and we basically sort of copied it. The other two we just got together there.'

'No Time for Games' remained a live favourite for the next two decades thanks to Jim's extraordinary guitar solo towards the end, which was different each and every time they played it. The recording was done at the idyllic Music Farm studio outside Byron Bay, where they were visited by Cold Chisel for a jam variously remembered for Ian Moss's volume, Jimmy Barnes's incredible voice, and the copious consumption of alcohol and local herb.

In November 1980 the *Bird Noises* EP was released and Martin's gently strummed 'Wedding Cake Island', inspired by the reef off Sydney's Coogee Beach, became the band's unlikely first chart success. It reached number nine on the day John Lennon died and was in the singles charts for three months. Although the song was released as an instrumental, it originally contained a stream-of-consciousness rave from Pete that included the lines 'red sails in the fucking sunset', and the only vocals to remain in the song, 'lines of swell round the Byron Pass, mate'.

The decision to record such a different-sounding song was part of a philosophical standpoint. Jim: 'Well, we bought this Ovation guitar and had it when we did "Wedding Cake Island". We just started using it and it sort of implied this whole other way of working where you can bring other instruments in and do other things. I was always keen to do that, and Martin was a willing accomplice. "We're going to try different things and evolve along some path." I think you can't be bored with what you do. And so we went down that road.'

That road led to the manicured wilds of West Sussex and the *Place Without a Postcard* sessions. *Postcard* was a watershed recording for the band musically, and once the tape-speed issue was solved everyone was extremely happy with the result. Pete: 'I flew back on the plane listening to *Postcard* and I was listening to "Lucky Country" as we were landing at Sydney airport, to the rave in the middle, "no conversation", all that stuff, and the way it broke into "Lucky Country", and I just thought, "This is the best record any band has ever made in Australia." I felt *very* good about that record.'

When it was released in November 1981 *Place Without a Postcard* reached a creditable number twelve on the charts, and 'Don't Wanna Be the One' snuck into the top forty. The album went gold faster than *Head Injuries* had and again attracted complimentary reviews, with one critic calling it the most important Australian record since Skyhooks' *Living in the 70s*.

●

But it was the band's next record, *10–1*, that really captured the public's imagination. Nick Launay had heard *Postcard*. 'I thought, "Wow, they're in tune, they can play their instruments", but for me it was too perfect. I was used to things being out of tune, out of time, and pretty nasty sounding!'

For *10–1* the band were in the heart of London, recording in one of the most celebrated studios of the time and living in accommodation above the studio complex. The Stone Room in the Town House had been the scene of recordings by the Jam, Phil Collins, XTC, Simple Minds and others.

Nick was determined to stir things up in the studio. 'My approach was not "Are the songs together? Are the arrangements together?" it was more "I want them to sound raw and louder than anything on earth, and I want it to sound different to any rock record out there. I want it to be original", and— I wasn't thinking of the words "cutting edge" but that was basically it. And it was just the right time, they needed someone to come in and mess things up, put a spanner in the works.'

Many of the songs were enhanced by the spirit of adventure, including the two top-forty singles, the extremely out-of-character 'Power and the Passion' and the permanently topical 'US Forces'. Nick: 'The drum beat for "Power and the Passion" was kick, snare, high-hat for six minutes. So we put that down and just built the song up. It wasn't done as a live song, to us it was a joke – we're doing a disco song. It was talked about like, "This will be really funny". They got into this mood of "Let's do something outrageous for the kids back home – let's shock them". That was the mood all around this album. "We're in London, we're doing something different." But we didn't like the snare sound, so Rob went out and played the snare and of course just him doing that suddenly made the whole song groove coz he plays ahead of the beat. His snare is always ahead of the beat, that's his kind of drumming, which is why all the Oils' songs have this magical thing that most drummers can't achieve, which is sounding like they are getting faster all the time. But they're not – which gives it that urgency. The snare drum is always slightly early and his kick drum is slightly late – that's a good thing. Charlie Watts – his snare would be late, all the time, to get that laid-back thing.

'So we overdubbed Rob's live snare, which immediately made the song happen, made it more urgent. I don't know who made the decision for him to do a drum solo, but I know I would definitely have been enthusiastic for the idea. We had the whole thing set up and he went out there and I pressed RECORD just where the drum solo was going to happen and he played what you hear, first take. That is it. Then he ended it with "drrr drrr drrr ttshsh!" and then in came the rest of the song. I remember that the whole song was all fun and comical and laughs. The only thing we added was that breaking sound that finished it. We found this big light bulb, like one used in theatres, which didn't work and was lying around in the studio. And the floor of the "Stone Room" was – well, it's stone! So Rob just dropped it.'

Nick was particularly impressed with Jim and Martin's guitar-playing. 'As individuals, they are the best guitarists I've ever worked with – and I have worked with Eric Clapton. They are amazing, incredible – not only original, not only great at playing and coming up with ideas, but just the way they finger, the way they hold the guitar, on every level, technically just . . . They know how to play a guitar in a way to make it loud and raucous and spirited, and that's all part of it. It's how you strum and how you take the pick and how you strike the strings. And they both have their own way of doing it.

'One of the things we definitely came up with, which became a Midnight Oil thing from then on, was this whole thing of getting big acoustic guitar sounds that sounded unlike any guitar sounds out there. It's most audible on "US Forces", and how we did that was with Jim on a Fender acoustic and Martin on a Martin acoustic (I think!) – both are great-sounding acoustic guitars. They both played at the same time, facing each other, looking at each other. I pushed RECORD and we went from beginning to end and they both strummed all the way through. Then we went back to the beginning of the song and they swapped guitars and did the same again. Sometimes, depending on the song, one of them would play a dobro. It has a very clangy sound, so on "US Forces" particularly that's what we used. So there were four acoustics. Sometimes we'd go further and there would be six, I think "US Forces" is six, a combination of three different guitars, twice. And they play so tightly, so consistently with their strumming, that . . . ! Later on, when I recorded other bands with two guitarists, I would go, "I've got this great trick" but it would never work. I'd copy the whole idea, and of course it's very difficult to do. Any tiny change or little skip in the strumming from one take to the next and it would sound like shit. It has to be identical, every time. That's the only way it's going to sound like one huge big acoustic instrument. And that's what we wanted on "US Forces". We wanted it to sound like this big acoustic guitar that one person was strumming. And it does. And the reason it does is because they are so good.

'They are both different guitarists, though. Martin tends to be more aggressive, and what I recognise as the Martin thing is that bending of a guitar solo – well, you wouldn't call them solos. In "Only the Strong" there is a guitar solo and that's very him. In a way it's a Stonesy thing, but Keith would have done it more laid back, less aggressive. Martin is more on top of it, he's like – bending between notes and there are all these spiky kind of things. That's what he does. Jim's thing is more like playing the unusual notes. He's played on other records that I've done. He played on Silverchair's *Neon Ballroom*, and as soon as he picks up a guitar and starts playing it's just – Jim. Daniel Johns is really into weird notes too, and he'd play and then Jim would come on and do his thing, and Daniel would go, "Wow". No one plays like Jim.'

When it came to getting the best sound out of Pete's voice, Nick occasionally used a not-so-subtle approach. 'Sometimes we'd make him sing a lot until his voice fucked up, and then have a little break and he'd come back and have this great voice. His pitch isn't the best, and sometimes that would take a lot of effort. It's just one of those things. Peter is always willing, always wants to do his best. He knows he's not a natural singer, so he gives it much more effort than most.'

Nick recalls 'US Forces' undergoing major changes. Firstly the title: 'If anyone talked about a single while we were making the record, it was going to be that one. And it was originally called "The Next Big Thing". I thought, "That's great. The radio will say, 'Here's the next big thing by Midnight Oil!'", and as soon as I said that I could see them all going, "Uh-uh, we can't call it that".'

But the bigger problem concerned what key it should be

recorded in. 'We spent a lot of time getting it right. We had put all those weird sounds on it that took a long time to get right. A *long* time – all day. I remember spending six hours on one thing: the catchy percussive bits in the chorus that you can't work out. "Is it a guitar? Is it a piano?" – it's a piano with a brick placed on the sustain pedal. Rob then hit, *with his drumsticks,* the strings! That takes some accuracy of playing. And it's such a fast beat. This was before sampling, so we couldn't fake it.

'We got the song so it sounded so cool. It was completely finished except for vocals, it was late. We went to do the vocals and Peter was struggling with it a bit and Jim had a "This isn't working" look. But Peter only had one attempt at it. So next day I come in happy and up and "Here we go" as always, and they are all very quiet. "Nick, we've got something very awkward we need to speak to you about." I thought, "Oh my God, someone's died or something." We'd all been so happy the night before with "US Forces". We'd built the song up and it was sounding fantastic. They said, "We need to record it again – the whole song – in a different key." "Why?!" "Peter can't sing it." "Well, we'll get him to sing it!" "It's not going to sound right. His voice is in the wrong register." "Why? You bastards!" They knew how happy I was. It was completely finished and it was sounding incredible.

'As it turned out we didn't have to do the drums again because they are not key related. And the guitar stuff that Jim plays at the end – a genius guitar lick – I thought, "I'll never get that performance again!", so I worked out how I could pitch-change it. So I salvaged the guitar solo, and a few other things, that's why it sounds so weird. But Rob's piano thing had to be done again, and everything else as well, at one or two semitones higher or lower. The verses went lower and the choruses went higher, from memory. But it was a bloody good reason to redo a song – playing in the right key for the singer. "What key, Mr Sinatra?" Every singer has a preferred key. So I don't know who fucked up, but the key is very important.'

The album closer, 'Somebody's Trying to Tell Me Something', features some fabulous bass playing from Giffo among the fairground piano, knife-edged guitars, torrid drumming and a chilling scream from Pete. Nick: 'Giffo at his genius best. He contributed great bass lines; he's an incredible bass player and a natural musician.'

But Giffo's influence occasionally went beyond his bass playing. 'This violin player, Gisele, came down to do that stuff on "Short Memory" and no one knew quite what she was going to play – it wasn't that worked out. Jim had some ideas and we were working it out. And Giffo came in, drunk off his head, stumbling drunk, and sat in the back of the control room. He started saying, "I reckon she should do this, I got this idea." Then he went out into the studio, grabbing hold of her and trying not to fall over, with this idea. I'm thinking, "OK, we'll let him do his bit. Hopefully he'll fall asleep somewhere and we'll get on with it." Then she plays his idea – and it's brilliant! It's what's on the record, it's totally him. That violin part on "Short Memory" is all his choice of notes.'

Giffo: 'I just had a different idea how it could go. So I went, "It should go like nyear, nyear, nyear nyear", and Jim said all right and made it into musical sense. I had quite a lot of input into "Short Memory" – the little riff in the middle, the bass line, the whole swagger of it. I was really quite passionate about that song. To me it's one of the better songs Midnight Oil have written.'

Nick: '"Short Memory" ends with a guitar solo and piano solo playing off each other, then in come the big drums. It needed some crescendo; it needed to go somewhere, especially after that emotional middle bit. I didn't feel like big guitars coming in and rocking out, that would have been corny. So I got this big drum sound and Jim helped fill it up with a sound like a siren, and because it had a great beat Peter got inspired and went out and did his rap rave thing. It wasn't called rap back then. Was he the earliest white rapper?'

Nick was more like a whirlwind than a breath of fresh air, a radical challenge for the band. Giffo preferred the Glyn Johns approach to recording. 'I could relate to Glyn a lot. He's more natural performance based, which I sort of liked. Nick was a bit different, Nick chopped tape up into two-inch lengths and stuck them all back together. He was fearless when it came to messing around with the knobs, but he was more a technical sort of person than a musical person. So you had plenty more time to muck around with stuff with Nick and experiment more. Whereas Glyn wanted a performance, a live band playing – and that's what he got. Nick worked with everything coming in components and then being reassembled. I think *10–1* was really the turning point for the band. It was a fabulous album and my recollection of it is that it wasn't too hard to make, except for the usual thing – I'm still struggling with trying to be a competent studio musician. I'm just not one of them!'

Jim: 'The approaches for the different songs changed as we went into the studio, but the songs were written. It didn't feel like we were doing anything new; we just happened to be in the right place at the right time. Nick Launay was this young guy with all these ideas and wanted to try them out. So there was always a sense of adventurous spirit.'

The sessions are remembered fondly by all, but the experimental and essentially risky process they were involved in did add pressure to the situation and Rob was acutely affected by it. Jim remembers Rob going to hospital one night very mysteriously. Rob: 'It was an anxiety born of being separated from friends and family for a long time, and an anxiety as to whether the band was ever going to get out of this giant financial hole we found ourselves in after making *Place Without a Postcard*! *10–1* was the album that *had* to succeed. I remember walking around London with Jim and him saying, "I'm going to leave, the pressure's too much." It was getting to everybody. It was a real make-it-or-break-it thing with Nick – which is very good for a band, but also incredibly stressful for the people in it. So anyway, I started having anxiety attacks in that time, in the claustrophobic environment of living above the studio in Goldhawk Road. So much so that I was having the classic anxiety symptoms of sweaty palms, racing heart, feeling of lightness in the head, and I was unsure what it was. "Am I going fucking mad, or not?" Finally I get to see a doctor who said this was born of anxiety. "De-stress, go for long runs, see the big picture, and if it gets really bad cup your hands and breathe carbon dioxide back and you'll feel fine again." It's the classic "fight or flee" reaction. Once I realised what it was it didn't bother me any more and it wasn't such a problem again.'

Nick: 'To me the *10,9,8* stuff was a fantastic meeting of minds – my naive mind and their overly brilliant musicianship minds all meeting in this strange middle place – very special. In the States it was one of the biggest college radio records. It was huge, number one on college radio. And I still to this day get work from *10,9,8* because those people who were at those college radios are now A&R people, and they loved that album.'

Pete: '*10–1* is *not* a punk record. It's not a wild anarchic record at all; it's a highly arranged and almost intellectually performed record, which at its gut has got this visceral, driving energy. So it actually combined the two sides of Midnight Oil's heart and Midnight Oil's head probably as well as any record. Nick was this wild young alchemist who knew how to put his fingers over the album. I stayed behind to mix *10–1*, so I trusted him absolutely to the wire. I very much enjoyed making the record and enjoyed doing that work with him as well.'

For David Fricke, who was hearing the band for the first time on this record, the album was quite different-sounding. 'It's sort of a funny record to be introduced to because the first thing you hear when you put it on is that kind of weird dreamy reverie thing at the beginning, and it's like, "This guy's voice is really kind of strange, the song isn't really a song, I'm not quite sure what this is." Then "Only the Strong" blows up in your face, and it's "This is incredible!" Right there, the intro to "Only the Strong", that was it, that's where it started for me. When I first heard them on *10,9,8*, particularly what the double guitars were doing – hey! The funny thing is they're not really playing riffs and they're not playing straight chords or simple melodies, either. It's quite intricate. They're both playing counter-melodies, almost like a network of – "licks" doesn't even sound right, it sounds so dopey. They've created this unusual hybrid of riff and actual melody and then done it in a way where they sort of interlock, so it always sounds like four guitars instead of two. And that sound had a lot to do with the power they had, because you had this melody and force in what they were playing. It's colour and stab, which is something you don't get in a lot of guitar, even double-guitar, bands – it's really unusual. It's so intuitive, and so natural, and yet it's really aggressive. It's also quite beautiful, because there are melodies in there. And they're not just hooks, they are actually involved. It is a drama that then is elevated because the vocal melodies are so good.'

David is also a fan of the scream. 'That scream in "Only the Strong"! Oh, man! That was the other thing about them – everything in "Only the Strong" was like, "OK, this is why I love that band". If I was to point to one song that summed up everything I wanted out of them, and that they gave me, it was that, because it was the first one I really heard and it was the total package. It was melody, it was commitment, it was noise, and it was so intense, just so inclusive as well. Only the strong survive – there it is, there endeth the lesson!'

Jim: 'I think *10–1* has to be a favourite of mine because I really got on with Nick and I really love what he did, and it was so new and creative and wonderful and just sounded so good. It was a lot of fun and a laugh and that was great.'

Nick: 'Jim and I have always been on the same page, going back to *10,9,8*. We were the ones that stayed up after midnight and did all the weird stuff, and the next day it was always appreciated. But it was always like, "Now we've gone over budget, you idiots!"'

•

Budgets proved to be a big concern during the next record, *Red Sails in the Sunset*. Sony were about to buy CBS/Columbia and were very interested in a western rock band making a whole album in Japan, which had apparently never been done before. They ended up working at Aoyama studios in Tokyo – rehearsing, writing and recording in this top-of-the-line recording facility. So they were in an expensive city, in a very expensive studio, with a batch of only half-formed songs. Pete was absent from the studio quite a bit preparing for the likelihood of NDP duties and researching Japan's nuclear experience, so his role in the band as time and money monitor was being neglected a bit and the band stayed much longer than planned. They were all staying at the same hotel and walking to the studio, where a normal day lasted from noon to midnight.

The studio management organised a meeting on the first day, a weekend, with all their staff. It was a big organisation, four floors of studios. Nick Launay was producing again. 'They normally make an album in three days. It's all budgeted hour by hour. We were going in there with the idea of being there a month and a half, knowing that it could be longer. So there's all these people there, and everyone is bowing and the Oils are all sort of tall and sweaty, and I'm jetlagged with a cold or something and my nose is running. I felt terrible coz the Japanese wear face masks even when they haven't got a cold and I'm sneezing everywhere. So we arrive there and we're not taking anything that seriously, but they want this serious meeting in a circle with all these chairs. They introduce "the number one recording engineer in Japan" and "the number one arranger". They've organised that we will use all their engineers and arrangers, and I'm like, "No, I engineer it, and I produce it."

They thought that was one person doing five people's jobs, but after a while they got it. "OK, so this is different."

'The songs weren't fully formed, they were kind of un-together, and we're in an eccentric place. The most influential record in my mind at the time was the Art of Noise's album. So I'm walking around Tokyo with all this imagery, huge television screens and anime characters, all that going on, walking through Jap-anese gardens listening to the Art of Noise on my way to work with Midnight Oil. Added to all that was Peter. He worked, but he was disappearing to do his political thing. I think he thought he wasn't needed, but it didn't work that way because somehow we spent longer doing things, things got out of sync. He thought he would go away and we would work on the songs and arrangements and get the recording done, and then he'd come back and do his vocals. But in order to work out the music, we had to have a vocal to work around. If you try and do all the music hoping the vocals are going to fit, forget it. So Rob did the vocals, at least on the ones he wrote, and he was really good. I'd never heard him sing a lead vocal before. It was good – especially "Kosciuszko". So eventually when Peter came back he heard it and said, "I don't need to sing that." And it wasn't as if he was being lazy in not wanting to sing it; as we know, Peter is not a lazy man! It was a genuine thing; he thought Rob's vocal was really good. So that's why there are a few songs on there with Rob singing. They were in an "anything goes" frame of mind. "We're not going to bend to anybody's rules, let's break all the rules. It worked for us with *10,9,8*; let's push it further." That's what that album's all about.'

Pete: 'I wasn't particularly happy with the whole way everybody wanted to produce and record the album – I thought it was all a bit overdone, getting too tied down into the studio and studio effects. I mean, some of them worked and some of them didn't. In hindsight people may say they missed my participation, but no one was particularly interested in moving any quicker. We were coming off the back of an extremely successful record and the producer, plus Rob and Jim, felt that this was what they wanted to do with this record and they had a very clear view of it. Their view was clearer than mine, because I was starting to think about other things at the same time. So away they went.'

Jim: 'It was bizarre what we did. I mean, it was truly bizarre to go to Japan and make a record anyway. But I think the reason we went there was coz we didn't want to go to Rhinoceros and get that big, crashy drum sound that everyone else was getting. So we thought, "Let's go to Japan – they'll have different gear and different everything else." And we turned up and of course they had the same gear as Nick was used to working with in England.'

Rob: 'We felt we were pushing every song into an area we hadn't been before. We deliberately set out to put the quirkiest sounds on there, to make the most unusual album. And I think that was partly because of the environment, Tokyo in the mid-eighties, which was so full of youth and colour and possibilities. We were swept along by a culture shock, but also by the youth of Japan for the first time having money and cars and independence and clothes and attitude. And we were in the middle of it. I think a lot of that, a sense of "the possibilities are endless" ended up on *Red Sails*. We might have made a very different album if we'd stayed in Australia or done another English album. In the back of our minds I think we might have chosen Japan for that reason. We thought, "Let's really throw ourselves at somewhere that has no reference points to where we've been."'

Giffo also found Japan pretty stimulating. 'Going to Japan was the most amazing experience – it's one of the most interesting places I've been in my whole life. The culture is so different. We've grown up with a culture of the Japanese being these people who did all this stuff to our Aussie soldiers in World War II – and it's true, they did – so I was a bit nervous about going to Japan for a lot of reasons. What I found was the most amazing experience. They were so friendly as people, but tough at business – of course Pete did the business and he said they were pretty hardline business people. I found that we were treated incredibly well – they were just courteous people. I never expected it. In such a place, with such a population, you felt incredibly safe. Millions and millions of people jammed into a really small spot and there was no real crime or aggression. The place wasn't even grubby!'

Nick thinks Giffo really came into his own with his playing on *Red Sails*. 'Unbelievable stuff he played on that, just genius stuff. He's such an Aussie beer-drinking bloke, quite quiet and happy and gets on with his bass playing – does his bit, as bass players do. Giffo is one of the most amazing bass players I know. I honestly rate him as one of the best. His parts are very imaginative.'

There was one more record before *Diesel and Dust*, and it's one that many regard as essential in any Midnight Oil collection. The *Species Deceases* EP was recorded very close to where I worked. To get there from the Triple Jay studios you had to descend in the lift before passing through a gaggle of transvestite call girls who made the foyer and footpath their own after sunset. Then it was a quick dart across William Street, dodging the cars that slowed down for the 'regular' girls, and down into the darkness of Woolloomooloo and Paradise Studios, which had been built from the proceeds of Billy Field's monster hit 'Bad Habits'. A discreet set of buttons on a warehouse wall let you into a moderately sized version of rock'n'roll heaven, with all the clichés – spa, latest computer games and a stocked fridge (but no scantily clad women or lines of coke that I saw).

A disinterested-looking New Yorker, producer François Kevorkian, was at the controls as some fabulous rock'n'roll was recorded. I was privileged to be there when the band said they needed an extra voice for the chorus in 'Progress', and immediately accepted with the enthusiasm of a starry-eyed fan rather than the cool demeanour of a DJ who had just casually dropped in after a shift. With Jim, Rob, Martin and Giffo, I shouted 'Progress' three times – we all wore headphones and were gathered around a single microphone – then 'That's progress' another three. 'That's fine,' said François over the intercom and that was it. The band moved straight on to another task, but my involvement left me with a lifetime of nervously trying to anticipate where my bit starts each time I hear the song.

The EP contains a supercharged foursome of relatively raw rock'n'roll songs: 'basic, powerful, unadorned', one critic wrote. Pete: 'It's a great little rock record. I think the boys were red hot, playing-wise. Can't remember why, maybe we'd just finished a tour. I know that the songs, when we wrote them and rehearsed them, which all happened pretty quickly from memory, just sounded like red-hot live tracks and that was the intention. I know I was really keen for us to do stuff that wasn't too over-arranged and was more spontaneous and wilder and "live-er". I'm not saying it was only my idea, because I'm sure other people had that idea as well, but I was very pleased that that's what we were doing. I know that Rob had to go and get François up every morning at eleven o'clock and found it very difficult working with him, but I actually thought he was great to work with. I thought he got onto the takes really quickly and picked the eyes out of them. There wasn't much overdubbing, and he mixed it really well. I thought it was great fun.'

François was a lateral choice as producer. He later became known as François K and is now widely credited as the father of house music. He was initially attracted to the Midnight Oil job when he heard Rob's drum solo in 'Power and the Passion', but found himself facilitating this full-on guitar attack, and not percussion-based music as he'd anticipated. He lived on takeaway pizza and when he wasn't in the studio barely left his Kings Cross hotel room just up the hill. His trip had been soured by losing all his luggage on the flight over from New York, and although Rob took him to Gowings and kitted him up he never seemed to get over it.

Gary thought François was a great choice as producer. 'The thing about François was he was one of these people who was off the wall and not predictable, and also couldn't be controlled – the right kind of guy to work with the Oils. They should have gone more that way. He was good.' François probably doesn't see his work on *Species Deceases* as a highlight of his career, but 'Progress', 'Hercules', 'Blossom and Blood' and 'Pictures' still sound like they were recorded this morning. The disc is a scorcher.

Diesel and Dust, by comparison, was a slow burner in its feel and its road to commercial success. The scale of international touring over the two years following its release was completely unimagined. They lost Giffo just before they headed out, but Bones took his place and fitted like the fifth finger of a glove.

By the time the band returned from touring the *Diesel and Dust* album at the end of 1988 it was time for the follow-up record. They decided to work with Warne Livesey again and set up in Sydney's Rhinoceros Studios, owned by INXS, their former stablemates from the days when Gary was the manager of both bands.

Blue Sky Mining had no title for most of its recording – in fact, the song 'Blue Sky Mine' was virtually the last track to be recorded. It was created in the studio from a remnant of a song of Jim's that went back twelve years. Bones: 'The great thing about the band is that everyone has ideas and you just sort of pass them across and take them on board because it's all about people pooling their talents. Most of the songs for *Blue Sky* were co-written by Jim and Rob. Pete was never really there. He came in, did his stuff and then left. I remember one day we all gathered around the ping-pong table and it was like, "This is not working, let's knock it on the head." And I thought, "You mad bastards. Here you are in this fantastic studio with this English producer, making a record, and what do you mean it's not working? It's fucking brilliant!" But in almost every album we got to the same spot; everyone would stop because "It's not very good". I thought it was crazy, but it's just the way they are with each other. I mean, Jim's a musical genius, Rob always has a big folder of notes, it's weird. They just got to a point where they didn't think they had enough songs and, well – "Blue Sky Mine" came at the very end. It was the very last track. We'd cut it together from this thing that used to be called "Drought". They thought we were short three or four songs till the very end. Maybe it was the pressure of being the big follow-up album – "Have we got a single?" I didn't feel any of that pressure coz I was just having fun, floating around this place, and on Friday they'd serve mango daiquiris and there was catering, and it was all cool to me. In the INXS pleasure dome twelve hours a day. We were six months in the studio, ludicrously long. I mean, if you spend half a year then obviously you do get to a point where you wonder if you're doing the right thing.'

Rob remembers Pete initiating the discussion around the ping-pong table. 'This bombshell from Pete happened about two-thirds of the way through, although he'd expressed discontent before that. I think the rest of us could already hear a very strong album, including Warne and Dave Nicholas the engineer – all very positive. It was taking a long time, but we thought we were making something really great.'

The band had already recorded some fabulous songs, like 'Forgotten Years' and 'One Country', but Pete wasn't convinced the record was going to be strong enough. 'It didn't really have any song on it that really summed up what we were doing and what it was about. It had a lot of slow and medium-tempo songs on it, which didn't seem to me to have the urgency that was needed for the situation. By that stage I really did have two very full-on, full-time lives, and I think I was working as hard as I've ever worked and being fully committed on political fronts et cetera. I probably did hear it a bit more clearly when I came back in – where the sessions had got to and what we needed to do to try and lift it a bit. I think one of the upshots of the meeting was "Blue Sky" itself, the song, to get that up, and I think maybe even "King" [of the Mountain] came more to the fore. I certainly came back in to spend more time in the studio and do more writing and more singing.'

Pete does acknowledge that there were already some very strong songs recorded. 'We just didn't have enough of them. I mean, you need ten "Forgotten Years". I've always thought it was a really, really good song. It's not a case of doubting "Forgotten Years". It's a bit warlike, "Forgotten Years". It's got its place in that sort of "Blossom and Blood", slightly more serious, sombre kind of thing to it, so while it was a really good song, it needed stuff sitting around it. It's just a mood thing. You listen to an album, it's a weighting thing; how you weight it. "One Country", for example, is another pretty fine piece of writing, the way it unfolds. It summed up a lot of what we were doing, and Jim's whole initial thing was beaut – and then where we took it, it went to some place. And by the end of it there's all sorts of good things in it. But you need ways of counterbalancing deeper moments with moments that are storytelling, or moments that have a bit more of the breath of life in them.'

Jim missed Pete's presence in the studio. 'I actually felt like we'd done all that touring, we had all this huge success and suddenly it wasn't feeling like a band any more, it was feeling like a bunch of individuals. And I rang him and said, "Come in more, we need you more than you probably think we need you." I think Pete's input is always very non-specific but it's good, it's always a really good vibe. He gets people not getting too intellectual about stuff – he'll always get people to just fuckin' well play! You know – go hard, go wild! That kind of stuff, which is very important, and I think he was feeling that it wasn't very wild, what we were doing.'

So as a result of the meeting around the ping-pong table Pete committed to being there more often and there was the impetus to create a new song based on the twelve-year-old Jim composition named 'Drought'. Rob: 'The original chords and stuff were part of "Drought". But the verse melody changed, and the lyrics changed, and the chorus wasn't there, and the central riff was in a different key, et cetera, et cetera, and it was a completely different arrangement.'

Jim: 'We kind of grafted them into some sort of arrangement and then ripped the arrangement apart, which Warne did actually, a really good job! And we worked and worked and worked on it and I remember sitting in the corner reading Ben Hill's book about Wittenoom and going, "This is such a great issue, such a great subject for a song. Why not?"'

Rob: 'That, probably more than any other song, particularly any other radio song we'd ever done, was collaboration. It's not a Jim song. The original thing it was based upon was added to by my chorus, "Who's gonna save me", all that stuff, and the middle eight, "And if the blue sky mining company". The verse lyrics were completely written by Pete after being directed by Jim to *Blue Murder*, the book about Wittenoom. The intro riff and stuff was actually a contribution by Warne, I think, which he took no credit for. The harmonica played over the top was Warne's idea. It was truly a collaborative effort, that song.'

Rob suggested the title of the album after a meeting with their accountant, who referred to a couple of companies they shouldn't invest in as 'blue sky stuff'. 'I just took the mining idea of Wittenoom and put them together to get the title. "Blue sky stuff" meant "The sky's the limit but the floor can fall in on you as well" – totally speculative stuff.'

Warne: 'It was particularly rewarding that something that happened in the studio and came together in a slightly haphazard way, with a very high creative energy, actually did sort of become the pivotal track on the record. It became the biggest single off the record and inspired the album title. It's kinda nice when that happens, but it doesn't always work, of course. That sort of freedom of being able to work like that was neat, was really cool.'

Since the band had worked with Warne on *Diesel*, Giffo had left and Bones had arrived. One of Warne's skills and passions is capturing and arranging vocals, so he appreciated the flexibility that Bones' voice brought to the band. 'Bones is probably more versatile vocally, and that was probably the biggest difference in their contributions. The majority of the backing vocals on *Diesel and Dust* were done by Rob, but you now had two people in the band, in addition to Pete, who could really sing very strongly. They've both got quite good ranges as well. Bones can really get up high as well as sing in a mid-range pretty strongly, which is always great from a backing-vocal point of view because obviously you're trying to get above the lead vocals, so it's good to have that strength up in the higher register. Bones is perhaps slightly more melodic with his bass playing and Giffo is a bit more of a driving-straight-ahead kind of player, but they're both great and it worked well with either of them, really.'

Bones: 'On *Blue Sky Mining* Rob and I worked tremendously hard on the vocals. Warne was right on, and being a musician himself he put us through the hoops, we'd be in there singing until we rasped. When I listen back to it they're the best records – *Capricornia*, *Diesel and Dust* and *Blue Sky*. Pete has never sounded better to me. That's Warne going, "Nah, you didn't do it properly, to my standard." Pete would come in and just sort of fire it off and "Right, that's it." Pete can be very nasal, but Warne made him sing, and the guy *can* sing. I mean, it's hard being the singer, you don't play an instrument and the recording session goes on and on, and you're not needed for the first two or three days. The rhythm tracks are down, overdubs are done, the base of the song has been built up, and then you come in and do your part a couple of days later. Vocalists just don't tend to be there all the time. There's nothing for them to do, they just get bored. Even I got bored, being there from midday, and it was 9 p.m. before I was called to do anything. It's a long day to sit around playing table tennis and reading trash magazines.'

Pete: 'I don't know that Warne affected the way I sang a great deal, except he probably got me singing more in tune. He brought high levels of musicianship to the process. He was pretty picky about pitch and phrasing and those sorts of things. It was a good discipline for me to work my way through songs like that. I think he was a good communicator, and even though he was adept at helping sort arrangements out, he was also quite good at cutting to the chase. I've always believed that getting stuff down reasonably quickly is better – it's more human, it's more live, it's got more living quality. But sometimes what you're doing isn't particularly inspiring, and you've got to work at it and keep on going, and he was good at that. And by *Blue Sky* he was good at pulling more consistent, modulated performances out of the singing. All the singing, the backing vocals as well – everybody did tend to get backing-vocalitis at times!'

Chris Moss: 'Once the *Diesel* success had happened we went into the next record with the whole world wanting it. The world had tasted and loved and was looking forward to whatever the band had to offer next. That was a really heady experience for me, to be a part of that. You spend most of your career on the international front walking around the world begging, grovelling, trying to get people interested in your material, trying to encourage and enthuse them to participate in it, and you get knocked back quite a bit. Then all of a sudden you're confronted with every territory in the world ringing, going, "When's the album coming? When are we going to get it? When's it going to be released?" And it went phenomenally well! The first single, "Blue Sky Mine", was just awesome. The feel of it, the song and everything else, to go out the gate with that, well, it just took the whole *Diesel and Dust* thing to another level. It just went way up there. The imagery over in Kalgoorlie in the salt pans, the subject matter and the harmonica, it was amazing, such a great feeling. And it was embraced around the world. It was everything that everybody thought they were going to see and hear – it was absolutely brilliant. Part of what made it so successful was the way it tackled the subject matter – "In the end the rain comes down and washes it all away" – if everyone does the right thing there's a future. Visually, in the video, it told such a sad story, but it was portrayed in a way that was uplifting.'

Despite the subject matter of the 'Blue Sky Mine' single, the album was not generally railing against corporate malpractice. It took those concerns and expanded their application to more universal issues. Pete: 'It's a greenie record, and a spiritual record. I think that's where we were heading as people. We were moving away from simply wanting to say stuff like "Big corporations are ruling the world, they're pretty greedy and horrible, and they get away with blue murder poisoning people in Third World countries" or whatever, to reflecting on some of the deeper changes that were under way in our lives and some of the things that were happening around us – a new, evolving awareness about the importance of the environment and what it meant. That's starting to come through in those songs. I think we were getting greener.'

Chris: 'I always thought that every record they did was distinctly different from the one before it. *Red Sails* was totally divorced from *10,9,8*, as was *Diesel* from *Red Sails*, as was *Blue Sky Mining* from *Earth and Sun and Moon*. That was one of the key things. If you look at any successful act, those that are very successful are artists who are able to reinvent themselves every time, and do it with the same calibre of creativity as they've done on each previous occasion. That's the characteristic, for me, that really defines a great act.'

After *Blue Sky Mining* there was *Earth and Sun and Moon*, then *Breathe*, then *Redneck Wonderland* and, finally, *Capricornia* – all marvellously individual recordings connected to, but not necessarily in step with, perceived global music tastes. On the way they released the live album *Scream in Blue*, the *20,000 Watt RSL* compilation, and *The Real Thing*, a collection of 'unplugged' recordings with three new songs. Some of those records were more polished, some were rougher, and some were more in synch with other sounds around at the time.

Many fans will argue that these later recordings contain examples of the band's best work, but the industry, particularly in the USA, had moved on, or lost faith, or found the band's relatively unconventional ways too difficult. Musical progress was a primary plank in the band's overall philosophy, and being in the studio was when they had the opportunity to actually do it – to progress. Jim was always happy when in the studio, despite the pressure, Martin too, and Rob as well to a lesser extent. For these three, nothing was too much trouble if it meant a better end result – and they were always aware of posterity when creating their music. Jim and Martin and Rob took a very long-term view of all their recording sessions. Pete was less happy in the studio environment, and less inclined to spend as much time on things. He was happy to do his bit, but would get restless if asked to sit for extended periods. Giffo absolutely hated recording, and Bones was bored by large chunks of it.

Each record was a step forward; each was either a chance to capture a song that had proved itself on the road or to write and create together. The band also drew from bits and pieces of unrecorded songs from their long history. No idea, once offered, was immune from butchery and reworking some time in the future. This was one of the band's real strengths. In general they approached the studio and its processes and the songwriting tasks at hand with a relative lack of ego and preciousness, totally in the spirit of creating the best music their collective skills could manage. However, making the record is only half the deal; the next obligation for the modern musician is going on the road. And that road can be endless.

six

into the black

Once *Blue Sky Mining* was released, a huge year started to unfold. The band's 1990 calendar was looking busy. First stop was for shows in the UK and Europe, with a short break from playing during the French leg to make a clip for 'Forgotten Years' in Verdun. Then on to the USA and Canada for a three-month visit, including three nights at Radio City Music Hall in New York and a gig at the Los Angeles Universal Amphitheatre at the end of June to finish. Then back to Europe, where the band were to have their first taste of the huge summer music festivals with performances at Roskilde in Denmark, Turku in Finland and the Isle of Calf in Norway. An extensive tour of Australia was also being planned for their return at the end of the year.

Nineteen-ninety loomed large for Pete especially, because at the same time as the band's international touring commitments he had to manage his first federal election as president of the Australian Conservation Foundation. The Labor Government needed the ACF's endorsement of its environmental policies and Graham Richardson, the Minister for the Environment and the man given responsibility inside the government for their re-election, was keeping the pressure on. His advisers were regular visitors to the Oils' Glebe office, there was a power breakfast or two, and Richardson even appeared backstage at an Oils gig for a photo opportunity.

In some ways, despite the fact that Pete had to take his political responsibilities on the road with him, it was a relief to be leaving the country. But there was no easy escape from his public profile. When the band boarded the plane there was a big display of the in-flight magazine, with Pete's face on the cover, on the wall of the entranceway. As they made their way down the aisle to their seats it seemed like everyone had a Pete mask on as they read the magazine. Then they were welcomed on board by a captain whose name was Gary Morris! It wasn't a good sign.

The band faced the job of going around the world and playing the new songs with a mixture of excitement and anticipation but also with some dread. Different members had different degrees of each, but touring is an inevitable consequence of making a record – especially an expensive record with all the attendant record company expectations. 'You're an entertainer, you go into a studio for incredible amounts of time and make a record, then you go around the world touring it – it's just part of the job,' says Bones. But for the Oils it was the hardest part of the job.

Before every tour the band has to gather and decide on all manner of matters, from the set design and level of light show to the size of the venues in each country and the amount of press and publicity they will do. They also have to do extensive rehearsals, depending on how big a gap there has been between tours. Bones: 'You're not gonna want to come out and be mediocre Midnight Oil. It always takes us two to three weeks to hit our stride once we go on tour after a large break. You go into rehearsal and then you do a few warm-up shows and the pain factor kicks in, the blisters, your ears start ringing, you sweat, and then after two weeks of that – match fit.'

He recalls the standard pre-tour rehearsal process. 'Rob and I used to go into a rehearsal room before a tour and just play coz we decided that there was no point in the rest of the band coming along until we had our shit together, and then we'd bring the guitar players in, and then finally Pete. I changed my style a bit when I joined the Oils. Rob's a powerhouse; I never used to play in that kind of fashion. It was hard, the hardest bass gigs I've done, because you're just powering it so much. It's so "on" and the tempos are so fast in a lot of the songs, and quite complicated parts. Certainly if you lapse, well, it's the engine room: if you blow a cylinder in a car, it starts blowing smoke, and the O ring goes, and next minute the top end of the engine's gone. It's kind of like that in the rhythm section of a band. It's like a Sherman tank – hard, but incredibly good fun at the same time.'

The band had never anticipated America as being a likely market for their music, let alone as the place for their international breakthrough. Gary: 'They had an attitude problem with the US: they felt US culture was suffocating Australia. Not until the end did they realise that they liked America.' Midnight Oil had always presumed the British would be more receptive. *Diesel and Dust* did well in the UK, certainly better than any previous album. It was a breakthrough hit there, but nothing compared to the scale or enthusiasm of the response in the USA or France and Germany. The English record company, A&M, had a very parochial attitude from the beginning and nothing much changed over time. *Place Without a Postcard* was 'too Australian', they said, and then *Diesel* wasn't loud enough. In England there was always a significant cult audience for the band but barely any mainstream profile. When it came to Australian music the Brits preferred Rolf Harris or the Seekers (and, later, Kylie), or, at the other end of the scale, the Saints, Nick Cave and the Bad Seeds or AC/DC.

Originally the band had felt much closer to the English music scene typified by the Beatles and the Who than to the scene in America, and their lack of success in Britain was a source of frustration and bewilderment. They didn't feel close to America and had serious misgivings about American culture in the way it manifested itself via foreign policy, media and music, seeping into – if not flooding – Australian culture. The Oils – with Gary smoothing (!) the way – were generally seen as too brash, too colonial and too much trouble in the UK. Even when they played full houses at some of the most prestigious venues in London the record company would say, 'Yeah, but it's full of Australians.' Nevertheless, they did get to play Glastonbury a couple of times and the Wembley Arena, they supported the Who in Birmingham, and there was a big London CND show at the Lyceum in 1983. They also performed legendary stands at the Marquee and Zig Zag clubs, and headlined at the Hammersmith Odeon. But over time, for commercial reasons, they had to shift the emphasis to North America. Over the next few years they were forced to consider that in lots of ways Australia had more in common with the ex-colony than the ex-colonial power.

From *Blue Sky Mining* onwards their main practical contact and facilitator at Sony in the USA was Mason Munoz. Mason had been working in LA running the Sony/Columbia international office when he met Denis Handlin at a convention in the UK. Denis invited Mason to come to Australia later in the year, and while in Sydney he was at a club and heard 'The Dead Heart'. 'I called my boss the next day and said, "I heard this undeniably amazing song last night. It's going to be huge – Midnight Oil, 'The Dead Heart'." The reply was, "Mason, it'll never happen. They're too political." About a year later I got a call from my boss at Columbia Records in New York: "If you come back I promise I'll give you Bob Dylan and I'll give you Midnight Oil."'

Mason became the band's label manager, responsible for liaison between them and the record company. The Exxon gig was one of his first exercises with the band, and it was the start of a relationship that Gary came to depend on. *Blue Sky Mining* was an amazing time of stress and triumph for the band. They kept their heads down and toured hard as Gary and Mason sought to keep them in the public eye, performing live in front of as many people as possible, as often as possible. On the surface of it, life was stimulating; it was certainly busy. All around them was a world of differences, and there were times when the tours were enlightening and culturally broadening. They enjoyed playing the songs and feeling the energy of the audience, but realised that the touring life was risking their lives with their families and they needed to draw the line somewhere between their own sanity and the endless, relentless sameness of the view from the stage. Being on the road risked their connection with one of the elements that made them different: their commitment to and love of home.

Everything about 1990 had been planned to run like clockwork, with major shows at significant venues, plenty of advance promotion, record company support at the retail level, a tour bus with all modern conveniences – all systems were go. This was theoretically the high life, and it certainly had all the superficial trappings of international success, but the band began to find that much of the day-to-day life just wasn't pleasant. Most hotels, most buses and planes and most venues look exactly the same from the inside. That time at night when the fans were smiling and the band were firing was all they looked forward to. In America they would have stadiums dancing, and the French and the Germans would buy the record in unprecedented numbers. Momentum and enthusiasm for the band and the new record were universally strong, but still the time and energy the tasks at hand absorbed would take their toll on the band members.

Their first trip to North America was a brief non-playing visit in 1981. Zev Eizik was still managing the band and Connie was the band's tour manager. She recalls: 'They'd never been to America, and came to LA on their way to record *Place Without a Postcard* in England. I remember us flying into LA and the first thing that happened was Peter *had* to drive us from the airport – he was like, "I'm going to drive." "OK Peter, whatever." We had a station wagon and you gotta remember, here we drive on the other side of the road, and the steering wheel is on the other side of the car. So he pulls out of the car park and immediately hits a bus! Straight out of the parking area and takes a mirror off the side of a bus! Then we get to the hotel – we were staying on Sunset Boulevard – and we're all feeling a bit jet-lagged, but Rob decides to go out for a walk. He goes up to Hollywood Boulevard, a street away, and walks into an armed robbery. There were two guys with sawn-off shotguns! So by the time he got back to the hotel he was like, "You'll never guess what happened to me!" And I'd been telling them America was really nice, because you know what they're like about America – they weren't real gung-ho about going there. Then Peter hits a bus, and Rob walks into an armed robbery!'

Connie also guided the band on their second visit to North America in 1984, when they took didj player Charlie McMahon with them for eleven dates in New York, Los Angeles, Montreal, Detroit and Chicago. Their third visit was an unlikely pairing with British pop reggae band UB40 a year later. By then Zev was no longer the band's manager, and although Connie had gone with him she agreed to return to help on the American tour. 'There was a parting of the ways because Gary came back. I stayed with ACE but Gary called and said, "Why don't you come and tour with us? We're going to America." We worked with UB40, who I'd worked with already on their tour of Australia.'

UB40 had sympathetic politics and were good people. However, the Oils' music scared the pants off their crowd, and the way the tour had been organised was problematic as well. The band had to do a lot of flying rather than using a tour bus, and this proved very taxing. 'You just didn't get any sleep,' Michael Lippold remembers. 'You got an hour, an hour and a half a night. We'd leave the gig, usually have to travel an hour to the hotel, check in to the hotel at 2 a.m. or 3 a.m. then have to get up at five or six, go to the fucking airport, and catch a plane and get ready for the next gig – fuck no! At least in a bus you can sleep. Half our time was travelling to hotels or airports; it was fucked. I used to insist on getting into bed and having some sleep even if it was only for an hour and a half. Wormy, our lighting guy, wouldn't take his clothes off. He used to sleep with his shoes on and never even unpacked his bag. As soon as that door got knocked on in the morning he was up and walking out the door. And I'd be going, "How does he do that?" It took ages before I knew how he did it. I just thought, "Fuck, he gets ready quick! Why can't I do that?" I'd go and get on the bus to the airport and he'd already be asleep, because he wouldn't even have woken up. He'd just move from the bed to the bus. He was so good at it!'

During the first of the US *Diesel* tours in 1988, Grafitti Man opened the show, then Yothu Yindi performed with their dancers, and then the Oils. The members of Yothu Yindi had never left tropical Arnhem Land when they were invited to join the Diesel and Dust to Big Mountain tour, and there was some trouble when the temperature dropped. The touring group encountered some extremely cold weather and Yothu Yindi lit a fire in the bus. Bones and Michael both remember the incident well. Michael: 'Yothu Yindi's bus driver was a redneck who had a scar from his ear to his mouth, and a pistol. He was going to shoot them!'

Bones: 'They lit a campfire in the back of a forty-five-foot motor home, and the driver was very upset. In the back lounge, on the floor, a half-million-dollar motor vehicle and there's a fire in the back of the bus!' You can get cold and homesick on a tour bus, and according to Jeff Apter's biography of

Silverchair, *Tomorrow Never Knows*, the young Aussie boys from the beachside city of Newcastle also succumbed to the freezing conditions on their first tour of America – they lit a kerosene heater in the main lounge area of their bus.

That first *Diesel* tour had a vaguely calamitous ending, too, as Bones remembers. 'We were playing somewhere in California in '88 and Pete leapt off the stage to run down and slap hands, press flesh with the punters in the front row. He came back and Michael crouched down in front of the stage so Pete could step onto his back and get back up but at the same time some security guy got confused and thought Pete was just some guy trying to get onto the stage. Pete flung him off but the security guy hit the side of the stage and knocked himself out. Unfortunately he was a cop. So Pete's knocked out a Californian policeman. The show ends and we're in our little mobile dressing room and suddenly there's sirens and we're completely surrounded by police, can't move. It was the last show of the American tour: there's the champagne on ice and Sergeant Something is getting heavy talking about assault charges. It was great!'

The band always preferred that Gary didn't go on tour with them. Some of his duties on the road were taken by the tour manager, whose job it was to make the whole show run. Connie was fantastic, and her most successful successor, Willie MacInnes, was equally gregarious and competent – and almost as good a dancer. He cushioned the ride as best he could and kept at bay those who sought to disturb or intrude on the band. He was their protector and provider, and on those occasions when they needed particular mothering he would FedEx in their favourite chowder from a restaurant in

Boston. His hotel room, wherever it happened to be, was the party room – 'Willie's Bar & Grill', as Rob titled his 2003 book about the band on the road in the USA.

Willie was a charm machine, with a very convincing Prussian accent that he launched into when it was necessary to move people urgently. He was the captain of the touring ship and officiated at all levels, from early morning wake-up calls to moving a party of twelve into an already fully booked restaurant, or arranging parking for two semitrailers and three forty-foot coaches.

Willie could make things happen when they were most needed. On one occasion, when the band were due to play at one of the big European festivals in front of a crowd of fifty or sixty thousand, they were caught in a major traffic jam making their way up the mountain to the festival site, seemingly close to the venue but far enough away to make achieving their stage time an impossibility. Willie jumped out of the bus and disappeared, heading back downhill on the back of a motorbike. He returned several minutes later with a helicopter. By then Jim and Martin had panicked and grabbed pillion rides, each holding his guitar case with one hand and the jacket of his unknown motorcycle chauffeur with the other. Willie used the miraculous helicopter to airlift the remaining band members to the festival site in enough time to see frozen-blue versions of Martin and Jim arrive on the bikes. Already late, they had no choice but to go straight on stage and perform. Jim says his fingers didn't thaw properly until after the show.

By the time of the *Diesel* tours in 1988 the band had high-quality and well-placed support on both sides of the Atlantic. Everywhere they went the 'Beds Are Burning' single had preceded them and that meant bigger venues and bigger crowds. Rob remembers the change in their status in France. 'We were suddenly elevated from the Elysée Montmartre club, which might hold 1000 or 1200, to the Zenith Theatre in Paris, which I guess holds between six and ten thousand people. We were supported by a fairly unknown band at the time, the Red Hot Chili Peppers, and I remember Bonesy coming backstage and going, "There's four guys out there in penis socks!" That appealed to Bones immensely.

'The next time we went back it got bigger again. We played at the Bercy Auditorium, which holds maybe 16 000. Then the dominoes fell all over Europe. A similar situation happened in Sweden. There we had done a little club the first time that only held two or three hundred people, a tiny little club. The next time we went back we played at the Globe Arena in central Stockholm, which is an indoor venue with a huge dome over it. You can see it all over Stockholm. It holds about 18 000. The ceiling is so high that the Swedes told us that clouds form at the top of it. They have cloudy days inside this thing, it's so big! So suddenly there in 1988–89 the band was catapulted from club or theatre level into the very top level.'

In the latter part of 1990 extra European shows were added to the tour and the band did another run through France, with shows in Béziers, Fréjus and the Bercy. Despite the rigorous demands of the touring lifestyle the band only cancelled a couple of shows in their entire career. Rob: 'No one wanted to let the other members down, so you had to be pretty crook to do it. It's a cliché, but the show must go on. You're performers; it doesn't matter how crook you are. There were only a couple of times, like when I was running a really high fever and had the beginnings of pneumonia, that I actually couldn't play, when it would have been dangerous. But our band has traditionally had no sympathy for that whatsoever. There was always enormous pressure from band members and/or management and/or record company and/or agents to play because— we've got costs, have to pay the crew, have to pay for the trucks, have to pay for the lights, have to pay for the tour.'

A lunch in Lyon with Salomon Hazat, the band's French promoter, almost caused a cancellation of their huge Bercy show. Every time they came to France Salomon would try to teach them something about French food. 'I would take them to the provinces, where there is real food. Once we went to Lyon – this is the place to go to eat really French. Some of the food is not very attractive if you say it, but when it is cooked very well . . . ! Things like the balls, like intestines, ears, brains – offal. Some of the band were vegetarian at the time, but I said, "We are in a major restaurant in Lyon and you will eat something, but I will tell you what it is after." And I ordered everything they would never eat. They were all, "Well, it's very strange, Salomon, but we have to say it's quite good. What is it?" I said again, "After, after." We had very good wine and everything was great and then the dessert arrived, and I told them. I thought they would cancel the show, they were so sick! It's funny because you don't realise how you can give something to someone and when you tell him what it is, then mentality works stronger than anything else. They were sick. And I have to say that one or two did not want to speak with me ever, nearly ever, because they were pissed off. "How could you let us eat this? It's terrible. How could you do that? We will never do restaurant time with you ever. I'm sick now. I cannot play the show." But fuck, I thought they were adults. It was an experience that made me laugh – after they played the show! Rob was always the most excited, with Peter, to go to a restaurant to try. Rob was the one who laughed after this miserable experience, but Peter was so pissed off you can't believe. I think he was the one who was the most sick, because at the restaurant he tried everything! But when he realised what he'd eaten . . . ! It was so great – but not at the time. They came 10 000 kilometres by plane and they were very curious and into the idea of doing local things to get to know the stranger. To appreciate the stranger you need to live like he does. France is still a bizarre place for a lot of people.'

America is also a very bizarre place for a lot of people. And it is a very large place, with 290 million people at last count. There are thousands of radio stations, and it's not an easy place to succeed – in fact, it's unbelievably difficult. A hit in the USA is the pinnacle for most musicians, and when a band has one, they have to hang on for grim life. Success at that level has a lot to do with being in the right place at the right time, and 'Beds Are Burning' certainly had a little of that. Like most overseas territories it was *10–1* and then *Red Sails* that had started to build legendary status for the band in the States, particularly among the people in the know, and that helped to open the door for *Diesel and Dust,* and then *Blue Sky Mining,* and all the touring that surrounded those records.

But touring America is like playing in fifty different countries – the east coast is light years from the west, and in the centre there are other quite different cultures, each with millions of subscribers. The environments are different and the accents are different, but inside the big venues they are all people in T-shirts drinking Bud. On the bus the band had a chance to see the differences only fleetingly. The journey waited for no one, and when you are tens of thousands of kilometres from home, the bus is all there is. Bones: 'We all varied in how we dealt with it. At different periods of time different people would crack – you're going to get homesick and it doesn't all happen at the same time. So someone will get a pack of sad for a few weeks or a few days, but the rest of you identify what's going on. Maybe they want some space, because you're living very confined with each other. You just lend them a bit of moral support. Everyone would rather be at home than having a bum night in Pittsburgh. But it's only one night, and then you move on to somewhere else. In fact, touring is really boring apart from being on stage, because you're always in transit, on hold. You're in a van or a plane or a bus. Obviously going to places like South Africa or South America seem highly exotic after you've been around North America and Europe endless times, because it just becomes so repetitious.

'Pete would get frustrated because the time changes and stuff would put out his ability to deal with the other issues in his life. It's only been in the last few years that there's been satellite phones, laptops and email. In the eighties it was like being on a ship at sea. There was no contact from the time you left one venue until you arrived at a hotel the next day. And really enjoyable for that. The last few years with cell phones on the bus, you know, we could ring each other in our bunks! Laptops and stuff mean the outside world isn't far away. You can get a call from home about the guttering. You're on the road between Phoenix and somewhere else trying to deal with a guttering problem on the other side of the world. I kind of preferred it when we were ships at sea.'

Touring in 1990 was very challenging, but because they were older guys with many years' experience as a band, they managed to survive the exhausting life on the road without falling victim to the pitfalls that often trip up younger bands enjoying the sort of worldwide acclaim that the Oils now were. Bones remembers a mature attitude prevailing. 'When you're in a young band you get on your shaggin' boots, your drinking glove, you smoke roaches and off you go, and you get that out of your system. Oils were much more laid back – there was none of that hurrah going on.'

By the time of *Blue Sky Mining* there were quite a few Midnight Oil children (nine, in fact – eight girls and one boy), so naturally the band had a preference for shorter tours. But shorter tours are less economical and logistically more difficult, and in the pressure-cooker environment of the time they were not an option. The rationale was always that the longer you toured the longer you could stay home, but it was never as straightforward as that. In the middle of the tour new dates would be added, the tour would be extended, trade-offs would have to be made – a couple of weeks at home in exchange for extra tour legs. They were big tours, although not as big as Metallica, who do two years at a time, or even U2 and REM, who can appear to tour constantly because of being based in the northern hemisphere.

Gary was always pushing the band to move operations out of Australia. In 1981 London was his preferred choice of headquarters; at *Blue Sky Mining* time it was New York. 'I've always felt that in order to be relevant to the northern hemisphere the band should have moved their families either to New York or to somewhere in Europe, so that when you're in the flow of things that are happening you get invited, you participate, you cross-cultivate with other artists, managers, promoters, you're actually on the coalface of idea inception. You can have input into collective entrepreneurial activity. Back in Australia you've got time-zone issues, the tyranny of distance, you've got the whole sort of momentum of getting fifteen people on an aeroplane and getting production on an aeroplane and then moving across and living out of hotels and all that expense. So to really kick-start the Midnight Oil machine, to get into an activity that's northern hemisphere based, you've got to have your roll-out pretty well sorted six months in advance. And if you're going to be rolling out something six months in advance and focusing and planning all of the necessities for that, you're pretty fixed – you're not very flexible. And you've got to go and do your six-month tour or your three-month tour or your one-month strategic hit that's all been planned six months beforehand. You're focused on that, you budget for it, and then you go and do it.

'In contrast, if you actually live there, in that environment, your ability to turn things around is very quick. The ability to attend to activity that is germinating is more efficient: you've got crew on the ground, you've got production on the ground, the band living at home, and it's nothing to get on a flight or a train or whatever and get to where you want to go.'

But with children in school, homes being established and the band's continued commitment to being essentially an 'Australian' band, they resisted Gary's strategy and remained steadfastly based in Australia. *Blue Sky Mining* was a big record, selling over two and a half million copies in a relatively short time, but it was not quite the success of *Diesel and Dust*. To make this one as big, the band would have to tour for twice as long. The campaign for airplay by the record company was also more fraught, and according to Gary the playing field had gone from flat to bumpy again. 'Once again payola was back in place. The boogie man of US anti-trust investigation had moved on to other things and America was back to business as usual. So the "magic" that was around *Diesel and Dust* wasn't there. It was business around *Blue Sky Mining*. It was all business, and you had to make it work, and put the bucks into it, and roll it out, and direct it and control it, and produce it. There was a lot of hard work in selling half the amount of records.'

The pressure from the record company and the public and from Gary was hard to resist. After *Diesel*, Gary had negotiated new contracts for all Midnight Oil's recording, publishing and merchandising. Substantial amounts were made available against the band's future costs. Gary: 'There was nearly six million dollars that came in on advances after *Diesel and Dust*. The band were at that platform where you have this sense of infallibility, immortality, high priority on everything you do and say, and I think it then became no longer a coordinated accident that worked. It became an enterprise, a business, and it had to be run efficiently and accountably, and it had to have proper decision making and planning, and all of a sudden everything became very serious.'

●

Through the *Diesel and Dust* period and into *Blue Sky Mining* a new person became head of Columbia Records in the United States: Don Ienner. He proved to be a man who loved the potential of the band but had his own very distinct ideas on how to capitalise on it – but these ideas could change very suddenly. Needless to say, he was (and still is) a very powerful individual, and Gary was forced to negotiate almost everything with him. At first the similarities in their personalities made them a good team and things hummed along, but as decisions became contentious serious difficulties began to arise.

Don desperately wanted Columbia to be perceived as a cool label – and there is a story that he went out and signed Toad the Wet Sprocket and a band called Poi Dog Pondering not because of the music they were making, but because of their names. He didn't care what they sounded like, he just wanted Columbia Records to be cool, and Midnight Oil were seen as a really cool band who were doing their own thing.

Chris Moss was Sony Australia's international marketing manager at the time and observed some of the goings-on at head office. 'There was a conflict with Donny, the momentum got lost. All of a sudden when we were meant to go to radio with a track, we didn't. In Australia we'd gone "Blue Sky Mine", "Forgotten Years" and "King of the Mountain". They were huge singles, enormously successful. He wanted "River Runs Red" as the second single over "Forgotten Years", so we went to "River Runs Red", and at the last minute he changed his mind and wanted to go back to "Forgotten Years". And it just put the whole thing out of kilter – the timing, the momentum.'

Then Don and Gary really started to lock horns. With so much money at stake, relations with international record company executives were always going to be challenging. The nature of the environment at the top level was established at one of Gary's earliest meetings at Columbia headquarters in New York. Before Don was running the company it was Al Teller. A story that Gary laughingly refuses to deny or comment on concerns a meeting with Al sometime in the early eighties. The story goes that Gary went into Al's office demanding support for the *10–1* album. Gary, being his usual not-so-subtle self, went in really hard and Al, who was apparently a bit of a wild card too, turned around and unzipped his fly. He put his penis on the table and said, 'Listen, Gary, if it comes down to a battle of whose dick is bigger, there's mine.' No version of the story records what Gary's response was, but that sort of behaviour usually only encouraged him. Welcome to the big time.

Generally Gary seems to have been able to match wits with the record company executives in the early days. He was supremely confident in the band's abilities and had certainly put a lot of time into the USA, setting the band up with the right people from touring companies to publicity organisations and even a high-level co-management deal. With Sony Australia's help he had brought in North American journalists and industry people to experience the band in full flight on home turf. Sony Australia's general manager, Denis Handlin: 'When people actually see them live and see the crowd reaction, that makes a big difference. It was a great thing for people to see what an *amazing* live experience it is. The band were their own best sales tool because they had the goods. I mean, they just had it.'

Chris: 'There was Steve Smith from the *Hard Report*, the most important industry tip sheet in America at the time,

Chips Moman from MTV – it was the early days of MTV – and some key journalists. We brought them down, there were four or five of them and basically they were in Midnight Oil land for five days with gigs and Gary – 'the world according to Gary', the whole thing – and it was quite amazing. They went back, as everyone did who came in contact with the band, completely smitten with what Midnight Oil was all about.'

Following up the multimillion-dollar sales of *Diesel and Dust* created pressure for everybody and Gary had challenges, too. He had enormous logistical concerns moving band and crew and gear around the world and balancing the demands of the record company with the desires of the band. But more important were the big sovereignty issues. Gary was struggling to maintain the band's control over their own affairs. This had never been an issue in their relations with Sony in Australia, but now the stakes were bigger and in New York the executives were committed but anxious. Not surprisingly, their priority was to maximise their financial return, and to do that firstly the band had to stay on the road, and secondly the record company needed to create a strategy for the release of singles from *Blue Sky Mining*. Decisions about which songs should be singles, and into which radio markets they should be directed, were now largely out of the band's control. Their profile was still extremely high, but despite the first and second singles – 'Blue Sky Mine' and 'Forgotten Years' – both charting strongly, particularly in Europe, the album hadn't produced another hit the size of 'Beds Are Burning'.

The record company felt they needed another candidate, a third single, for mainstream radio in America, and even though 'King of the Mountain' had been a big hit in Australia, 'Bedlam

Bridge' was chosen to be next. So while they were in New York a 'Bedlam Bridge' video clip had to be made.

The Australian Ambassador to the UN, John Dauth, is an old friend of Pete's and mine from college days in Canberra. Usually the band all stay at the Roger Smith Hotel on Lexington Avenue, but John's place is hard to resist as an occasional refuge for Pete in New York. The embassy is just a stone's throw from UN headquarters and a spit above FDR Drive on the east side of midtown Manhattan. Its spacious accommodation, expansive views of the river and spectacular Australian chef allow Pete to enjoy the smell of home and a relaxing environment that is otherwise difficult to find when on the road for months on end.

From the embassy windows you can see U Thant Island, which looks like a large piece of floating excreta in the otherwise relatively unpolluted East River. It's the size of a semi-submerged whale, and this improbably barren stretch of real estate seems perverse surrounded by the spectacular density of Manhattan. It is commonly referred to as 'Rat Island', and at about 2 a.m. one cold autumn morning in early 1990 Pete discovered why. A helicopter with a spotlight and camera on board was making a number of runs over the island while Pete sang different verses to 'Bedlam Bridge', a song highlighting the irony of so many poor people living in the world's richest city. Each time the helicopter completed a run the rats closed in – lots of them. Pete was singing and dancing predominantly for the clip, but between takes his noise and movement were all that kept the rats at bay. He had already put in six or seven hours doing other bits for the clip prior to the island effort. In the meantime, the rest of the band earned

$10 busking on the street, then hung around the Queensborough Bridge and wandered among the street people. Clip director Claudia Castle had to convince a couple of police she was not homeless herself. The shots on Rat Island were extra vocal shots. Pete was there with the rats for two hours but, in the Spinal Tap tradition of rock'n'roll fiasco, the whole weird (and no doubt expensive) exercise was a waste of time, and none of the footage made it into the final clip.

There were many unpredictable moments that kept the band on their toes as their touring took them to faraway places. Bones particularly enjoyed their visits to South America, Brazil above all, for the pure unpredictability of it. 'When we played in Florianopolis, which is an island, a resort kind of place, we played in this market. During the day there were fruit and vegie stalls, at night it was a venue. So they had just diesel generators for power. We were meant to go on about nine o'clock, but they put us back to a quarter to ten because people were still coming into the venue. They hadn't put into the equation that the show would therefore run forty-five minutes later so maybe they should put some more diesel fuel in the generator. So we go on stage and halfway through the show the lights go out, the power goes off, it's pitch black. There are four or five thousand people in this place in complete darkness because the diesel generator has run out of fuel. That sums up Brazil. We went off to the dressing room and there were a few things broken and a few harsh words spoken. Eventually it was rectified and we came back on, but by that stage the damage was done. Pete had smashed his in-ear monitoring; it was a rotten vibe.

From the photo shoot for the cover of Australian *Rolling Stone* of April 1986. The band almost made the celebrated cover of the US edition in June 1990, but were displaced by Bart Simpson *(Adrienne Overall)*

Jim, Martin, Bones, Rob and Pete don face masks at an intersection in São Paulo, Brazil in 1997, as a protest with Greenpeace about the city's poisonous air quality *(Gary Morris)*

The band always felt more comfortable in outdoor settings for photo shoots. Here, Bones, Rob, Pete, Martin and Jim pose in Sydney's Hyde Park in 2000 *(Karin Catt/Sony)*

Bones (far left) really helped boost the band's vocal strength, but they could all sing if required. Martin (second from right) is singing in this shot from a Melbourne gig in 1993, so it's probably the chorus for 'Sometimes' *(Susan Alzner/Columbia)*

Ready for action in a room at Albert's studio in 1987 are some of the guitars used on the *Diesel and Dust* album *(Jim Moginie)*

Martin and Jim, guitars absent but probably not too far away, wait for the overnight bus in a salubrious hotel foyer in St Petersburg, Florida, in July 1988 *(Susan Alzner)*

Gary Morris and a friendly olive python in Port Keats, Western Australia, on the 1986 Black Fella White Fella tour *(Jim Moginie)*

In a break from filming the clip for 'Blue Sky Mine' in 1990, Rob poses on the salt pans near Kalgoorlie *(Ken Duncan)*

George Rurrambu ('Djilaynga') from the Warumpi Band joins Pete on stage in Broome for a dance and a sing at Stompem Ground 1998, during NAIDOC Week *(Robert Duncan/The West Australian)*

When Pete removed his beanie in the cool evening air at the Tanelorn Festival in 1981, the steam from his head had a chance to escape *(Joe Murphy)*

Martin, Pete and Rob in full swing at The Venue in London in 1987 *(Jim Hooper)*

The band made the 'Dreamworld' film clip in 1987 by the sea at Coalcliff, south of Sydney *(Ken Duncan)*

On the verandah of a house in Newtown, Sydney, in 1998 for a *Redneck Wonderland* photo shoot *(Andrzej Liguz/moreimages.net)*

At the closing ceremony of the Sydney Olympic Games on 1 October 2000, the band sent a message to a global television audience of about 3.7 billion. The famous SORRY suits are now in the Powerhouse Museum in Sydney *(Narelle Autio/Fairfaxphotos)*

'We only toured Argentina once. We didn't go down very well there because they wanted Marlboro sponsorship and we made them take all the banners and stuff down. In fact, we never did very well in any Spanish-speaking country. We only played Madrid once, a curious scene for us. But Brazil was great. You hop off the plane after flying fourteen hours and you look up and there's the Southern Cross and red dirt and it feels like you haven't gone that far from home. But it's an incredibly wild place. We had some very strange experiences in Brazil. In Cococabana there were these exercise bars out front of the hotel where everyone was Mr Atlas, doing their chin-ups, totally waxed. Totally weird for rock'n'roll. I sat there wondering where they kept their keys and credit cards.

'The incident in Rio where those guys died was tragic. The place we played was about a 6000-capacity room. There had been torrential rains and floods and mudslides and the place had been flooded forty-eight hours before the gig and they'd pumped the water out. But there was one exit underneath the auditorium that was still full. They just put a couple of sheets of plasterboard over it to stop people going down. And these two guys left their seats by hurdling a barrier to go down to the dance floor. They landed straight on this plasterboard and one went through and was electrocuted, and then the second one went in to save his mate and he was electrocuted as well – the place was full of wires. It wouldn't happen anywhere else in the world. No one stopped the show or turned the house lights on, and we didn't even know until afterwards.'

The band continue to stay in touch with the families of the boys who were killed, and help them financially. Michael Lippold was the band's production manager at the gig and still feels very bad about the incident. 'I remember talking to a detective afterwards and he asked me a few questions and I said, "What now?" and he said, "Don't worry about it." I was confused; I didn't know what he meant. But that was what he meant – don't worry about it, it doesn't matter. He said, "The football's on tomorrow, we'll lose ninety." They were really blasé about it. Every time I think about it I cry. For a good month or so after, I'd be sitting on buses or planes and I'd just start crying. At the end of the day there was nothing I could have done about it. The local council was at fault. But I was the production manager and public safety was my responsibility, the safety of everybody there was my responsibility, and two kids died. That really hurt. That was hard. It was a hard place to be on the road.'

Bones: 'I think the week before that the soccer stadium just behind our venue had a stand, or a section of a stand, collapse. There's no funding. There's no money. It's a Third World country. Bizarre things happen in Brazil. You travel with an accountant who is armed, an ex-policeman with a gun. At night you can run red lights, just sort of pull up slow and flash your lights, work out with the other drivers who's going to have the right of way. You don't stop in case a confrontation happens, like a carjacking. No one wants to stop at night. Even in the daytime people come up to you – women with babies or infants, people with tumours like the elephant man – all asking for money, gathering at the intersections in the afternoon.'

Michael: 'There were lots of dodgy places, always shit going on. The whole nation was coked to the gills. In Port Allegra a doctor had to be called in because Doc [the band's drum technician] was in his room with the curtains closed for two days suffering from a major migraine. The doctor came with a translator, a forty-year-old guy covered in sweat, and he's talking to Doc. "Do you do cocaine?" and Doc goes, "No", and the guy says, "You should! It'll get you out of bed in no time!"'

On tour, most of the time between gigs was spent travelling. Mostly the band were lucky if they had a few hours free to have a look around and see where they were, but there were some spare days. Bones: 'Our usual thing was Jim, Martin and I would hang out together. We'd arrive in a city and if we didn't have a gig that night we'd go off and look at a music shop. Rob would go to an art gallery or do something else. I don't know what Pete would do – we wouldn't see him till the evening. If you needed space you went back to your room and slipped into something more comfortable, like a coma. Got a bit of shut-eye.'

Every now and then they had a proper excursion. Bones remembers their visit to a South African game park where the band rode around in roofless Range Rovers. 'We were driving along at about 35 k and there was this thing called a dung beetle that eats elephant shit and rhino shit – this *huge* insect. It was flying in one direction and we were driving in the other, and it hit me in the forehead! I had crap all over my face. "Man, you been hit in the head by a dung beetle!" That was pretty funny.'

Michael and the crew also went exploring during their time off. 'Every time you got to a new place you'd always get an A4 sheet of paper from the local promoter with a map of the place, showing the hotel and local restaurants and then this big grey area – "Don't go to this area". We'd always go to the concierge of the hotel and say, "See this grey area, how do we get there?"

But there are some cities where you should believe in the grey area – Johannesburg and Rio de Janeiro are two cities where you've really got to acknowledge the "Don't go to the grey area"!'

Over the next few years the band visited and played in some other exotic places – an ancient bullring in France, a natural amphitheatre in the cliffs and caves of an American Indian settlement, beer halls in Germany, muddy fields in Britain – and after 1990 they barely missed the European summer festivals. They played impossibly huge crowds in South America, ecstatic crowds in South Africa, and there were various other unique examples of cultural exchange and interaction.

The band played the European summer festivals regularly as part of their typical touring year. These festivals run over three weekends in June and July. They are huge and extraordinarily well organised, and feature stunningly impressive line-ups. At Roskilde in Denmark in 1990 the headline acts were Bob Dylan, the Cure, Midnight Oil, Sinead O'Connor, Ry Cooder, Nick Cave and the Bad Seeds, The The, the Jeff Healey Band and Little Feat. Further down the bill were the Cramps, the Red Hot Chili Peppers, Faith No More, Lenny Kravitz and Sydney's long-lamented Hummingbirds. Bones: 'Roskilde was over four days and it gets a bit blurry as to who played what night, but I remember Jim and Martin hanging round outside Dylan's dressing-shed thing with this smell of sinsemilla wafting out. I think they got caught coz someone handed them a pre-rolled joint and said, "This is Bob's pot." It was so cool; we were high on what Dylan was high on! And it wore off and I realised he was just a boring old fart like us, but he had good pot.'

Michael was watching from the catering area when Dylan was led to the stage. 'Everyone had to clear the walkway between the dressing rooms and the catering area and it was "Don't look – you're not allowed to look at him." But I did, and he looked like a vegetable.'

Bones: 'For the *Earth and Sun and Moon* world tour Jim decided he couldn't cover both guitar and keyboards, and there were all these parts not being represented, so we got Chris Abrahams for a year and a half playing keyboards, which was great. He became a friend of mine. The *MTV Unplugged* "Short Memory" piano playing is exceptional, and that version of "In the Valley" is better than anything we ever recorded – just him, Pete and Jim on a harmonium. We'd spent weeks chasing that song around in every key known to mankind to try and make it work for the album. Eighteen months later, and the best version we've done is minimal.

'Chris was great to have on the road. We were staying at the Sheraton in Rio, and right next to the Sheraton is the biggest village of slums – hundreds and thousands of people. There's the Sheraton, then some guy who owns a TV channel, his huge mansion, and then the slum; they're side by side, it's totally ironic. The people all come down the side of the hill and go swimming at the beach while everyone at the Sheraton stays in the pool and swims around in the protection of the hotel. Chris decided he was going to the beach. I remember watching him; he went down, took his clothes off down to his Speedos, and 30 000 people cracked up laughing. He was an outta-shape white guy wearing a pair of Speedos, hadn't been in the sun for nine months. It looked like a white seal had been washed up on the beach.'

The oxygen that was first used in '78–'79 in the packed Australian pubs was still carried by the band, but for different purposes. Rob: 'It was used occasionally in shows where the altitude added another demon, or health hazard, for example, the Johannesburg show when we finally went and played Ellis Park, which is a mile in the air, and shows in Denver. Places like that, where the air is very thin. You're supposed to acclimatise over a couple of days if you want to do strenuous exercise, and we'd just fly in that afternoon from some swampy lowland and suddenly we're a mile in the air wondering why we can't breathe.'

Touring was an extreme activity and there was pleasure and pain, just not in equal proportions. Bones was the one who was most immune to the pain. 'I loved being on the bus. I got to see the world, got to play music, and I got paid for it. It's what I dreamed of as a kid. I couldn't have been luckier in any way whatsoever. Sure I would have bitched and moaned over a few sleepless nights or a couple of thirty-hour flights. After a while everyone whinges, but you never forget how lucky you are.'

Touring was hard for the others, who were married and settled in Sydney. Jim: 'As soon as we all had young families we'd never worked harder. We went on the road and became road warriors. My daughter didn't recognise me when I came home from one tour. One year I think we worked a tour ten months basically straight, and it was murder.'

The *Blue Sky* touring schedule was particularly gruelling and much more open-ended than the *Diesel* tours. The public was ready, the record company was ready, but Pete knew it was a big ask for a band like the Oils to undertake this sort of tour. 'For all of us, with the exception of Bones, being away from home for long periods of time was always challenging. And once we decided we didn't want to go and live overseas – that we were going to stay in Australia – we all had different takes on how we could do it. Some people would fly back and forward all the time, and Gary would try and figure it out with touring schedules. I mean, in terms of our mental and spiritual and social health, we were not really particularly well set up to be a never-ending touring show: "Aussie political rock comes to a stage near you – see the big bald guy jump up and down, listen to the acoustic guitars and watch the drummer stand on his drum stool", and all that stuff. It was fun, and we could go out and shake it up and enjoy it, try and say a few good things at the same time. But we were never going to be able to do it endlessly, and there was always that tension, and when you get into a *Blue Sky* scenario that's when you start to feel it as a band.'

As the year progressed, the pressure of delivering the sort of shows the band always delivered was proving taxing. The record was still selling, tour dates kept on being added, but the rocket they were riding started to feel like a rollercoaster, and then a sped-up merry-go-round, and each phase was less pleasant than the one before. At various times, as a way of countering homesickness, the band would fly their families over to join the tour. Rob: 'By *Blue Sky Mining* time we could afford that kind of indulgence, and our psychological health was improved by taking the families on the road whenever we could.'

But the solution was inevitably temporary and largely unsatisfactory. As Jim recalls, 'We all had nannies with us, and all the kids, and it was just a disaster really. Kids and nannies and tours and music don't work.'

Bones: 'That was a peculiar year. We had twelve children and about five nannies. I think we were a touring party of thirty-five people around North America and Canada. It was fucking mad. Gary even employed a special security guard, this guy who was Michael Jackson's bodyguard. All he did for us was lug luggage. I remember one gig, I think it was Calgary Speedway, something was going on in the audience he didn't like, so he jumped in wearing his Armani suit with his walkie-talkie system and stuff. All I remember seeing was his shoes and shit going everywhere and he came out half-dressed and said, "I'm never fucking doing that again. I quit."'

Eventually, despite the obvious consequences, they needed a break, a big break. The act of reproducing your art every night runs the very real risk of dulling the very talents that helped you create the art in the first place. One of the major ironies of being a musician is that creating music in the studio is not enough – you must go out and re-create it in the live arena night after night, while at the same time trying to keep yourself musically stimulated. As Joni Mitchell once said, 'Nobody ever asked Van Gogh to paint *A Starry Night* again – and again.'

But the band had an enormous repertoire of songs to draw from and that certainly helped to keep them interested and the performances varied. According to Bones, Pete was always the first to not want to play particular songs. 'He'd come in and say, "Let's play this instead", and I'd have to go through the CD collection and scrub up a song we hadn't done for seven years. We'd jump up on stage and I'd struggle a bit through it only to realise that he didn't know the words anyway! But the band has over 100 songs, so there's no way you can remember every note, chord and lyric. I remember one night in America and Pete didn't want to play "Beds". Afterwards I heard a punter complaining in the toilets and I understood how he felt. OK, so we played the song five nights a week for, well, how many years, but for the punter that lives in Winnipeg the band may only come around once a year, if that. They want to hear it. I think that is the hardest thing for a band who tour – to keep it fresh.

'Towards the end we devised a method of slotting in wild cards. We'd rehearse them a couple of days before and know they were coming up. The chocolate wheel tour was one of my brain-cell-frying experiences. There were twenty on the set list and sixty on the wheel! Somehow the radical ones never came up that much when the wheel stopped spinning. "Read About It" would always come up – it was like it had been rigged, but it hadn't.'

Bones does have a different take on touring from the rest of the band and speaks as a journeyman player. 'The road is the life and soul of it. You get together in a garage (not that I was in their garage, I was in another garage), learn to play and perform your songs in front of people, and eventually you get records out, and you keep touring. It's immediate; you're on stage getting off on the buzz and the adrenaline of performing. The audience is right in front of you. You can see it, it's instantaneous. It's not like recording, where you go and spend a lot of time in isolation from people, you put this thing out, then you wait and see what happens. A gig is a lifeline; if you don't play, you're not a band. Once you stop playing, there's nothing.'

But there is a difference between playing gigs and endless touring. Playing is obviously life-sustaining for musicians, but the big tours required at the level the band were now performing were another matter entirely. Being on the road for that long was a danger to their health and just too much time away from home. It's not as if they didn't want to pay their dues: they had toured constantly in the twelve years up until then. They certainly hadn't been afraid of getting out and playing. In addition to the regular Australian tours, there had been routine visits to the UK for London and regional shows, a few small tours in Europe, several trips to New Zealand and six to North America. They loved playing and touring in Australia, where they were never too far from home, but after more than a decade of international touring it had ceased to be fun. Rob: 'The playing every night, playing that hard, and for me singing as well, it was like running a marathon every night, without enough time to recover before you did it again. Not enough time to eat properly, not enough sleep, throw in jet lag.'

The decision to stop touring was made with a full appreciation of the possible economic and career consequences. Rob: 'We just needed to defuse. I mean, how could it be any other way? You've got people in intense situations and circumstances, all living in each other's pockets, for months at a time. Of course you're going to be at each other's throats unless you have time off. It's hard enough to keep two people in a marriage in an ordinary domestic situation, let alone five men – plus Gary occasionally dropping in – in an intense situation like that. I think we did pretty well. Long breaks were the key to our survival – that and Bones' humour.'

Mason Munoz wasn't laughing when he heard the news. 'At the end of the tour I remember Peter saying to me, "We're going to go away for a few years." I was like, "Wait a minute. What do you mean? You can't do that." "Yes, we can." "How? You know you're riding the crest of a wave right now – who knows what's going to happen two years from now? You guys need to go home and take a break for a few weeks, then start working on another record." And they didn't. They went home and took a few *years* off! I certainly learned something from that – these guys had their own agenda and their own timetable and they didn't care about anything else. They were willing to accept whatever the consequences of their decisions were.'

David Fricke saw the band's fortunes change. 'The decision they made certainly cost them a lot of commercial momentum – and time goes by. After that their touring was eccentric at best: weird time periods and lengths of tours. But again, it's why do you do it? You have a choice. Which will you sacrifice, your career or your family? That's the point where you decide what the rest of your life is going to be like. They had been on tour here in the US, and they had been touring Europe at the same time. You know, exhaustion sets in. And one of the things – and this is a constant recurring theme – America is huge! It involves an enormous commitment and you've got to be willing to give up so much. Just the notion of being on tour for eight months to a year, just in the US – and then dealing with Europe. Also, they were flying from a lot further than just England or London. And I know lots of *British* bands that can't be bothered! The highway is littered with British bands who thought they could tour America, do twelve shows, and be acclaimed as the next big thing. It can't be done.'

Chris Moss agrees that the momentum is easily lost. 'You've got to base yourself at the centre of it, put yourself on the road, tour constantly, be in everybody's face – because if *you're* not there, somebody else is. It's as simple as that, really; it's the nature of the business. There are very few acts – if any – that can get away with doing that. The bands who are the most successful are the ones who put the yards in. You do have to say that Midnight Oil have built their whole career on defying conventional wisdom. Everything that everybody thought was the norm, they did exactly the opposite. It had worked very successfully for them in the past, so why shouldn't it now? If you tempt fate by falling into line and doing what everyone wants, then you may be agreeing to do the very thing that destroys you.'

Towards the end of the *Blue Sky Mining* touring, Rob remembers most of the band members being desperate and determined to stop. 'There was a really strong anti-touring ethic in the band by then, although I remember Martin being keen to keep the momentum going. I think he was concerned that the momentum was being lost and that we couldn't take for granted that there would always be an audience overseas for us if we left for too long. The other camp was saying, "Look, we have toured relentlessly ever since *Diesel* came out and it's starting to take its toll. We've got to recharge the batteries. We've got to come home, re-establish our roots and spend some time with our families. And if there *is* going to be another album it should be an album full of songs that are written at home rather than songs written on a bus somewhere." And all of that was valid. Martin's attitude was true – the momentum *was* lost. People came and went from record companies and we lost our contacts. We moved from being a "player" and became increasingly sidelined. But the other thing was true as well – we *were* burnt out, we *did* need to recharge the batteries. It's much harder for Australian bands to overcome this dilemma. In Europe you can take time off and it's quite easy to get going again, you can respond to festivals and offers like that. We always felt like we had to mount this juggernaut of a tour and go away for months and months to make it viable, and that was true as well. It was difficult just to go for a weekend, although that occasionally happened.'

When the band came home from the *Blue Sky* tour in 1990 there wasn't anything that could tempt them out, least of all the glamour events of rock'n'roll. MTV had been early supporters of the band through the 'Dead Heart' and 'Beds' clips, and with 'Blue Sky Mine' and 'Forgotten Years' it once again had the band's music on high rotation.

Mason: 'They had become one of the darlings of MTV, but they couldn't embrace that. You could see they had fun making those videos, but I also know that they didn't have a whole lot of respect for a lot of the programming and imaging on MTV. Towards the end of the *Blue Sky Mining* project the band had an amazing run on MTV – they were one of the core artists. This was in the first few years of MTV's big New Year's Eve gigs. This guy named Abby Connor who was running MTV called me one day and he went, "We want Midnight Oil for New Year's Eve." And I told him, "Abby, I don't think that's gonna happen, but I'll ask the question." And he went, "See what you can do for me." Well, the reply was, "No, we won't do this. We don't like MTV. We don't like what they represent, we don't like what they have to say. We don't understand why other people watch MTV. The answer is no. We're not going to come over from Australia to do this."

'And I had a conversation with Abby and diplomatically

and politely told him it was a no. And he said, "Why?" I said, "Well, maybe if you told me who else was on the show it might help." He said, "We got Madonna and we have Aerosmith." So I believe I had a conversation with Pete, who said, "Mason, we don't like those acts, we don't like what they stand for, we don't want to be part of this." And I went back to Abby and told him that and he said, "Well, tell them they don't have to come over here, we'll do a remote from Australia." And once again, I was told no. At this point I had to say to Abby, "Look, they really don't like MTV. They don't respect what a lot of the artists have to say and the way they market themselves. They just don't think it's healthy, they don't think it's right." And he went, "Mason, tell them they can say that! They can say whatever they want. They can say in front of the camera, 'MTV sucks', whatever they want. We just want Midnight Oil." And they *still* said no.

'Now one of the conversations I know we had was, "Take advantage of this forum. It's a worldwide forum and you're speaking to a young audience. Tell them how you feel. He's willing to let you do that and he's not going to censor you." So I really had mixed feelings. I can't say in retrospect whether or not that was a lost opportunity; it's hard to say. The mercenary in me really wanted them to do it, because I knew what the upside was. On the other hand, how can you not respect someone who's strong enough to turn down that temptation? But here was an opportunity to say something profound that might open some people's eyes. To this day I have mixed feelings about it.' The decision within the band may not have been easy or unanimous, but there had always been a generally accepted view that events of that kind would not be done.

Blue Sky Mining came out in March 1990 and in December the band finished their touring commitments. The year was a bit of a blur, but at least for the final stretch they were touring at home. They started in North Queensland and then made their way around the country, playing full houses in the biggest venues in all the major cities. They played to over 200 000 Australians in just under eight weeks.

Gary felt there was a general malaise slipping over the band during the whole *Blue Sky Mining* period. 'I think everybody started to get a bit too precious about what they'd become. Everybody in the band, the crew, everybody was looking to try and protect what really wasn't theirs to protect. Yes, we were part of it, we were part of something that was happening. If you try to control that, direct it, protect it, somehow you lose that innocence, you lose that formidable poetry. And I think that's what happened to Midnight Oil. Things weren't as visionary and unanimous after *Diesel and Dust*.

'We kind of rested on our laurels a bit after we'd copped all this massive amount of money. We did our record contract, our publishing contract, our merchandising contract, then we had to try and do things to make all that work. So we had to come up with ideas to try and illustrate the "us against the world", the "us against the system", the underdog and all the injustices. The band were trying to formularise what the next record would become. Therefore *Blue Sky Mining* had to have these themes, and the band had to do these things that had social commitment to them. And in some respects they tried to manufacture a yang moment when in actual fact it was turning out to be a yin moment – it was all under control, it was all under wilfulness. There were lots of arguments within the band and lots of disgruntled opinions about whether they'd made the right record or whether that song was the right song to play in this set.'

Gary was not happy with the band's decision to stop touring. 'The Oils took a couple of years off when we should have actually got out there and done some serious touring and some serious interfacing with the new audience. '*Blue Sky Mining* had the professionalism of everybody now – the band were professional music-makers, there was a professional management system that understood how to work and move through the business globally, there were professional production people who knew how to interpret Midnight Oil requests and put them down. There were great, technically perfect shows – sound, lights, the whole thing was running perfectly – but there was something missing. And it was this heart moment, this *life*, this *uniqueness* that Midnight Oil have had lots of through their career. Somehow that flame was dimming in the whole *Blue Sky Mining* process. Call it success, call it the sickness of being successful – call it the music business. It never got as good again.'

seven

kiss that girl

The rise of punk in the mid-1970s forced contemporary musicians to revisit the rock'n'roll roots of it all. It was plain for all to see that the bloated world of corporate easy-listening rock had taken over, and that record company obsessions with seventies stadium rock were affecting all aspiring musicians. This was the root cause of the punk backlash, and the reason for punk's success. The appeal of punk was its directness and honesty, which had also been at the heart of rock's fifties origins. Those themes started to re-emerge in virtually all forms of modern music as a result of the global new wave of the punk aesthetic.

Despite Midnight Oil having blistering turns of speed and extreme volume, and on occasions venomous lyric delivery, they were never punks in terms of musical format. They never had a two-and-a-half-minute song in 4/4 time. Right from the beginning each of their songs was quite distinctive, and the song arrangements were diverse and often complex. The songs may have had cohesion within the context of a particular record, but they exhibited individual style and subject matter. Every album, with the possible exception of *Diesel*, contained a number of major stylistic gear changes. David Fricke: 'The sound is really unified in the sense that it's all them, but there are also a lot of genre steps – "US Forces" does not sound like "Power and the Passion", "When the Generals Talk" is not the same as "Kosciuszko". The albums are amazing compendiums of everything they can do.'

Every song tells a different story, literally, and will be interpreted in a different way by each listener. My interpretations are my interpretations; even the co-writers' interpretations are sometimes different from each other. But if there is a common message in Midnight Oil songs, through all the variety of words and sounds, it is an overwhelmingly life-affirming and hopeful one.

Inevitably songs are open to misinterpretation, and certainly Midnight Oil were regularly described as 'aggressive' when 'angry and determined' would have been more accurate. Similarly, the band's mistrust of the establishment and its processes could be mistaken for the related feeling of paranoia. However, their major themes were unambiguous. Subjects like peace and progress, integrity, social responsibility and incitement to action have often been revisited, with growing musical skill. Each new record has been like a refining and re-examining of the world according to Midnight Oil while also seeing them determined to tackle new areas and new ways of expression.

As a general rule songwriters are too coy to talk about their trade. And most are too circumspect to reveal anything much about the process. It's too convoluted, too fluky or too boring, they say. Most are unwilling to take the ambiguity out of the lyrics or to impose a meaning on them that may limit people's enjoyment or interpretation of the song. Often the subject matter is too personal, too prosaic or too 'deep'. The nuts and bolts of how a song is constructed in a musical way, or evolves lyrically, may be interesting to us, but in the songwriter's opinion that sort of information is counterproductive because it risks eroding the very thing we enjoy about a song.

In the Oils there are many ways in which a song can come to fruition. Essentially, Jim or Rob presents songs or song starting points to the full band. Jim usually produces his at home in his studio and has them on tape, either with or without words. Rob initially had a little keyboard, then later an acoustic guitar, to accompany himself as he sang his ideas to the band. Although Martin contributed songs to the first couple of albums his role as a song contributor subsequently diminished. However, his role in the songwriting *process* became even more important. As time has progressed he has become the filter or honest broker through whom all songs must pass. Rob explains: 'In the demo process, although Martin isn't a major writer he is absolutely invaluable in his contributions to which parts are valuable that Jim and I bring in and which parts aren't. And it's often what Martin *doesn't* say that is exactly what you need to know. There is no way of pushing something through if Martin doesn't like it. Before we even enlist a producer it kind of falls on Martin to be in that role because he can be objective about everything. He can hear all this new music being brought in, and Jim or I might be really wedded to a part and try to stick it in a song and then it will reappear for another song, and "How about we try it here or try it in F sharp or E or whatever?"

It won't get through Martin. If he doesn't like the part, it just isn't going to get through – which I understand, because it's done for good musical reasons.' The raw songs then proceed to a further stage of work and input from the band.

During Pete's time in the band he did almost all his co-writing with Jim. On the few occasions when he and Rob are credited together, it usually means Pete added to or adjusted Rob's lyrics. Because Pete was the one who delivered the lyrics, he inevitably had final say and often made changes to them regardless of whether the originals were his own or Jim's or Rob's. Changing them spontaneously in the studio with the tape running could be a source of silent tension for the other writers. Rob was the more sensitive to this, but he says Jim shared his view to a degree. 'We tried to resolve it by pleading with Pete to have lyrical input much earlier than the day we were actually recording the song. We didn't think the best lyrics were obtained ten seconds before you sang them for the final time, although we understood that Pete's spontaneity was a great asset. It was better if he was at least working constructively over a period of months in the demoing process, but lyrics being replaced on the day of recording without notice was difficult to take. I should add that sometimes at the nth hour Pete would come up with some brilliant stuff, but the brinkmanship that was employed with that process drove me, and I think Jim as well, to a point where we were concerned about the balance between Pete's lyrical freedom of expression and trying to be objective about the quality of the song that resulted.'

Pete: 'Sometimes with songs there'd be lines or verses or ideas which didn't quite gel with me. I'd either suggest a change, or change them. Other times a song would come along absolutely as it was from somebody and I'd think, "This is right on, let's just go with it." And there were shades of grey in between. I always looked at the song and my ability to connect with it as the first step in the process, and if it worked at that level then it didn't matter where it came from. Rob and Jim are both very good lyricists and quite often with the songs that came from them I was, "Let's record it."'

While recording *10–1* in the hothouse of experimentation in London in 1983, producer Nick Launay noticed tension over Pete's rewriting of Rob's lyrics. 'Rob and Jim would write the songs separately. They'd come in with their songs and Peter would either like the lyrics or not, and very often rewrite them. What he often did, which was kind of disrespectful to Rob or Jim, was write new lyrics and not discuss them at all. He would have them, no one had ever seen them, and when he went out to do the vocal he would just sing his lyrics – and with "Power and the Passion" his lyrics completely ignored Rob's lyrics. Rob had a whole thing worked out for that song, so he was extremely upset and affected by this. I remember it was a major anxiety thing, to the point where Rob got very ill and stressed out and it was kind of unpleasant. I didn't see any argument between them; it was just this silent thing.'

Nick remembers being asked to arbitrate on the matter. 'I think I said, "Well, I like the first verse of Peter's, the choruses of Rob's" – actually the choruses were always Rob's, Peter didn't change them. The third verse was definitely Peter's. "Big Mac, Pine Gap, no one goes out back" – I thought that was great, it was funny. Somehow a compromise was reached, and it's probably fifty-fifty Peter and Rob.'

Pete doesn't recall any particular reaction from Rob about going into the studio and changing the lyrics. 'No more than he did in other circumstances. I just thought what I wrote was better than what we had. I actually think "Power and the Passion" is the most fully realised song on that album. It's a classic example of combining, where the sum is greater than all of the parts. The first verse was, I think, Rob's original idea, and then of course you've got his chorus, and the rest of the verses, which I wrote, I think are pretty good.'

Nick: 'It was an issue with other songs, too, where Peter came in with his own lyrics and didn't share them with anyone. For Jim, being a very passive, easygoing person, it was more like, "Well, my lyric is what I wrote, but Peter's written his lyric – it's all good."'

Most Midnight Oil songs end up being collaborations in some sense, regardless of what the particular writing credits on the liner notes show. Songwriting credits can be misleading. On Midnight Oil records the first credit listed is usually the instigator of the song, but not necessarily the person who contributed most. Significant lyrical or musical input also earns a credit, in most cases. Compositions that are credited to the entire band usually indicate the jamming nature of the song's origins, or multiple sources for the song's component parts, or a philosophical decision to do with sharing the wealth or presenting a united front in difficult times.

In most bands the song credits are financially crucial: publishing royalties are a musician's major source of income. Selling records is the only way to survive and the people who write the songs make the most money. New songs are the life blood of a band, and an industry, and songwriters are undoubtedly its most precious resource. The writers are not just rewarded for their talent and effort: they also have to deal with the pressure to deliver when the band needs new material.

Bands can break up for many different reasons, but matters of ego or money are invariably central. Both these factors are involved in who gets credited with writing a band's songs and whose songs go on the albums. The more democratic bands try to find ways of allocating songwriting money among the members for the sake of band unity and longevity. For example, the Talking Heads specifically recognised the role of arrangements in their mathematical formula for dividing songwriting royalties: one-third for the musical arrangement, one-third for the top-line melody and one-third for the lyrics, with each of those categories divided by four to accommodate the possibility that all four members contributed in each category. The money was allocated in twelfths. More traditionally, the melody and the words are allotted half each, especially in bands where there is one wordsmith and one tunesmith. But all bands who perform their own material have different ways of assembling and creating songs and therefore of distributing songwriting royalties.

The arrangement of a song is often crucial to its effectiveness, and in Midnight Oil, where a new song might be the end result of the combining of elements from several bits of unused band songs, it is particularly important. Those who doubt the value of arrangements should listen to the early version of 'Down Under', the worldwide Men At Work hit. There was a sax solo in place of the flute, and the leaden style is totally at odds with the lyrics – it's certainly not the bright and breezy pop song we know today. It was a very ordinary song until it was rearranged and re-recorded to emerge as the biggest-selling Australian single of all time and a number one on music charts all around the world. Because of Men at Work's particular publishing arrangements, that financial bonanza didn't translate to making all the members of the band equally rich; some were left more than a little disgruntled. Crowded House notoriously fought, and eventually split, over the distribution of their songwriting royalties.

Crediting an album as 'All compositions by Midnight Oil' certainly helped the band be perceived as a collective enterprise, but it also acknowledged the often complex birthing of a song and the importance of its arrangement. In the band's legal set-up with their publishing company, Sprint Music, the songwriting royalties are not necessarily split according to the song authorship as credited on the albums. This document is secret, but I have heard no complaints from any of the principal players and it seems that a workable and equitable formula was worked out many years ago. The codified arrangement, apart from recognising the collective songwriting methods of the band, also acknowledges the way Midnight Oil operates as a business, where the costs of making the records and the film clips – in fact, everything – are shared. Therefore, it is reasoned, so should the income that is derived from them.

Jim and Rob were constantly writing, particularly when the band weren't on the road. When it was time for a new record they could be counted on to provide a surplus of songs. Right from the very earliest days Jim was presenting an enormous amount of material for them to work on. Bear says that every few months Jim would deliver a tape with forty minutes or more of new music. Some songs also came directly from the band jamming together. Bear: 'We would develop song ideas from jamming, but I suspect that Jim had already been working on some of the chordal and riff ideas. Rob's strength was in melody. His lyrics at that early stage were fairly hormone driven, and often alluded to physical pleasures.'

Most of the material on 'The Blue Meanie' was written by Jim and Rob, with significant contributions from Martin. Jim effectively co-wrote everything on the album, and on most of the albums to come, but 'Nothing Lost, Nothing Gained' was the first song credited totally to him. Jim is in effect the band's musical director, and his contributions and ideas are often central to the records' overall direction and sound. Rob has had a few songs that are purely his own through the band's career as well, but it's the combination of his and Jim's talents that is crucial to the band's usual way of working.

Pete was not really involved in the songs for the first album apart from some lyrical input to 'Surfing with a Spoon' and 'Dust'. By the time of *Head Injuries* his input had started to increase, but it was not a case of him only feeling happy to sing words he'd written himself. 'I never had a concern about singing other people's words, no problem at all. I always saw myself as a conduit between a consciousness, which I described as "Midnight Oil", and an audience, which I saw as our extended family. I would have done an album of covers happily, and wanted to do one for many years. I think songs stand up on their own whoever writes them. If they're good, they're good. In the Oils I also recognise that I was a character in the band. I had ideas about things so on different occasions

I would try and put them in songs or work songs up for them. Plus, we had to record albums, and we needed songs.'

By the second album Jim had started to pass songs to Pete in a partially formed state and Pete was attempting to complete them. This technique proved very productive over the years. 'Is It Now?' from *Head Injuries* is the first example. It's a song with the desperate gathering velocity of an out-of-control carnival ride, on the rails, but only just — a totally wild piece of music, especially live, with one of Pete's most blood-curdling screams. It's a song that can take you to the very edge. Pete also initiated a song for the first time on *Head Injuries*: 'Koala Sprint', which has something of the mood of wider Australia about it. The first album had been very much an urban record and most of this one was too, but 'Koala Sprint' was really the first song that hinted at a broader cultural picture of Australia. Martin contributed a couple of songs to the album, but most of the tracks again stemmed from Rob or Jim. However, musical contributions from Martin, sometimes major ones, could come at any time.

After 'The Blue Meanie' Rob started to deliver songs with more immediate appeal than the songs on that first album. His strong feel for melody and growing 'pop' sensibility came through on *Head Injuries* in songs like 'No Reaction' and 'Cold Cold Change' and continued over the next few years. 'Don't Wanna Be the One' and 'Written in the Heart' from *Postcard* and 'Only the Strong', 'Short Memory' and 'Read About It' from *10–1* are all examples of his growing ability to write with Pete's voice and range in mind. According to Rob, Jim's approach to Pete's voice was different from Rob's own. 'Jim's attitude was to present everything and hope that Pete would be able to come to grips with it, no matter what key, no matter what lyric, whether it was a really tricky melody, whatever. I didn't see it quite the same way. I actually always tried to write something I thought Pete could sing – and I was sometimes successful, sometimes not. Right from "Powderworks" I thought, "Yeah, he can sing that"; "No Reaction" – "Yeah, that sounds like Pete"; "Only the Strong" – "That's Pete". This wasn't as tough as it sounded, because Pete and I were both driven people – driven for different reasons, but actually quite similar in terms of being determined to get to a point, I think because we were both interested in politics. When it worked well, it fitted like a glove. Songs like "The Dead Heart" and "King of the Mountain", the stuff that is powerful and self-affirming, there wasn't going to be a problem.

'I also had this thing of storytelling, and I increasingly enjoyed ambiguity. These were areas Pete was less enthusiastic about – but not always. A story like "Jimmy Sharman's Boxers" was something he probably remembered from his childhood like I did. But as you get older things become less black and white, and ambiguity and textures and shades of grey become more part of your life, almost as an inevitability of seeing contradictions, loss of family members, marriage break-ups, heartaches, whatever. The arrogance of youth is shed almost always, and with it comes another interesting area: music becomes more personal and soulful and ambiguous and interpretive. These weren't things that were part of early Midnight Oil, but they were increasingly part of the *men* of Midnight Oil as we went into the nineties.'

Pete identifies a couple of ways the band's songs evolved: 'I think we created a set of songs over a period of time that sometimes reflected the band's work and sometimes were songs people brought to the band that summed up what the band was about. And 90 per cent of those songs required a level of further involvement, whether it was editing or arranging or lyrics or just a general contribution, to move the thing on, to bring it up – to be the song. All of the members who were writing were generally very musicianlike in their approach to the business of songs. As a consequence, there wasn't generally a great deal of preciousness, not on my part, and not on the others' either, I think. There were specific instances on specific albums. But generally there was much more of a communal "This is what we can get to work in this instance", even if it was just changing a word in an intro of a song or something like that. And that would make the song, which maybe has one person's name or two people's names on it, come to life. A very good example of this would be "Armistice Day" [from *Postcard*], which Giffo probably forgets his contribution to, but which I think was quite significant. Now, his name is not on the credit, but it wouldn't sound like "Armistice Day", and wouldn't have the force of "Armistice Day", and wouldn't be nearly as good, if he hadn't made the contribution he did.'

The pooled talents of the five band members took a song and then added bits of songs from somewhere else and fashioned them, sometimes over years, into a new piece with several parts interwoven. A single song could contain multiple melodies, changing and complex rhythms, and sometimes the canvassing of several serious subjects. There was plenty to keep mind and body occupied. Pete sang the songs with unfailing conviction, and as a result, regardless of who actually wrote the words, he was always presumed by fans and by both types of critic – the media and his political foes – to be the author. Pete was aware that's what people thought but from his point of view there wasn't much he could do. 'I always took it from when I met the band – they already had fifteen or twenty songs – and if I was willing to sing those songs (which I really liked, I thought they were really good songs) then that's what being in a band was all about. I had two particular and specific things I wanted us to address in our career as songwriters. One of those things was what I would describe as our real Australian experience, as opposed to trying to model our experience on, and package it and sell it as, something from America or elsewhere overseas. The second thing was a reflection of political and social and environmental awareness, of some degree. I thought it was important for us to have songs like that because that's what we felt, that's what I believed very strongly. I actually didn't much mind where they came from if they managed to do that job.'

For 1981's *Place Without a Postcard* the band had quite a bit of material written before they went to England, but they were often stuck at producer Glyn Johns's farm while he was away in London and had plenty of time to rework songs in readiness for his return. Many of the songs benefited from more work, including Rob's 'Don't Wanna Be the One', which at last, having missed the cut for *Head Injuries*, made it onto a record after input from Pete and Martin and Jim. It became the new album's single. On *Postcard* Pete was more involved in the writing than on most other records. 'Partly because we wrote some of the songs there – we were living together and had to write a lot of it on the spot, partly because we thought it was a really important record – the next record! – and partly because there was more time to do it and the others wanted to do it.' Moginie/Garrett credits first started to become a regular thing on *Postcard*, with 'Brave Faces', 'Burnie' and 'Ned Kelly' falling into this category. 'Lucky Country' was Jim's original idea with significant lyrical contributions from Pete and extra music from Rob.

Giffo summed up the way it worked when he was in the band. 'Jim and Rob together wrote great stuff and it was their thing, you know, they were the songwriters. And Pete would go in and do lyrics but it was a Hirst/Moginie effort really, that was the guts of it. It's not that they weren't open to it – you could throw in bits of stuff – but it's a gift. With Moginie it's a gift. Rob's a very hardworking fellow, he works so hard to get stuff, and he and Jim were just so dedicated to the whole thing.'

Pete saw Rob's songs as usually heading in a definite direction. 'You could hear what the song was trying to do. Jim's songs kind of had more entrails – you could take them in many more different ways. Rob wrote pretty much from listening to the band's sound, with my voice and what we were on about in mind, how it might do and where it might sit in the pantheon of tunes. Rob was more cerebral and Jim was more intuitive in their basic approach.'

Rob: 'It was always kind of tough contributing songs to Midnight Oil. It became tougher in the nineties, but it was tough right from the word go. Because you bare your soul when you bring stuff in. You're not sure whether it's the greatest load of horseshit anyone's ever heard or it's fucking genius – you don't really know, you're just coming up with this stuff. *You* might like it, but everyone else might think it's a load of bollocks. But you bring everything forward. Sometimes it would be stony silence, or Pete would say something like, "That one's best left for the solo album", and that's the only feedback you'd get. So you have to be fairly thick-skinned, and I don't think songwriters generally are. I don't think people in creative fields are generally – that's why they need bulldog managers.'

When the band went to Tokyo to record the *Red Sails in the Sunset* album, they intended to use the studio as an integral part of the song-creating process, like they had on *10–1*. They wanted to experiment again with Nick, but circumstances were different. For a start they didn't go into the studio with very many songs. Pete: 'Writing in the studio is not really a good idea – I think any musician knows that. Sometimes you come up with good stuff, but you usually tend to get better results if you've got them ready before you go in. Lyrically the album's bloody good, most of it, but with all respect to Nick, the production was just a bit overwrought. Apart from that I think it's a very fine record. "ICBMs, SS-20s, they lie so dormant", with the falsettos "they got so many" [from 'Minutes to Midnight'] – I could go to my grave after doing that.'

Jim: 'We had about five or six songs beforehand. We were very ill prepared, but we had a lot of time in Japan.' With Pete concerned with political activities a fair bit of the time, it fell to Jim and Rob to create the bulk of the material. Martin's inevitable antennae were always up, and his riffs and licks always available. Pete did make significant lyrical contributions to several of Jim's songs on *Red Sails*, particularly the hauntingly beautiful album closer, 'Shipyards of New Zealand', but also

'Minutes to Midnight', which followed up the nuclear theme of 'Maralinga' from *10–1*. The wryly amusing and cheekily produced 'Who Can Stand in the Way' is a Moginie/Garrett composition. It has injections of comic relief but also contains some of their darkest lyrics:

> *We killed all our first born and we slashed and we burned*
> *And we sold off the paddocks and we raped and we gouged*
> *On the wings of a six-pack*
> *Will we ever learn?*

This song, along with 'Harrisburg' and 'Minutes to Midnight', touches directly on the shadow being cast over society by the nuclear threat. It ends with a Pete rave:

> *When the spinifex hit Sydney it was the last thing we expected*
> *When the desert reached to Gladesville we tried to tame it*
> *And when the emus grazed at Pyrmont it suddenly*
> *dawned on us all*
> *Hi everybody, the world was silent and the door was shut*

In 'Bells and Horns in the Back of Beyond' Pete's words reveal a wistful nostalgia mixed with his love of the simple life:

> *I get home, I see Matt*
> *I drive down, I look out*
> *I see those lines and lines and lines of swell and smile*
> *Coolangatta, what's the matter?*
> *Paradise is surfer's worst*
> *With flashing lights and real estate and one last wave*

*Get up and run 'cause there's a beach lies quiet
near the open sea
And a car park lies stretched where the bindies used to be*

Suddenly a futuristic surf-guitar instrumental breaks in, augmented by a ghostly vocal chorus. The whole thing ends abruptly and then there's the sound of Pete – or is it Rob? – laughing. 'Harrisburg', 'Bells and Horns in the Back of Beyond' and 'Shipyards of New Zealand' are an extraordinary threesome to finish the record. Jim and Nick pulled out all the stops in moody and colourful studio soundscaping on the album. It's sometimes simple, often weird, and on occasions totally moving.

Red Sails in the Sunset was the start of Pete, and the band, taking politics very seriously – only 'Sleep' and the instrumental 'Bakerman' seem untouched by the subject. Paradoxically, there was much more of a sense of humour and playfulness in the production than on other Midnight Oil records. Nick: 'The sense of humour was totally Tokyo, it was nuts! Everything about it was crazy. It's hard to make sense of Tokyo, but you try. Everything is very colourful. Everyone was wearing colourful clothes, bright colours. We all ended up wearing pink-and-green sneakers. There were no other foreigners there. We had two assistant engineers, and one day I came in early to find them putting all the microphones back on the stands. I said, "What happened?!" They looked puzzled so I said, "Why did you take them off? Why did you take them all down?" We'd been there for about a month and it seems that every night they took all the microphones off the stands, wrapped them up and put them away, and every morning they would come in and put them all up into position again! They had Polaroid photographs of every microphone position. I'd seen them taking photos but thought it was for some magazine. I asked again: "Why?!" Apparently the moisture in the air affected the capsules. I mean— OK, but it doesn't seem to bother anybody in America or England! They were incredibly efficient and had a great sense of humour about things.'

Nick remembers that it wasn't just the microphones that came in for conscientious maintenance. 'One morning after we worked late they had these white towels wrapped around their heads. They looked like turbans and we thought, "Maybe it's some religious day." After a while we asked why they were wearing the turbans. "We didn't go home last night," they said. We thought maybe it was some sort of tradition: you don't go home, so . . . you've got to wear a turban. They didn't speak English, either of them, very, very little. "Not clean" were the next words they said, and we realised they hadn't been able to go home and wash their hair, so they were covering it! We must have seemed so big and so smelly to them.'

The band were surrounded by and immersed in an unfamiliar environment, which influenced the record in all sorts of ways. Nick: 'When it came to doing "When the Generals Talk" – I'm not sure that the song even existed before the session – the original plan was to do the chorus with Japanese girls singing. Rob and Giffo went out and sang like they thought Japanese girls would do it, which is why it is the way it is. So it was supposed to be Japanese girls and I don't know why we never did it for real – probably because it sounded pretty good with Rob and Giffo! Jim had also written a brass part and we wanted a school band, so we got a Japanese school band to come down and they played it way too well. It was supposed to be more out of tune; we wanted it to sound a bit wonky. In "Best of Both Worlds" we got in a horn section: a trumpet, trombone and saxophone. It was all written out; Jim had arranged it. We got these Japanese people and they came in and played and it sounded awful. We tried different microphones and did it again – just the same, terrible. We tried to explain to them via an interpreter, who was an American sumo wrestler and a journalist for *Time* magazine who was so musclebound he couldn't put his hands together. There was all this eccentric stuff going on. No wonder the album sounds so silly. Jim and I said, "Can you ask them to play more raw? More rock, more out of tune?" They were apparently the best players in Tokyo – these guys were so good they could hit really high notes and not strain – and suddenly the penny dropped: "Ah, more rock'n'roll!" So we ran the tape again and this time it was perfect – out of tune and out of time. To distort an acoustic instrument you have to play a certain way, and they could do it, but the magic words were "rock'n'roll".'

The studio effects were a significant part of the songs on the album, and that's why quite a number of the tracks failed to make the grade in the live arena. 'Kosciuszko' and 'Best of Both Worlds' proved to be the live standouts, and were also the tracks that eventually attracted the most radio airplay. Perversely, there were no actual singles released from the album, but 'When the Generals Talk' was the first song delivered to radio. Because it featured Rob on lead vocals, there was some confusion and speculation in the press about Pete's future.

The album had a strange fate. It was released amidst Pete's political campaigning, and although some observers whispered that the political campaign was a publicity stunt for the record, the record was almost certainly not helped by all the distractions. The band's decision not to release singles was in part influenced by not wanting to appear to be using Pete's other activities as a commercial springboard.

Red Sails in the Sunset is a very aberrant Oils record in lots of ways. For a lot of fans it is their least favourite, but there are also many for whom its eccentricities make it very special. It was the same with all of the band's most extreme musical turns, particularly 1996's *Breathe* and *Redneck Wonderland* from 1998. But even *Diesel and Dust*'s acoustic sounds, when they were first heard, perplexed many a diehard fan. 'Dreamworld' was brilliant, and 'Sometimes' was a spectacular example of the sort of material the fans expected, but it took some people a few listens before they slowed down enough to appreciate the ride and the totality of the experience. *Diesel and Dust* was a visionary recording, and like all their records – including *Red Sails* – was brought about by an ongoing commitment by the musicians to follow their hearts. On *Diesel*, however, there was a clear road plan, and an enormously collaborative songwriting process took place. Over half of the songs on the album are credited to the entire band, as befits compositions that were largely strummed into existence around the proverbial campfire.

Between *Red Sails* and *Diesel* the band released the explosive little *Species Deceases* EP. Jim says it was an antidote to the huge process of making *Red Sails*. When they entered the studio, 'We had it all written, and we'd written it very quickly.' All four songs seem cut from the same quality cloth. They are all sharply political, simply arranged and absolutely full tilt musically. 'Hercules', inspired by the sinking of the *Rainbow*

Warrior in New Zealand some months earlier, is one of the band's most muscular and desperate pieces. 'Progress' is a Pete-and-Jim co-write with tough lyrics and huge, propulsive energy. 'Pictures' is very much a band composition and a further slice of grim determination wrapped in galvanised rock. There are echoes of Japan in Rob and Jim's 'Blossom and Blood' as it evokes Hiroshima and Nagasaki and the deadly tide of intergenerational score settling.

> *All people with dreams, all mothers with sons*
> *All people with dreams never woken at night*
> *by the sound of guns*
> *Like a child that's born on a moonless night*
> *Like a child that's born, we parachute down to an unknown fight*

Crunch time for the songwriters came with the *Blue Sky Mining* album. It seemed as though everything on *Diesel* had been a hit: there was hardly a song that hadn't been played on the radio, at least in Australia. As the recording of the new album progressed there was plenty of material, but song selection was difficult. There was a mild stress about, and Pete had a sense halfway through the process that they didn't have the right mix of songs, which probably reflected a bit of the pressure to match the success of the *Diesel* collection. Rob: 'It wasn't so much a debate with Pete about what he was saying, but a determination not to call the album off, which is what he was suggesting, halfway through! He was genuine – this wasn't just an ill-conceived throw-away comment, it was something he genuinely believed. And I think history proves him right, because around that time the grunge explosion happened big time in America and music changed, but we were too far through an album of melodic pop, or whatever it was, to change horses in mid-stream. We would have had to completely rewrite and start again.'

The fast-tracking of 'King of the Mountain' and the extraordinary creation of the song 'Blue Sky Mine' – a miracle of musical cut-and-pasting – emanated from that emergency band meeting. There was a change to 'King of the Mountain's lyrics, when 'Say you're Jesus, say you're Paul/I'll put you up on my subway wall' became 'You can say you're Peter, say you're Paul/Don't put me up on your bedroom wall', but otherwise that song was relatively ready to go.

'Forgotten Years' also underwent lyrical changes, but its processing took much longer. Along with 'Beds Are Burning', 'The Dead Heart' and 'Blue Sky Mine', it was one of the band's most commercially successful songs. It was a chart topper in 1990 in France and Germany and several other European countries, and still receives regular American airplay. The song had been in Rob's and the band's collective folder for ages. Rob rewrote the main lyric several times through three different titles. Originally called 'Prayer for Peace', the second verse went 'If our sons should ever be soldiers/Our soldiers may never have sons/This is a prayer for peace/These are the children so precious so young' with the chorus 'But it reeks of politics/Aches like tetanus/Old signatures stained with tears/These need not be the broken years.' In a later version, now renamed 'Jacob's Ladder', the second verse became 'Our sons will never be soldiers/*Our daughters* will never hold guns' and the chorus changed to 'But it aches like tetanus/Reeks of politics/*No signature* stained with tears/These must always be *golden* years.' In the final version of the song, the second verse resolved itself as: 'Our sons *need never* be soldiers/Our daughters will never *need* guns' and the chorus delivered another little change, and the song its new title: 'Promises torn at the edges/*Old* signatures stained with tears/Seasons of war and grace/These should not be *forgotten* years.'

The big tours from 1987 to 1990 took a major physical and emotional toll on all the band members, and after the final tour they took a break from Midnight Oil matters for all of 1991. Well, almost. At the end of year they started compiling some live tracks for *Scream in Blue*, an album that features songs recorded at five different concerts over a ten-year period. It was partly a contractual fulfilment to deliver an album in that year, but typically the band were determined to make the record as good as possible. They certainly spent many hours of their 'time off' going through live recordings and picking the choicest cuts, indulging in only a little judicious remixing.

Scream in Blue captures quite a bit of the sounds and atmosphere of a Midnight Oil performance, including several classic raves from Pete. It also illustrates how some songs grow and evolve once they've been exposed to multiple performances in the live arena. Pete: 'I liked it. A little too much reverb, but otherwise it's a beauty. Live records aren't usually very inspiring, partly because most bands who do them aren't necessarily that inspiring live. But I think "live" is one of our fortes, so it was worth having a shot at.'

But live albums have a reputation for not selling; new studio songs invariably do better in the marketplace. Sony accepted that it was unlikely to sell a lot of copies of *Scream in*

Blue. Chris Moss: 'The album released in the year-off scenario was an absolutely phenomenal album – as a document of the band it's still one of my absolute favourites – but it was a live album, and live albums don't really sell. I think we probably sold about 800 000 worldwide.' By contrast, the band had sold two and a half million copies of *Blue Sky Mining* by the time *Scream in Blue* came out in May 1992.

By October the band were ready with new songs from their sabbatical year's writing, and they went to Megaphon Studios in the southern Sydney suburb of Tempe to commence recording *Earth and Sun and Moon* with Nick Launay. They made an unheralded appearance at a Tibet benefit gig at the Annandale Hotel the week before and took the opportunity to road-test the new material by treating the assembled inner-city activists to a set of all-new songs.

The *Blue Sky Mining* songs had emerged from the post-*Diesel* pressure-cooker environment in 1989, which meant it was almost three years since demand for new material had needed to be met. This had advantages and disadvantages, as David Fricke notes. 'It meant that the Oils had time to write and really craft things, and I think *Earth and Sun and Moon* is an amazing record, *highly* underrated. "Drums of Heaven"! "Truganini"! They were making great music, writing really good songs. At the same time, one of the other factors, just at the time they'd said, "We're going home", that's when Nirvana hit. So not only was the band not here in the States, but the landscape changed overnight. It was not enough to be their kind of loud and their kind of sincere. Rock became much noisier, much more raw, and the Oils went the other way. They were actually putting a lot more finesse into their intensity.'

Like punk, grunge was a return to the more elemental rock'n'roll aesthetics of simplicity and emotional honesty, with a distinctive blend of full-on guitar thrash and calmer moments. It was often not very well played, and although it was no less enjoyable for that lack of technical finesse it sounded quite different to Midnight Oil's new record. *Earth and Sun and Moon* still had plenty of wild squally guitars (check the end of 'Bushfire'), but the grunge movement had roughness at its core and was lyrically much more personal. Grunge songs were about feeling miserable and trying to deal with the mess in your head more than the mess in the world, although bands like Pearl Jam and Smashing Pumpkins certainly dealt to some extent with those broader themes.

It was almost ten years since the band had worked with Nick on *10–1* and *Red Sails*. In the intervening time relations between Gary and Nick's management had become strained, but the band really liked Nick and the work he'd done, and he was talked into overseeing the new recording after negotiations on behalf of the band were taken over by Pete. Despite the progressive, technical nature of their two previous recordings with Nick, the band wanted to move back to a more old-fashioned way of working. They wanted to capture the sounds virtually live onto analogue equipment, which was a deliberate shift away from the relatively high-tech digital approach of *Blue Sky Mining*. They were prepared to sacrifice cleanness for atmosphere and Jim says the *Earth and Sun and Moon* keywords were 'groove' for the songs and 'raw' for the sound. 'We probably didn't go far enough in terms of being rough, because it didn't turn out rough at all compared to these new bands – which basically had a new sound. But it was a very honest album, and an album we wanted to make.'

Pressure to come up with the raw song ideas and component bits wasn't a problem for Jim, but delivering into an increasingly demanding business and marketing environment, with constantly rising expectations for 'hit' singles from the record company and others, seemed to make the approach more problematic for him. 'We'd had two albums that were in the sun in terms of the world, but personally I really couldn't have given a shit about what the world thought anyway. I hated that whole scene. It was like fascism, you know, delivering hit after hit after hit after hit. It was like— well, you know, I had to do that. I never thought the band was about that. I thought the band was about being the band – not a movement, or some sort of spokesman for a generation.'

The *Earth and Sun and Moon* album is full of songs inspired by and conceived in a relatively relaxed state. They had all enjoyed the year off, most of it at home in Sydney. Rob had spent time on his boat and enjoyed socialising and gardening again but also launched his musical side project, the Ghostwriters. Pete had been in International Greenpeace mode a good deal of the time, but found time for surfing and exploring the Australian landscape. Jim and Martin had still probably played guitar every day, but had significant family time and stopped to smell the roses too. They were all dads, with the exception of Bones, and contributed time to school tuckshop duties and neighbourhood child-minding schemes. They were all the fathers of girls – with only one boy between them – and, given the male-dominated nature of their work environment, the time with their daughters no doubt proved refreshing and rewarding.

Nick Launay: 'That album was "We're all mature, we know what we're doing, let's do it and have fun doing it", and that's pretty much what we did. They'd just had a huge hit album – a massive hit album – with *Diesel and Dust*, and then followed it up with *Blue Sky Mining*, which, although it was a great, great album, wasn't as big a hit. In America if you've had a huge album followed by a not-so-huge album you get the pressure. And it's stupid pressure. It's illogical. It's disrespectful. I'm sure they were getting that, but they didn't let it filter through.'

Fatherhood and its responsibilities seem to be reflected in the 'new-age-ness' of the lyrics and the rich, warm sounds of *Earth and Sun and Moon*. The title track is a beautiful piece of pure Jim. It's an eerie, awe-inspired tribute to the natural world, delivered with swelling emotion and love but with the lyrical suggestion that although the earth and sun and moon may survive, humans may not. 'Bushfire' is a deceptively simple piece that looks at life from the land's point of view – it welcomes the regenerative power of the flames. The character and nature of fire are displayed in the music, right from the song's tinder-dry acoustic start to its incendiary finish. The use of the word 'blazing' for the guitars at the end of the song was never more appropriate.

Possibly the most personally revealing lyrics Pete ever contributed are on 'In the Valley', in which he recounts his family story, including the death of his parents. The house fire that killed his mother is referred to as 'a stiff arm from Hades'. When he sings, 'She always welcomed the spring, always welcomed the stranger' I can attest to that – his mother was a wonderful and impressive woman, tall and strong and endlessly interested and interesting. 'In the Valley' may be alluding to the biblical Valley of Death, but it could just as easily be referring to the little cabin in Kangaroo Valley where Pete spent many of his free hours at the time, walking through the forests, weeding and writing. Or it could be one of Jim's lines.

Nick: 'The thing that grabbed me about it, and why I thought we should do it, was that it was very much a Peter song. It was him spilling his guts out. I did have a problem with his whole religious thing, because I think of religion as something that limits you. When I worked with Midnight Oil the first time, I'd seen this rebellious guy who would get up and swear and be outrageous, and when I first heard "In the Valley" I thought, "Oh my God, here we go, it's a religious thing." Actually, "Boring boring boring" is what I thought. But then I realised how passionate he was about the song – and that's a good thing.

'What I remember with *Earth and Sun* is that suddenly it was more important that Peter was in tune than ever before. To me that's never been a problem. On some of my favourite records the singer isn't in tune, and I love it. The obvious person is Bob Dylan, but Mick Jagger, too. They're not really in tune but they've got this great "Rrroaarr" performance – to me that is what it's all about. I remember doing vocals over and over again with Peter and sacrificing some character vocals for ones that were more in tune. It was definitely a concern of Rob's, in particular – he was very adamant that Peter's voice on this album had to be more in tune. And I understand that, because Rob can sing really well and in his mind – well, ask anyone, "Is it better to have it in tune or not in tune?" – it's better to have it in tune. But you've got someone like Peter, whose natural thing is not to sing that way. In hindsight I wish I'd let him just rant and rave, because that's what he does best.'

Rob was the most critical of Pete's singing. He considered Pete's inability to pitch notes reliably as the band's biggest liability, musically. 'Pete was our greatest asset for all the obvious reasons — amazing charismatic front man, superb off-the-cuff speaker, riveting performer, enormous active exploding brain. But a liability, because we couldn't depend on him singing the right fucking note! Well, that's not quite true. In the studio he often sang beautifully, and there were some songs where he was always great, and of course he always put in as a live vocalist, always gave it his best shot.'

Jim: 'I think something happened to the band in those days. There were a lot of external pressures, and I think "In the Valley" and certain songs like that, everything had to be a single. I especially felt the pressure of that. Well, *Blue Sky* too, but *Earth and Sun* was probably where it was at its most rife, because the band had just made two huge albums and we were about to make our third one of that series. But everyone had very young families. We were with Sony, who, quite frankly, didn't really want to know about that. And creatively I think the band was up against the wall. We wanted to be kind of rougher, like it used to be, but we'd kinda lost that roughness because we— I don't know. The world really said to us, "You know, you're the guys with the hats, you're the guys from the outback, you're the guys with the music guitars, you're the guys with the political message".' The image of the band from the success of their previous albums raised expectations that they would deliver the same sort of sounds and songs as before.

By almost any measure *Earth and Sun and Moon* is a very strong album, varied in style, beautifully produced and arranged. And for Oils fans it was full of those expected

Midnight Oil surprises: a love song of sorts in 'Outbreak of Love', Pete's very personal lyrics for 'In the Valley', and a song that touches on how the band were feeling about their career, 'Feeding Frenzy'. But its position as the long-awaited follow-up to the *Diesel* and *Blue Sky* albums meant its release in America was so tied up with the details of marketing, and with record company issues, that success was far from guaranteed.

Nick and the band thought 'Truganini' was the most likely single. It talks about redressing a situation that has been ongoing in Australia virtually since white settlement in 1788. It is a universally understood call for decisive measures in challenging times and for independence and freedom for all, but ended up being pigeonholed by most listeners as another song dealing with Indigenous issues. If there is a dominant theme, it would be the Australian republic-versus-monarchy debate.

There's a road train going nowhere
Roads are cut, lines are down
We'll be staying at the Roma Bar
Till that monsoon passes on

The backbone of this country's broken
The land is cracked and the land is sore
Farmers are hanging on by their fingertips
We cursed and stumbled across that shore

I hear much support for the monarchy
I hear the Union Jack's to remain
I see Namatjira in custody
I see Truganini in chains

The third and final time through the chorus, it changes: 'I hear much support for the monarchy/*I see the Union Jack's in flames*', then we hear Pete's ad-libbed yell from the near distance, 'Let it burn!'

Nick: 'We finished "Truganini" and everyone was like, "That's the single". I thought it was great. I did think it was a bit too much "about Australia", but Australia was very popular in America at the time and to be Australian was a cool thing – still is. If you're really gonna go down that road of trying to predict what people will think about lyrics, then you have to decide "Is the audience intelligent or are they stupid?" and if you really get into it, you're going to end up deciding they're stupid. And that's not healthy, because then you start making stupid records.'

Dumbing down the material to match or attract the latest vacuous but saleable trends was never an option. *Earth and Sun and Moon* reflects the band's extraordinary musical skills and their concerns as people, and as a band, as well as, if not better than, any other of their records. Its release was highly anticipated and it was tipped by all and sundry to go straight to number one on the local charts – but it went to number two. Not a bad start for the 'comeback' album, but less than expected.

It had been almost three years since the huge local and international profile of *Blue Sky Mining*, with very little touring in between. The record company hoped this new set of songs would satisfy American radio's needs and re-awaken the public to Midnight Oil. As soon as tracks were complete they were sent to the record company in New York and Sony began the process of choosing the right song for the right radio market and plotting its rise to mainstream chart success. How they did that happened largely behind closed doors and amounted to what Gary calls a loss of sovereignty, something he had managed to guard doggedly through the band's career. To counter this challenge to their control, Gary felt he had to move to America. Company boss Don Ienner was even more determined with this record than with the last that things would be done his way. Gary's powers of persuasion were legendary, but this task was looking to be his biggest challenge. Against the odds he was going to try and talk Don into doing things the Midnight Oil way. Back in Australia Gary had had the run of the yard, but in New York things weren't going to be so easy.

The ability of a seed on the forest floor to reach its full potential, or even to survive long enough to grow into a plant, depends on conditions being favourable and fortunate and the seed being of sturdy stock. Bands are like that, too, and so are songs – little seeds to start with, vulnerable to prevailing conditions, but sometimes lucky enough or inherently strong enough both to survive and to succeed. However, in the smoke-and-mirrors world of contemporary pop music it is also possible for bands and songs to exceed their potential, buoyed by the fluff and fiction of modern marketing and promotion. A big push can make a monster hit out of a modest song – sometimes – and some records don't even feature the actual members of the named band. Who can forget Milli Vanilli? Songs can be global successes for all kinds of reasons and dismal failures for just as many others. Split Enz's 'Six Months in a Leaky Boat' was about to become their breakthrough hit in the UK when the departure of the British fleet for the Falklands War put an end to any radio airplay.

Songs can 'make it' through quirkiness of sound or lyrics, clever chord use, attractive word combinations and, of course, repetition. It is because of radio repetition that we often have a love–hate relationship with songs. We love them, then we hate them or we can't listen to them. Songwriters are particularly hurt by this result of radio overplaying songs. Even though they seem to be the content on a 'music' station, songs are really the filler between advertisements. Radio uses them as a free and disposable way of attracting listeners to their business – not the music business, the advertising business. Songs should be treated much more sensitively than that. To the listener they can be highly significant, and to the writers they can be like children.

Songwriters generally can't explain it, but most acknowledge that their songs do not necessarily emanate entirely from within themselves. Songs, it is often implied, are like gifts from some sort of creative spirit to the songwriter – who is a simple conduit, in some interpretations. The artist may work hard at enticing and interpreting and presenting that spirit for public appreciation, and frequently resents the underlying exploitation at the other end of the process. Most feel that radio stations regularly ignore their best songs, but equally, if a song is 'rewarded' with airplay, no writer likes to think that their magic, nurtured and loved creation could be turned into an incitement for some people to turn off the radio.

Songs are precious things to all of us, but particularly so to their writers. For the members of Midnight Oil, the idea of their songs being used to advertise or promote something they don't personally endorse is anathema. Over the years substantial sums of money have been offered for the right to use their songs in TV commercials – in Australia and overseas – but the band have refused all such offers. Occasionally they have licensed songs for inclusion on compilation albums aiding particular causes or for use in movies and documentaries. Many of those licenses have been given gratis because they were for projects by people the band respected who would use the music appropriately.

'The majority of the band has a visceral negative reaction to the exploitation of our music,' says Rob. 'The short-term gains of pulling a quid for flogging the use of your music for selling something actually devalue the music, to a point that in the longer term those gains may seem small. So the more you treasure your music, the more you limit it to special causes. Music can then end up being precious rather than exploited, gutted and devalued. In our case it's particularly important, because most of the songs have a strong context and a purpose for which they were written in the first place. If taken out of that context, they are not only absurd but would turn the band into a laughing stock. For example, for "Blue Sky Mine" we had a big offer from a motor-vehicle company to use it for a four-wheel drive commercial, but the song was actually written about the survivors of a blue asbestos tragedy in Western Australia and has nothing to do with motor vehicles. The people who appeared in that film clip dying of asbestosis and mesothelioma, and the people who really believed in the song and got into the whole issue of the exploitation of southern Europeans and Aboriginal people working in the asbestos mines, would have been rightfully horrified to hear that song selling four-wheel drives. So it's not just our own consciousness and sensibilities that are at stake here.'

Radio can, and regularly does, kill songs – as can a TV advertisement – but it is also the lifeblood of contemporary music. Songs are described by record companies as 'radio friendly'. They are categorised by superficial criteria and fitted into different radio formats, and deliver particular demographics for advertisers. In the United States it gets very complicated. There are formats for every sub-genre and decade of music imaginable, used by networks with hundreds of stations, millions of listeners and playlists researched and paid for by the best and most brutal in the game. The final hurdle for all songs in the commercial radio arena is judgement of a thirty-second sample played down the telephone to random members of the public. Record companies use focus groups: handpicked cross-sections of 'the consumer'. It is these groups' responsibility to give the thumbs up or down, and it was one of these groups, in New York, that said 'Truganini' wouldn't work in America because the title was too hard to say. The Sony executives were furious with the band. According to Mason Munoz, upper-level executives were saying, 'Who the fuck do they think they are writing a song called "Truganini"? Nobody can say "Truganini". Fuck them. How dare they!'

But anyone who went to a performance of the song would have witnessed a room full of people singing along and dancing with wild abandon. It wasn't the song itself that was the problem, it was the packaging. After the title came the video. Mason: 'Unfortunately Midnight Oil delivered a very Australian video for that song, where they were on a bus driving through the outback. I remember a senior executive here in the US saying to me, "I'm tired of this shit. I'm tired of this—", and he started describing all the things that would be typically Australian to an American. "Enough, enough! Why can't we have a Midnight Oil video that looks like an American MTV video instead of one with the outback and the red soil and the kangaroos?" But the dusty roads were what Midnight Oil were all about, and that's how they were comfortable presenting themselves, and proud of it.'

It's not as if one video image or song could possibly represent the entirety of the band's musical styles or the range of their themes and interests. David Fricke praises the skilfulness of their songwriting. 'In a lot of ways, the way they sound and the way their songs are constructed is so artful, with a real attention to detail.' He compares their work to the Who's most acclaimed album. 'It reminds me a lot of *Who's Next*, certainly in the fact that there's exceptional integrity there. Townshend may have a been a bit more fictional in his renditions of his vision of the future – "Lighthouse" was meant to be this prophecy of the Internet – whereas the Oils were getting down and dirty with Greenpeace, American imperialism, the mess of nuclear waste and a threatening holocaust. But the architecture in the songs, and the drama they achieved on the record, and then the way they transferred that drama live without worrying about all the little prettifications you get in the studio, just like *hitting it*.

'A lot of the things they spoke about, even though they were current events then, still haven't changed. "US Forces" – hello! They're all over in Iraq now. And Afghanistan in "Short Memory". They played that song at one of the shows after 9/11 when they came through that October and played at The World over at Times Square. I remember thinking, "Afghanistan, that's where we are now!" The very thing that they were singing about was happening that day, even though that record was almost twenty years old. All the stuff about the nukes, about the environment, even the things as simple as the images in "Power and the Passion" – people being caught in this kind of stasis in their lives. Is that any different from sitting at a computer, or watching 200 channels of TV, or babbling away on a cell phone? All of the things they talk about in their songs are as bad now, or worse, than when they were written. When you talk about US imperialism you can go back to Vietnam, or the Philippines, or the Spanish-American war. What Midnight Oil did was to key their writing into a particular figure, like Reagan, or a certain issue, like Greenpeace, or write something inspired by a particular event, like the giving back of Ayers Rock. All these things reverberate still. You can listen to their songs and they are absolutely as contemporary now as when they were written, because they are about specific manifestations of universal themes and events.'

Most songs we hear on the radio are love songs. Love is the most universally inspiring and widely understood subject matter. It is also the least contentious. Other emotions, such as hate, lust, envy, shame, paranoia and the rest, only get a look-in as an adjunct to love. Songs about social issues and political concerns, outside of specialist areas of music like punk or folk or the blues, are most unusual. The love song is everywhere, and the word 'love' is everywhere, which would be a good thing if it made more of a difference.

Loving one another as brothers and sisters went out with

sixties lyrics, so 'love' has been left to refer to making love, or wide-eyed romance. The use of the word love to describe both of these creates what Frank Zappa, in his *Real Frank Zappa Book*, calls 'a semantic corruption' with a resultant 'shove in the direction of bad mental health'. Zappa thinks listening to love songs in general is bad for you. There is 'a subconscious training that creates a desire for an imaginary situation which will never exist for you. People who buy into that mythology go through life feeling they got cheated out of something.'

I don't know whether this philosophical line has ever been discussed by the Oils, but love songs do not feature in their repertoire. It isn't that they are anti-romance or misogynistic, they just think there are more important things to write about, and besides, doesn't the world have enough love songs? There are only a couple of exceptions. 'Head Over Heels' is the least convincing song on their first record, and 'Loves on Sale' from *Postcard* is about *everything* being on sale. Ten years later, on *Blue Sky Mining*, there was 'Shakers and Movers', with the line 'I can shake, I can move, but I can't live without your love'. At the time Jim commented on the use of the word love in the song: 'We've never done it before. Our fans will go, "Oh no, it's the beginning of the end!"' But the lyrics are generally interpreted as love of nature, or God, not romantic love.

On *Earth and Sun and Moon* in 1993, there was 'Outbreak of Love', which definitely sounds like a more conventional love song, but Rob's original idea was to remove the word 'outbreak' from its usual linguistic linkage with war or hostilities and appropriate it for more benign occasions. The *Earth and Sun and Moon* album deals extensively with truth and beauty and nature, so love isn't entirely out of place.

Love of country is a theme the band has dealt with quite a few times. 'Lucky Country', on *Place Without a Postcard*, simply glories in the eccentricities of Australian life. The song almost engages Frank Zappa's point with the line 'Love, it's so tough, coz it raises your hopes and then it makes you run'. Then there was 'One Country' on *Blue Sky Mining*, which seems to call for our love of country to extend beyond national boundaries and include the occupants of the rest of the planet. On *Earth and Sun and Moon* the band revisited this theme in 'My Country' and, to a degree, in 'Best of Both Worlds'. 'My Country' entreats people not to take love of country and national pride too far. It encourages the view that criticising your country, or admitting that your country has done wrong, is not a sign that you don't love your country – that 'My country, right or wrong' is wrong.

In the beautiful wood-panelled lounge area outside the main Festival recording studio Rob and Pete were rewriting lyrics together on the couch for a new song, 'Kiss That Girl'. Jim thinks that Rob wrote it about him, but given Rob's reputation among the fans as a serial flirter, or at least as the band member with the most immediate sex appeal, it was quite possibly a 'note to self'.

Rob: 'Jim instantly responded to the naivety and the joyful chorus in that song. The song worked for me in the end because you had this quite compelling, brooding verse, with a very interesting climbing melodic but unusual vocal line that would normally be an instrumental line, followed by a joyful sixties-pop chorus. It's always those unlikely combinations that I find appealing. By the time the chorus lyrics had been worked over and worked over and rewritten and tried to be made more "Midnight Oil", I wasn't sure what the fuck it was about! The song sounds really poppy and up, but if you read the original lyrics they are quite dark. And it has a warning. All the music I've ever responded to, the stuff I've liked most in Midnight Oil, has a strong melody and beat but is also capable of a walloping great threat. I love music like that.'

If Rob was trying to advise his colleague to stay in his marriage he certainly didn't say so directly to Jim. Like noticing prams everywhere when a birth is impending, Jim was possibly seeing more in the song than there was. (His relationship with his wife broke down at the time following prolonged difficulties, and he now lives with the girl he kissed.) Pete almost certainly involved himself in rewriting the lyrics because of his dislike of 'love' songs in general, but this meant he had to indulge in his least favourite type of writing: ambiguity. Pete preferred songs that could not be misinterpreted. 'There are instances of nice metaphorical and ambiguous writing through the career, and on some albums there are probably a few tunes here and there that fall into that category, but generally speaking, I don't think that's the case. And anyway, quite often the action made the ambiguous clear.'

However, songs are often not what they appear and misinterpretations can be widespread. Springsteen's 'Born in the USA' is not a song about blind American patriotism: it criticises the Vietnam War and the degraded state of the country. And 'Won't Get Fooled Again' by the Who does not incite revolution: it is *against* the concept. Pete Townshend has commented regarding the song that 'a revolution is not going to change anything at all in the long run, and a lot of people are going to get hurt'. Songs can be deliberately ambiguous, too – flights of fancy or acts of devil's advocacy or simply examples of artists' willingness to experiment with ideas. Just because you relate to one song by a particular artist doesn't mean you will agree with the sentiments in other songs by that artist. Pete points out that Australian prime minister John Howard used to claim to be a Bob Dylan fan. 'He is no longer, since he was made aware of the more controversial issues Dylan has sung about. With an artist you can abstract the art because art is abstract up to a point – you can draw stimulation from it, you can interpret it, you can be inspired by it, but you can also read into it something that was never there and that it was never intended to mean. And in fact humans, in all their diversity, will do that. And that's great, that's what art is.'

But the band sought to offer something more than words and music with their art – they added activism. Pete: 'Art in practice is having the art and then practising it so that you leave no doubt, or little doubt, in the minds of those who come to read your story, to listen to your songs and see what you did, as to what you mean, and what your art is actually on about. And I think that's why you've got to step out. Not because you can't reach people just by the song, because you can, but people can also take out of the song what was never in the song in the first place.'

'Kiss That Girl' – just the title had me intrigued. It sure sounded like a love song, but as I watched Pete and Rob on the studio couch the song was changing. Words were being altered for many sound and meaningful reasons. Bones: 'The lyrical debates were the greatest ones. A chord's a chord and a drum beat's a drum beat, but the guys would spend vast amounts of time getting lyrical stuff together till they were all happy with what was coming out on tape – what it meant.'

'Kiss That Girl' was in the final stages of preparation for

Capricornia, and the philosophical discussion about recording a love song, if there had been one, was in the past. A day or so later the song was finished. In the final version the verses deal pretty ambiguously with the choice between resisting primal urges and following your heart, but the chorus remains quite direct – if ambivalent!

If you kiss that girl you could lose the lot
Everything you've got if you kiss that girl
You can fool the world but can you fool yourself?
Can you sing the words like you're someone else?

This song is only typical of the Oils in that it was unexpected, like the disco move of 'Power and the Passion' or the restraint of 'Armistice Day' or the acoustic sounds of 'Wedding Cake Island'. A love song at this late stage of their career was a surprise, but it sounded so good that some people who heard it thought it could be a single. That must have been the kiss of death for 'Kiss That Girl'. It was dropped from *Capricornia* and has only appeared on some European versions of the album.

'Truganini' was a love song, albeit another in the 'concern for country' category, and it was as passionate and powerful and accomplished as almost anything the band had done. As they prepared for the international campaign for *Earth and Sun*, 'Truganini' looked like it had the commercial goods as well. Nick and the band were quietly optimistic. Nick: 'To me that song had everything that everyone wanted. It had a groove, a bass line, a political message – all those things that "Beds Are Burning" had.'

But love was in short supply at record company headquarters in New York, where the Sony executives had been waiting almost too long for the band's follow-up album. The opening track on *Earth and Sun and Moon*, 'Feeding Frenzy', seemed to face squarely the prospect of another round in the ring. Along with general commentary on the urgency and demands of the modern world, it stated, 'Here we go again, into the clamour of the feeding pen'. And later, with a fatalistic shrug, 'God knows, it's been fun'.

eight

outbreak of love

The band were happy with the songs and sound of *Earth and Sun and Moon* but Gary, at a strategic level, was not. He recalls a 1993 meeting in St Kilda listening to the album with the band and saying, 'Midnight Oil is a high-energy rock band. What are you doing with this record?' His theory was that the crop of US grunge bands at the time were inspired by the Australian rock bands of the eighties and at the very time the Oils were poised to claim their place as the root of it all with the new group of anti-establishment rock acts, 'Oils went soft.'

Jim: 'Gary didn't like *Earth and Sun*. He just didn't think it was the right record for the time. He wanted to change the cover even after we'd done it. He'd originally wanted it and then suddenly changed his mind. "It's the wrong cover for this album." At that time the whole of music had changed and when the album came out we were getting to a period where American music was starting to find its voice, with bands like Nirvana and Pearl Jam coming up. And here were the Oils, who'd been there for a couple of years and were well established, being challenged by these new bands. We weren't part of that whole new thing that was going on; we were outside of it. And we *wanted* to be outside of it as people. The wind kinda changed – there was real change in the air. I think Gary wished we were on the right side of that change, but we weren't. I really liked *Earth and Sun*, but we probably didn't go far enough in terms of being rough. Coz rough was the key word. It wasn't that rough compared to those bands.'

Nick Launay feels they were caught in a dilemma between wanting a raw sound, but not a rough one. 'I loved the Midnight Oil I first met, who were raw and rough and ready and "We don't give a shit what anyone thinks of us; we're going to tell them what *we* think. There are things that are wrong in the world and we want to point them out." That's what Midnight Oil was about. Midnight Oil was also about Rob playing drums better than Keith Moon, about him doing all those wild and crazy things better than Keith. To me, Rob is one of the most amazing drummers ever. If you've only listened to *Diesel and Dust* you wouldn't know that. Yet here we were, two albums later, making a record with some confusion. One message was "We want it raw, we want it live", and another was "Be careful, better polish it".

'The song "Earth and Sun and Moon" is amazing – great track, so moody. That and "Outbreak of Love", and "Truganini"! It's probably a much better album than I realise. I just don't remember it having as much passion as the other two albums I did with them.'

When, as an Aussie pub band in the early eighties, Midnight Oil made their first forays into the massive and unfamiliar

American market they needed all the help they could get. Rhonda Markowitz's job was to explain the Oils to the Americans. 'I basically said, "I have got this *fierce* rock band – these people are ferocious. They take no prisoners, this is *rock* and *roll*. They pick you up by the scruff of the neck, throw you down on the floor and stomp on you. You like rock'n'roll like that? I got rock'n'roll like that. And they're political, and they're smart, and they're articulate, and the music's got enough hooks to catch a rack full of fish. Oh yeah, and they're from Australia."'

This was part of Rhonda's thumbnail sketch of Midnight Oil. 'The Australian-ness didn't really matter, except in so far as to say, "They've got a different point of view than your average band because they are not American, they are not British; they are from a country that has been kinda shunted aside and used for American purposes, and they don't like that, and this is their take from that side."'

Rhonda was the band's US publicist from 1984 through to *Diesel and Dust* time. She was from the large multinational public relations company Rogers and Cowan and was part of the top-line support that Gary managed to arrange thanks to his connections with Gerry Weintraub's Management Three organisation. Rhonda: 'The first time I got to see the band play was in a rainstorm at Pier 84 here in New York, which is on the water. I'll never forget it, because the visual was so extraordinary. The Intrepid War Museum – a battleship – is parked right next to the Pier, and there was Peter in the driving rain with the battleship behind, screaming these antiwar songs. And that was astonishing enough, but I looked at them and thought, "Oh my God, thank you! I can sell this! This is not a problem – I *believe*." I was just thrilled to finally have a rock band with some substance. I could get into what they were saying. I loved their whole political stand. There wasn't anyone around who was saying things quite the way they were saying things.

'As a publicist, you get as much profile for your client as possible, by any means possible, through the press, through all the media. You ask for album reviews, you ask for photos and listings when the band is on tour, and of course you always try for interviews to expose them and their thoughts as much as possible to the broadest possible audience. You go for television – I got them their first stories on *MTV News*. And it all came together with *Diesel and Dust*, because we had some very strong videos and TV was really growing, and TV liked the videos. The record company was behind them, the music was unassailable, it all worked. It was the hooks, it was the music, it was all that – and the big tall bald guy silhouetted against the sun.'

The fact that Midnight Oil had high-quality publicity and promotion in place, plus production, touring and record company support in the USA all ready to kick in when 'Beds Are Burning' took off in the charts, was almost entirely due to Gary. The band members saw the business operations as a parallel but foreign universe, and kept as much distance from it as they could. It was Gary's area.

Gary lived bare-footed and bare-chested in the jungles of New Guinea until he was ten years old. 'We lived on a pineapple plantation. My brothers and I liked to hang out in the tribal village next to the plantation. We grew up as "lik lik piccaninny masters belong big fella one talk master". We used to like eating with the locals more than we liked eating at home.

Brilliant memories. Highly recommended, being feral for the first ten years of your life – gives you an independent outlook. You don't get that herd mentality.'

In the Australian suburbs as a teenager he had some of his innocence rubbed off, got himself off to school and virtually lived alone from age fifteen after his parents' separation. He learnt martial arts and golf – at fifteen he had a handicap of four – and finished school early to become a golf pro. After being fired and rehired several times, Gary quit. He added surfing and part-time bar work to his pastimes, and started to see some live music. 'That was it. I went from a straight, innocent golfer to sex, drugs and rock'n'roll. I was looking at going back and finishing off my final PGA exam but basically started with the Oils, and it just became like a rollercoaster of excitement and creativity and new frontiers, which really appealed to the type of personality I am.'

Bear remembers how the band's relationship with Gary started. 'This guy came up to us after a gig at the Antler and started talking to us about how great we were and what we should do. To me it was like he was talking in another dialect, in words familiar to those in the surfing and drug culture and possibly stretching the truth in places. From memory he was selling cars or real estate at the time, or whatever he could lay his hands on to sell. Initially, we decided that if he was willing to help us, then we were willing to let him help us. His name was Gary Morris Vasicek.'

Gary's work rate and involvement in the band grew massively over the following two years. He worked tirelessly, often doing lights at gigs as well as managing affairs, operating out of wherever his bedroom happened to be (this was well before the advent of mobile phones). He was doing eighty-hour weeks, and enormous progress was being made. The band's work rate was non-stop – playing four to five times a week, totalling up to 200 gigs a year. The independently operated Powderworks label was set up for the band's first recordings, and they started their own booking agency, built with the goodwill and infrastructure of Chris Plimmer's Nucleus organisation, which operated largely outside of the established venues.

The Oils' agency blacklisted twenty-two venues for reasons of bouncer violence, unreasonable conditions for the fans or the band, or extortionate financial practices by management. They just didn't play ball with those places. Gary and Pete made a formidable team in difficult situations. Their combination of tough and fast talking, plus the inevitable visual impact of their combined presence, made it quite clear to the people they did business with – independent venue owners and others – just what they wanted and how things had to be. They'd get what they wanted, or they wouldn't come back. As a result there were several places they played a lot, like French's, the Civic, the Stagedoor and the Royal Antler, and many more they only played once. But even the Antler tried to squeeze the band, and they barred the venue for a time until the management agreed to their terms.

The band were on a mission not just to play music, but to do it on their own terms and conditions, and with Gary on board this was always more likely to happen than not. Gary: 'We were sort of on a roll. Audiences were paying the money to come along. I was promoting the shows, finding new venues, and at the time the band – and I guess in some ways it's Midnight Oil's weakness – liked to have a lot of say. But when it came to doing anything apart from playing guitar or being in a studio or having a meeting, they weren't that pragmatic about the nuts and bolts of putting it all together or the energy level required. It really started to be left up to me to organise it and put it all together, and I came into a bit of friction with them because of that.

'I think they felt that they were now becoming successful on a local level, and there was always this sense you got from Pete that it was gonna be temporary – that Midnight Oil was just a flash-in-the-pan thing for him. It was like "I'll do it for as long as it suits where I'm at in my own life". And so there was this incredible contradiction. It was like having a gun held to your head: "Perform, or else I'll pull the trigger." And the gun was also held to his own head: "If I'm not into this, then I'm going to take myself out." So you were continually trying to make things happen that would come up to a bar, a critique, that would be acceptable. This is where Pete started to bring about those demands and that requirement that was upon every member of Midnight Oil and myself – his demand for perfection – but also his scant regard for people holding things precious. And I think that disregard for preciousness was with him for a long time. Later every aspect of Midnight Oil became precious to him. I think I was probably better off when Midnight Oil was a throwaway, because I could sustain a two-hour argument or debate with him and know that he'd walk away and just leave it up to me to put it together. But when it became precious, it was like two or three times on the phone every day. "Pete, it's all under control, leave me alone." "Blah blah blah." "Don't worry; it's all going to happen." "What about this? What about that?" "It's all dealt with!"'

Pete's telephone conversations with Gary over the years

have become legendary. There was the one when the band were literally moments away from going on stage at the Olympics, and out of the blue Pete, out of breath from retrieving the radio mike, was handed a mobile phone by a security guard to find Gary was on the other end with a since-forgotten last-minute piece of advice. Then there were the hundreds of marathon international calls from hotel rooms when matters of major concern had to be thrashed out (which seemed like every day). The band regularly held conference calls when they were apart, and they all remember the occasion when one by one they all quietly hung up, leaving Gary to convince nobody of his point – and nobody knows how long he continued. Pete often felt that Gary was restating his position unnecessarily, and in the middle of one telephone exchange went and made a cup of tea and rejoined the conversation several minutes later without Gary ever knowing he'd been away from the phone. A story told in Oils family circles involves one of Pete's daughters sitting on the floor with a plastic toy phone, imitating her dad and saying over and over again 'No, Gary. No! No! No!'

Gary says, 'A combatant but deep friendship formed between Peter and myself, which is still with us. You have to learn to work with each other through all kinds of disagreements, like in a marriage. If you're willing to work through them, then you begin to respect the other party for their contribution. And I believe that's what happened between Peter and myself over the history. We still have real, full-on arguments about things, and then five seconds later we're not emotionally affected and we can chat to each other about something completely mundane and of no account, be perfectly normal with each other. I think we argue about the principle, and really hone the principle until it shines as something neither one of us has invented. And then there are times when I don't agree with him, but I know he's right. Pete has insight and an appreciation of things.'

Just prior to the band's first tour of New Zealand in late 1979 and a couple of months before their second album was released, Gary underwent a religious conversion prompted by visiting a Billy Graham Crusade. 'I came into what I call a divine encounter and opened my life to the Lord Jesus. I remember after the Billy Graham Crusade going back to Selinas where the Oils were and they said, "Where have you been?" and I said, "I went to the Billy Graham Crusade." And they all started laughing. I said, "Well, he drew more than you guys did tonight – he had 18 000 people. And he had a much bigger production than you guys, with lights and sound and a Jands stage." That shut them up for a little while.'

Bear: 'I never really understood what Gary was on about at the best of times. He was always an extroverted evangelist for some cause, moving way into your personal space and staring at you with glazed eyes. I would just smile politely and hope it wouldn't last long.'

Gary left the band and was out of the picture for almost three years. During some of that time the Oils were managed by Zev Eizik, whose methods were much more orthodox than Gary's. With Zev the band managed to draw closer to the mainstream while still retaining their independent approach and reputation. Zev was a well-connected promoter, and during his time with the band they expanded their profile from Sydney to the whole country. They also lost Bear and found Giffo, and made their first foray overseas when they went to England to record the *Place Without a Postcard* album.

When Gary returned from his wanderings, he was significantly different but essentially the same. He rejoined the band by slowly proving his worth to them with his customary independent thinking, straight talking and ability to get things done. Whatever he and the band dreamed up, Gary was the one who actually saw the practical side of the process. If it needed building, he'd build it. His energy and commitment knew no bounds, as did his ability to step on toes. Gary butted heads regularly with lots of people in his role as the band's protector and business representative. He was tough, and hard to refuse. 'Pit-bull tough – sometimes pit-bull-on-crack tough,' according to Rob.

Gary and the band's lawyers negotiated a deal in Australia with Columbia Records, soon to be bought by Sony. 'We'd left Powderworks after *Bird Noises* and there was an interlude with A&M Records and Zev Eizik – that was in the time I left the band. When I came back we ignited a relationship with Sony and basically *10–1* was the first release out of that.' In the deal the band maintained complete rights over all creative issues, including track listings, choices for singles and all album and promotional artwork.

They also wanted to ensure a personal connection to the company through a single ongoing point of contact with someone they trusted. Chris Moss was designated the 'key man' in the contract, which meant his continuation at the company was essential for the contract to be binding. The record company had similar intent with their 'changes to band personnel' clauses, which left the contract null and void if Pete or Rob wasn't in the band. Chris: 'The way the band used to operate is that they didn't really have anything to do with the record company. Midnight Oil did their thing and basically gave it to us, and then we would do our thing, so to speak. Gary was always the strongest contact within the company, and rightfully so, management and record company. The band were in a domain of their own and – not that they were unapproachable or unfriendly or anything else – they were very serious about what they did and also very serious about maintaining complete control of who they were and how they were presented. We as an Australian company felt quite proud of them: "The Oils are the Oils, and they'll do what they fucking want." We were part of that as well; we went with that.

Chris remembers his boss at Sony Australia sticking up for the Oils when head office in New York wasn't happy with one of the band's decisions. 'One of Denis Handlin's great delights was when the band were at the height of their success and the Oils were invited to perform at the Grammys. There was all this pressure coming from the US label, and everybody else. "They have to do this. It'll kill their career if they don't." Denis went back to them and said, "Fuck off! They won't do it. Midnight Oil will do what they want to do, and we stand by whatever decision the band makes."'

Chris went from Manager of Australian Artists to Managing Director during his time at Sony, and on the way he saw a lot of Gary in action. He became a friend and ally of the band. 'Gary was always working on that visionary thing. It was always larger than life, everything he came up with. He would sit down with his grand pictures and it would be the core of the band who would bring them down to reality. The thing with Gary's ideas was you could only call 5 per cent of them gold, but that 5 per cent was absolutely visionary. It's like the 80/20 rule: you gotta come up with 80 per cent of rubbish to get the 20 per cent that makes the content. For Gary it was probably 95/5, but the 5 was absolutely blue chip.'

Gary's personal approach was also unique. Chris: 'Gary, probably more than anybody else, is someone who is able to function, at least outwardly, with absolutely no regard for the feelings or concerns of other people. He is by far the bluntest man I've ever met in my whole life – and it can be such a charming thing if you are within the framework of Gary. But, of course, if you're outside the framework of Gary it's the most confronting thing you can ever be faced with.'

The 'framework of Gary' is that immediate group of people he needs to make things happen, people with skills to advance the band's career. In turn he uses *his* skills as a talker ('motor-mouthing'), a provocateur in the grand Aussie tradition of stirring, and a natural motivator, to generate the best work out of people. He is a big-picture player who has the enthusiasm and energy to match his vision. Add his piercing eye contact, suntanned good looks and intimidating physical presence, and he can be very persuasive and completely fascinating.

'Outside the framework of Gary' means you are of no importance to his plans. Outside the framework, it would be generous to call his general manner in encounters 'brusque'. More problematic was being in his way, like the misguided backstage security guard at the Bercy in Paris who refused to recognise Gary without his access pass. The incident escalated to fisticuffs (well, one blow each). Gary may have needed a few stitches – grumpily administered without anaesthetic by a doctor woken after midnight – but the security guard lost his job. Salomon Hazat was the gig's promoter. 'It became a game between two boxers and we could not interfere. You've seen Gary, how big he is – well, the other guy was bigger. So Gary tried to punch his face, and the other guy, well, he was trained to fight and he hit Gary once. The result was an argument for an hour. I sacked the guy and didn't pay him, but in private I said to Gary, "Why don't you wear your fucking pass! Who cares? It's only a pass!" It was the first time I'd seen a manager get punched, and afterwards that was quite funny.'

Giffo: 'I liked Gary. I've always liked Gary. A bit of a ratbag sometimes, but he's an inspired fellow. Zev was just a commercial businessman; he was the wrong person for the band. Gary was the right person. He was as inspired a manager as the band was a band. Pete and Rob would heap shit on Gary and it was a constant battle about things, but Zev was really way off track. Pete was always battling with Zev and I always thought it was much healthier to be battling with the Narrabeen surf rat, Gary. It was much better and much more in keeping with the band's whole philosophy. If you're going to be fighting with a manager, then it's much better to be fighting with someone who thinks along the same tracks.'

The battles between the band and Gary were not observed by many people, but Michael Lippold was witness to some exchanges. 'Gary and fuckin' Garrett were at each other all the time. It was an ego and a mind game. I think Gary did it more just to gee 'em up. He was always interfering. I used to tell him, "Don't talk to the crew. You want to tell the crew things, then talk to me – I'll talk to the crew." But he wouldn't. He had no idea how to do stuff like that.'

At *10–1* time Gary was fully back in the swing and helped the band to new heights in every department. Gary: 'The Oils were stoked that they had control. They felt empowered, and things were happening under their direction, and they had a representative who was a symbiot – somebody who had a symbiotic relationship with them – and able to implement these ideas that were sort of germinating out of all of us. At a Midnight Oil meeting no one could really claim an idea to themselves: it was the result of what distilled out of a six- or eight-hour debate, and if you were to try and go through "Whose idea was that?" it would defeat the spirit of what was going on. Even though some people had more input than others, those who didn't have a lot of input could still have an amazing impact when they did open their mouth with an idea. Everyone would shut up and the room would be silenced and everyone would know that's what we would go with. It would be something that came out of a very thick process of debate, conjecture, criticism, and whatever ideas survived they emerged out of this crucible of intense heat, and they were great ideas. As a result of going through all of that process I knew what to do, I knew what to represent. That's how I became Midnight Oil's manager, just representing this crucible of ideas.'

But Gary's way of putting the ideas into action involved contact with the real and ruthless world of rock'n'roll and real people, who occasionally, perhaps often, found Gary's approach difficult to deal with. Pete: 'I think there are a couple of major differences between Gary's management style and other people's management style. One major difference is his position: Gary is a part of the band. He isn't separated from the band in terms of, firstly, our arrangements with him and, secondly, in terms of how he sees the band. Most managers keep their bands somewhat at arm's length, and work with the industry to try and get the band where they want to go. Gary tends to work with the band, as well as the industry, to try and get the band where the *band* wants to go, even though the industry may or may not agree with that direction. He does that very ably.

'His personal style, though, is a different matter, because he can be very, very abrasive (abrasive may not be quite the right word – single-minded and determined) and some people can construe the way he talks and acts as intimidatory. He doesn't intimidate me, but I think he can have, and has had, that effect on others. But rock managers need to be pretty tough and pretty intimidatory in the work they're doing. He also has quite an original, quixotic streak for ideas, which sometimes he brought to the band and on some occasions they were great ideas and we went on to use them. I think he plays quite a valuable role, even when he comes up with an idea that is so off the wall that no one can follow it or go with it. He'd inevitably get us talking about something, and we'd head down another road as a result of his intervention. I think "catalyst" is a pretty good description for Gary.'

With the huge local success of *10–1*, Gary at last had chart-topping record sales as well as the band's enormous live reputation to try and make a bid for the American market. He has a number of pithy little sayings, and when it came to taking the band into the US arena it was 'Sell the sizzle, not the steak'. He explains: 'You send the scent and make sure you've got a really good barbecue happening, and then you wait for the wind to move in the right direction. So basically I sent the scent of the Australian barbecue of *10–1* to these managers, who basically wanted a piece of that steak. In order for them to get that steak they had to get us a release. Whoever got a release with Columbia I would then enter into a co-management agreement with them for Midnight Oil for America only.'

However, it took a while – about six more years of hard work and maintenance – before all the elements fell into place with the release of *Diesel and Dust*. Gary had sent the scent to the managers who looked after all the biggest acts on the Columbia record label. He reasoned that they already had the contacts with the record company that would be necessary to get to first base for a deal. Several major American management agencies responded to his package of information about the band's successes in Australia. Of these, Gerry Weintraub's Management Three looked the best. 'Basically I felt Management Three were going to give me the kind of freedom and sovereignty to work with Midnight Oil. And Pete felt good about Management Three.'

Weintraub was a high-profile manager looking after high-profile artists, Bob Dylan among others. He was also involved in producing films and promoting some big live concerts. Gary: 'He had this incredible infrastructure over there in LA that could deal with it all. We were suitably impressed.'

And Weintraub, along with his two top associates, Sal Bonefetti and Arthur Spivak, was impressed enough with Gary and Midnight Oil that he offered to do the deal. But that wasn't enough for Gary. 'I wanted them to fly down to Australia and actually come and see a Midnight Oil show. Weintraub said, "I don't get on a plane for John Denver or Bob Dylan. What makes you think I'm going to get on a plane and come down there and see Midnight Oil?" I told him, "If you don't come, we're not going to sign." That was fairly suicidal talk, but it worked. So he came down with his contingent, with Sal and Arthur, and took the top floor of the Regent Hotel in Sydney. Then he flew his entourage first-class down to Melbourne to see Midnight Oil at the Entertainment Centre. I can remember standing behind Bonefetti, Spivak and Weintraub, and there was, like, an 8000-capacity crowd filling the Melbourne Entertainment Centre, so the whole thing had incredible Midnight Oil atmosphere. And I overheard Weintraub turn to Arthur as the Oils were kicking into gear on stage and say, "What can you see, Arthur?" Arthur said, "Record sales and dollars," and Weintraub said, "Nah – it's stadiums."'

They wanted to sign a deal there and then, but Gary said no. 'I said, "Look, I want you to do one more thing. I want you to get Al Teller to send some people down to Australia to see the band while we're on this tour. If you can pull that off, we're definitely going to sign with you." He got a bit angry because he'd come all the way down and wasn't going back with a deal. I said, "Look, we want to do the deal, but I want to see that you've actually got some weight." It was sort of like the young buck telling the old buck, "If you've still got some potency, prove it." The Oils were pretty happy about how all this was going and they felt pretty independent and strong about it all. Then the word got around, and the industry said, "Wow, here's this heavyweight manager coming over to see Midnight Oil and he went back without signing the deal!" That sort of stuff was going on. Anyway, Weintraub rang up Al Teller and said, "I want you to give me an undertaking that you're gonna release this record."'

Eventually the deals with Management Three and Columbia happened and Gary ushered the band and himself into the upper echelons of the American music industry. He had a novel technique for dealing with this foreign and unfamiliar situation. 'I'd talk to these people about anything except the music business. I'd talk about golf, surfing, Australia, anything except music – because I didn't really have a clue about music! For some reason they thought that was pretty cool, that I knew more than I was letting on. I guess I was just this interesting personality who was representing this *incredibly* interesting *bunch* of personalities who could put out this amazing music in live performances. And the one thing I did learn very quickly was that by not talking about music, by not talking about other people, by not name-dropping and not giving anything away, and not wanting to talk deals or get money, they'd actually want to do business with you more and more. They became insatiable in their curiosity about what you were holding back. Because you were involved with this high-level network of people, well, they'd wonder, "What connections has he got?" And if you never told them, it would make them even more curious. So rolling that out and playing that game was a part of my management process with Midnight Oil. And not letting on that I didn't have a clue what I was doing at the time. All I was doing was hanging onto our sovereignty. You could call that the management ethic.'

Shortly Tommy Mottola took over from Al Teller as the head of the record company, and he made Gary feel they were on the same wavelength. 'He let me know that he was going to look at dealing with Midnight Oil at that same level, giving me the kind of access to sovereignty issues over our marketing and promotion and artworks and things like that. He was just reaffirming that attitude to me. That worked well.'

But neither *10–1* nor *Red Sails in the Sunset* did anything more than light a slow-burning fuse at college-radio level. The band concentrated on the campus circuit and started to pick up airplay on college and alternative radio.

Chris Moss watched their US progress through those years. 'They really were in a niche market within the US, and I think in total *10,9,8* and *Red Sails* sold about 20 000 copies each, which in American terms is a pimple on the backside of an elephant. But outside of the record sales, the impact they had in the marketplace and on people overall was dramatic, to the point where you would have thought they were a much larger act than they were. The word of mouth within the artists' and critics' communities was really large. And it was basically their live shows.'

David Fricke: 'By the time of *Diesel and Dust* the Oils had toured quite a bit in the US behind *10,9,8* and *Red Sails*, so there was an understanding with a core, cult audience of what they could achieve on stage. But *10,9,8* and *Red Sails* were not American radio records. College radio is a whole different beast. It's meant to be. When you go left of the dial that means you can be left of centre.'

Chris describes American radio as being like the spokes of a wheel. 'There's alternative, college, AOR and the rest, and they all go towards this point in the middle: CHR, contemporary hit radio. It's the top forty. That's the holy grail of having a hit record in America – CHR.'

When *Diesel and Dust* was released, the network Gary had been setting up finally swung into action. The 'Dead Heart' single opened the way with very strong results on college and alternative radio, and 'Beds Are Burning' followed in its path, only it went further. When it hit the top spot of those formats it crossed over and went all the way into the top ten of CHR. Due to the record's organic rise, the record company didn't need to tamper too much with the process. The single's success was unprecedented for an Australian act operating out of Australia, and a triumph for Sony Australia and its relations with head office. It all worked like clockwork.

However, the band's relationship with their record company in the USA didn't allow them the same level of control as in Australia. By the time of *Blue Sky Mining* the head of Columbia in the USA was Don Ienner (he had replaced Tommy Mottola), and he was getting personally involved. Chris wasn't surprised by this involvement. 'Once the success of the band in America had happened, it was the age-old story: the Americans wanted to participate in what took place. Selection of singles, track listings, which songs would go to radio, all that sort of thing. Don Ienner took a very strong, active participation with the band. He believed in or saw their potential and brought Mason Munoz in as their label manger. Don is a person who has very distinct ideas, and he's a powerful individual. You'd have to say he's a very Gary Morris sort of a guy: defiant, knows what he wants, makes the decision, that's what it is, if you don't like it you can fuck off.'

The stakes were high, sales expectations were high, there was a lot of money involved and it was becoming harder for Gary to keep on top of things. But the band clung to their own formidable and unique way of expressing themselves, and certainly weren't going to compromise their politics or their Australian-ness in the process. Mason: 'There are many bands who, probably for financial reasons, try to conform to what they believe will play well to the American public. In the Midnight Oil situation, what they wanted to write about and champion were things that were near and dear to them, things that were part of the fabric of their lives, the soundtrack to their lives. That was part of their appeal to the people who embraced the band early on. It was the fact that they were unique and wanted to walk their own path instead of following the one everyone else was on. They are the only band I can think of who came out of Australia and really made it here who were so uniquely Australian. INXS were a really good band, really good songs, but they were singing about the same things every other rock band who wants to sell records to teenagers was singing about: sex, drugs, girls. I don't hear any of that in Midnight Oil songs.'

During the American *Blue Sky Mining* campaign there were plenty of discussions, disagreements and stuff-ups regarding the release of singles. Gary wasn't one to compromise or kowtow to unreasonable demands, but marketing their records in America required the band to be more flexible. They survived all the last-minute changes to scheduling, but the problems between Gary and Ienner grew. Thankfully, an almost three-year hiatus between *Blue Sky Mining* and 1993's *Earth and Sun and Moon* allowed frayed egos to heal a little.

'Truganini' was agreed by the band and the record company to be *Earth and Sun and Moon*'s first single. The band, as usual, were responsible for making the video clip, and the finished product was sent to New York. Gary had moved to the States and was based an hour or so north of New York in Connecticut. He was determined to oversee the release of the record and to hold on to the band's rights as best he could. However, the first hiccup had happened before he even left Australia. Mason remembers having to call him from New York. '"Gary, we're not going to release this record in America unless Midnight Oil come over here and do a month of promotion prior to the street date. This is when we need you to come." He said, "Mate, we can't do that – we've got a sold-out Australian tour." I had a conversation in New York and called him back and said, "Listen, Gary, they don't care whether you've got a sold-out Australian tour. If you're not going to come over and do this pre-release promotion, we're not going to put the record out." So they cancelled the Australian tour, refunded all the tickets, got ready to come over here and I had to call them in Australia and go, "Whoops! That *Saturday Night Live* we had for you wasn't confirmed, so we don't need you to come over right now. I'll call you back when we've got *Saturday Night Live* confirmed, because that's going to be one of the anchors for the promotion leading into the street date." There were a couple of other false alarms and then I called Gary again and said, "Gary, we've confirmed *Saturday Night Live*. We need you guys to come over and do this promotion, do the video and all that other stuff." And they did.'

The initial part of the campaign looked good. Chris: 'The American reaction to "Truganini" was terrific; they loved it. Don Ienner loved it. He did insist on some sort of slight remix of the song, but after that was finished, it was all set to go. Then he decided he didn't like the band's film clip.'

Gary: 'Ienner was going to roll out all these budgets and get behind the band and stuff, so he wanted to see his mark on Midnight Oil activity. It wasn't enough for him to take our interpretation of "Truganini" and release it properly – no, he wanted to get a hit video producer and pay 250 grand and do it his way. He wanted Midnight Oil in the landscape of New York, and he wanted all these New York people dancing around a big bonfire and Midnight Oil playing live and making it almost tribal. Ienner was wanting to be creative, to play manager, producer, film-clip maker, and he was the big record executive! He was in the bottleneck and blocking our career out into the other side. There was no way around him. So we conceded to letting him spend his 250 grand, although the one thing I did negotiate was "OK, you want to spend 250 grand? It's not recoupable against our record base. That's the only condition under which we'll let you do it." And so he said, "Yep", and 250 grand was spent and none of it was recoupable against our royalties. That was the only reason we let it happen.' The new clip cost more to make than the entire album.

The band were committed to doing what was required to make the whole process work. In many ways they were more compliant to record company requests and mainstream marketing demands than ever before. They agreed to the refilming of the 'Truganini' clip, but Rob was very unhappy about the whole situation. 'If I had to look at a moment when we were at a peak and started sliding down, then that indecision about which mix of "Truganini" should be used, how long it should be persevered with in terms of radio promotion by the record company, and what song should follow it – should it be "My Country", should it be "Outbreak of Love", what should it be? – that was the watershed moment. The second "Truganini" film clip I found absurdly extravagant and culturally insulting. When we were dancing around a bonfire on the side of the East River, I felt like we were dancing on Truganini's grave. Then when I heard that this hotshot video guy had received a quarter of a million dollars for making an *extremely* average film clip, without any cultural reference to what the song was about, I knew we'd gone off the rails.'

The night of the filming was hard for everyone, including Rhonda Markowitz, who was now a reporter for MTV. She was there on the river bank to cover the shooting of the clip. 'I remember convincing *MTV News* to cover the video shoot, which was under the Brooklyn Bridge. After it was all over Gary said, "Peter's not in the mood to talk." I'm like, "Fuck you. I didn't come here with a crew and walk round in the mud all goddamn night and waste two hours for you to tell me he ain't talking to me. Get him over here!" And Gary's like, "Pete's on a ferry going back to New York." I said, "Get his ass back here, like, now – or die! Do not screw with me. I'm trying to help the band. What are you doing to me?" So he got the whole band over and Pete was like, "Grrr" and he passed the microphone over to Martin, who was like, "What are you passing it to me for?" And he said, "Jim?" and Jim was like, "Eh?" And I went, "Rob?" And Rob was ill that night, but he took the mike and went, "Well, Truganini was the last of the full-blood Tasmanian Aborigines . . ." and if it wasn't for Rob I wouldn't have had a damn interview.'

Eventually 'Truganini' was released, and it immediately did well on the radio. According to the tip sheets subscribed to by record companies and others, the statistical information on the song's airplay – 'spins' per week, and the rate at which new stations were adding the song – looked very healthy. Gary: 'It had been building for two or three weeks and had gone up to 900 spins and it was moving. It was going into 1100 to 1200 spins, which initiates a big kick, a big roll-out.'

Chris: '"Truganini" was an outstanding performer for alternative college radio. It went to number one on all those peripheral formats, and then there was the decision that it had to go to CHR. And Don Ienner, at the eleventh hour, after he had spent all that money on a second video, the Friday before the Monday they were going to walk it through the door at radio he said, "It's not the track. I don't want to take it to CHR." He didn't think it was the right track and he just operates that way, very definite in his decision-making.'

Gary: 'He let these focus groups sample it, and they came up with "My Country" as a more favourable song than "Truganini". So we were ready to roll out "Truganini" with the original film clip and that was changed. Then we're getting radio spins up to 900 a week and all of a sudden he changes his mind and wants to kill "Truganini" and go out with "My Country". That meant a thirteen-week lapse in our release schedule, a loss of momentum, because the band had to go and make a clip for "My Country" on the hop. We got Claudia Castle in, did it in the Mohave Desert and tried to put things together very quickly to come up with the clip.'

Saturday Night Live did go ahead, and the band elicited a minor roar from the studio audience when they performed 'Truganini'. They came on later in the show for a moving version of 'My Country', and even mingled with other guests for the farewell wave from the stage at the show's end.

Chris: 'But by then the momentum was gone. They fell into that dip and had to climb out and start all over again. You really don't recover from those things. That's where it all started to go haywire. And that's when the blues between Gary and Don began. That's where it started to go wobbly.'

By the time the *Earth and Sun and Moon* tour of the US started, 'Truganini's time had come and gone. 'My Country' was the new choice deemed right for mainstream America, but there were last-minute cold feet for it, too, and it was replaced with 'Outbreak of Love', the band's first real 'love' song. Unfortunately the old linguistic connection prevailed, and 'Outbreak of Love' provoked an outbreak of hostilities.

The band had agreed to a plan to meet and greet the fans after the shows. Gary's idea was that if the fans came to the show with the new single – a special cassette edition – that would be their backstage pass. The record company was not convinced it was going to work, but *MTV News* picked up the idea and all the radio stations that were playing Midnight Oil carried the story as well. The first night of the tour was at the Mann Center in Philadelphia. When Mason arrived the band was in the middle of meeting close to 1000 fans. 'Herbie Gordon, the local promotion manager of Epic Records in Philadelphia, said that the promotion in Philadelphia was the promotion of the year – the biggest, most exciting thing that had happened in Philadelphia. So the band started doing the meet-and-greets and they met from 500 to 1000 fans each night.'

After a couple of weeks' touring, Gary telephoned Mason with a question. 'He asked, "How many singles are there in

St Louis and Kansas City? We have dates there next week – we have 17000 advance ticket sales in St Louis and 12000 in Kansas City. I want to know how many singles are at retail in those markets." The incident that had driven Gary to call me and ask the question was, "We had 10000 in the audience at Gainesville last night and only seven people came with the single. What's going on?"'

The implication was that the 'Outbreak of Love' backstage promotion idea that had been approved by the record company wasn't being backed up – that the company hadn't actually serviced all the record stores. The fans had heard about the plan but couldn't buy the single. Mason: 'When I answered his question with "Not many", Gary said, "You guys must think we're really stupid." He got on a plane and came to New York for a meeting, and what I remember being said to Gary in that meeting was, "You were lied to. It shouldn't have happened, and it won't happen again." And if I recall the events correctly, the day before the show in St Louis, Columbia Records shipped a couple of thousand singles to the promoter and the promoter handed them out to people on their way into the venue. This precipitated another call from Gary saying, "What are you doing? The deal was that people had to go and buy the single. They're *giving them away* to people coming into the venue! That was not the deal."'

Mason's answer to Gary about the number of singles in the marketplace was seen as treasonous by Don Ienner, and Mason was sacked. His defence was this: 'Gary called me up and asked me a question – a question he was entitled to ask, a question it was fair to expect me to answer. I didn't divulge any company secrets. He asked me a business question and

I answered it. If it was an inappropriate question for him to ask me, I would have told him it was an inappropriate question to ask me.'

Mason was stuck between two very powerful guys. He had been witness to an example of their deteriorating relationship a couple of months earlier. 'I remember Gary coming to New York for a meeting with Donny, and he was kept waiting quite a while. I think Donny kept him waiting for two and a half hours. He flew from Australia and then was kept waiting for two and half hours. Gary had brought this beautiful putter. He's an avid golfer and Donny's a golfer too; Gary knew that. So he'd got this beautiful putter – a hand-made thing with a beautiful huge opal inlay in the head of the golf club. Donny came walking in and Gary stood up and put this thing over his shoulder and said, "OK, Ienner, where do you want it? In the head or between the legs?" And wow, that's Gary. He wears his heart on his sleeve. I don't want to get into all the other stuff that went on between those guys – truly unfortunate. And I know that when *Earth and Sun and Moon* came out the following week, the band were basically on their own.' Gary says the incident with the putter was a joke, but there was no doubt that relations between the two men did deteriorate rapidly.

Two other incidents illustrate the crossed purposes of Gary and the record company and their inability to get on. First there was a marketing meeting at the company's New York offices. Gary: 'I remember a meeting with the whole bunch of them in a room where I sat down and gave everybody a photograph of the band. I said, "What's this?" It was like a Morris moment, just to give them a reality check. They said, "That's a PR photo." And I said, "No. It's not a PR photo.

It's a photo of the family I am part of. Can you understand that?" And they went, "OK, OK, we'll go with that." And I said, "These are real people, and you have never met them. These people have got real history, real opinions, real talent and real achievements behind them. And I need to bring you up to speed with how you work with us." Well, that meeting blew everyone away – negatively. It was like, "You mean we have to deal with this manager who's representing these people and we can't do our thing, our Ienner man thing?"

'That's where it began, but I thought I had to take that stance. And if by doing that all of a sudden I had got people on side – who actually understood – then I would have had a rapport with those people. They would have gone, "Yeah, this is where music's at – with the artist. We're artist-focused, not product-focused." I wanted to get them away from the product focus to the artist focus, to convey to them the culture of Midnight Oil and how we work, and how we work with our alternative organisations and grassroots organisations and activist organisations, and how the company would have to apply their marketing budgets to facilitate this profile, building Midnight Oil in America around *Earth and Sun and Moon*.

'Well, mate, it was like water off a duck's back. They just looked at me and I could tell it was all too hard for them. They just went through the motions and I went back to the band and said, "Band, it's back to trying to do it our own way again. We've entered into the belly of the beast and some bad acid has come in."'

The second incident came some time later, when Gary heard that Mason had been kicked out of a record company marketing meeting in which Midnight Oil strategies were to be discussed. It was the final straw as far as Gary was concerned. 'Mason was told, "Get out! Don't come back until you're ready to represent this company." I got on the phone to Ienner and said, "Don, what's your problem? What are you on about, mate? Can't you ring me up and talk to me about it if you've got a problem?" And I thought, "Stuff it. This is it." I said, "Mate, I've got Italian friends back in Australia, and I know they're hotheads, and if this is you having an Italian moment [Ienner is Italian, from New Jersey] then I can understand that and I can accept that. But you've got to understand that I've been involved in representing this band, on their terms, for many years now. Don't you have any sense of that? Can't you appreciate that? And Mason is simply representing what he knows is Midnight Oil." Ienner goes, "Well, Gary, I'm running a successful record company here, and we try to accommodate our artists' requests and our artists' needs, but at the end of the day it's the way *we* make decisions that sells records." And I said, "Well, OK, Donny, if that's the way it's going to be then I don't know where we're going to go from here." And he said, "Yep, I don't know either." I hung up and went back to the band and said, "Guys, I think our US career is screwed."'

Pete is philosophical about the difficulty of the scenario and about the outcome. 'Getting a major record label, with a band whose album isn't particularly full of things the label can throw onto the radio, and trying to follow up on successes a band's had before by recasting the clip for the "Truganini" song – it was always going to be hard for all concerned. I mean, if the song had been something they had every confidence in, and all the people in the record company had thought it had airplay written all over it, then it would have got played no matter what.'

Maybe the record wasn't right, maybe the times had changed. Maybe the band were too accommodating and had lost some mystique. Maybe the executives at Sony lost their way, or maybe Gary was too close. Some might question Gary's personal style, but no one would challenge the fact that he represented the band diligently and fought valiantly on every single occasion. The release of *Earth and Sun and Moon* was always going to be hard work because of the time lapse since the band's last record.

Even the album title seemed to suggest a bigger universal canvas for the band's endgame to be played out on. It was an album about truth and consequences and human insignificance, and so Donny killing 'Truganini', 'My Country' missing the boat, and then 'Outbreak of Love' being sabotaged should adequately illustrate the band's point.

The record and its singles may not have sold as well as hoped, but the band could still pull an enthusiastic crowd anywhere in the world. They did start to feel marginalised commercially and that the ground was shifting beneath them, but the live performing was still enjoyable and the concerts were still spectacularly successful, with enthusiastic crowds wherever they played. The question was, which crowds? And at one point, which generation of punters? This choice had to be resolved when the band needed to choose between a spot on the young and hip American Lollapalooza tour and a spot at WOMAD (World of Music, Arts and Dance), which appealed to a more mature crowd.

Gary says he didn't try to influence the band's choice. 'I would just roll out the smorgasbord and the band would choose what they liked. My job was to recognise what they all liked and put it into action. Lollapalooza was more suited to the younger generation, whereas WOMAD was a musicians' experience and the band expressed a desire to be part of that. I supported them even though it was a less commercial event. It was a valid decision based on their desire for a cross-cultural experience.'

The choice wasn't exactly a fork in the road, or the last bite of the cherry, but it was significant, and maybe another of the so-called missed opportunities.

Begun by Perry Farrell in 1991, Lollapalooza was an annual travelling rock show that brought grunge and alternative rock together, with bills that included Rage Against the Machine, Porno for Pyros, Red Hot Chili Peppers, Pearl Jam and many other fine acts. At the same time they turned down Lollapalooza the band accepted a spot co-headlining with Peter Gabriel on the WOMAD tour of the eastern states of America.

Neither of these decisions was arrived at easily, and the band members still disagree about whether they made the right one. Pete downplays the importance of the band's choices. 'I don't think it would have made any difference at all to our career. Not a single bit of difference. I actually don't think these things are as important as people in the industry think they are. They are important up to a point, because otherwise the industry wouldn't put that much emphasis on them. But when you'd been doing it as long as we had, it was not actually about whether you did a Lollapalooza tour or not, it was *why* you didn't do a Lollapalooza and *why* you did other things. I think, additionally, we wanted to go where we were among friends.

Never mind whether the music was more sympathetic – the appeal was backstage. If you want to try and summarise it, my gut feeling was that I felt more aligned to Peter Gabriel than I did to Perry Farrell. *Earth and Sun and Moon* wasn't the kind of record we could go out and play to a Lollapalooza audience. I mean, we could have gone out and played stuff we'd played before, but by that stage I don't think you could apply the way of looking at and understanding what Midnight Oil did at an earlier stage and then jump it five or ten years. Gary quite often said things like, "What's wrong with going out and playing 'Back on the Borderline' and dah de dah? They're all great songs." And we'd say, "Yeah, but Gary, we've played 'Back on the Borderline' a squillion times, and it's the last thing in the world we *want* to play."

'There's a whole *internal* thing that goes with a band, where you're in a certain headspace at a certain time, where you've done a certain kind of record and want to play that record, or most of the songs, and you don't want to play the greatest hits or your rockier songs. You don't necessarily want to do what you've done before, or even behave in a way you have before. Bands can be quite contrary like that, but also I guess in some ways you're also trying to be faithful to whatever you're feeling at the time. To look backwards and apply the rear-vision mirror to the career from a business perspective, you know, "Well, this should have been the album. We went and did *Earth and Sun and Moon* and it hit at the time that grunge came, and we were one album before grunge" – it's all hindsight's wisdom! At the time you're convinced you're doing the right thing. Everybody is.'

Bones enjoyed the WOMAD tour, but in retrospect thinks

turning down Lollapalooza was the wrong move. 'We were asked to do Lollapalooza and we chose not to. We thought it would be good to be involved in a world-music event. The discussions went on over several days. It was us trying to pigeonhole where we sat, and I don't think we really knew that. The WOMAD tour was great; those kinds of things are really refreshing. Seeing all these different artists from all over the globe takes you out of the mundaneness and puts you smack bang in the middle of somewhere else. We did WOMAD in the States and then here in Australia. The American one was only on the east coast; they didn't sell enough tickets, so they cancelled the west. Gabriel, us, Lucky Dube, Gow Brothers (these Chinese guys playing Chinese instruments) – it was great. I liked hanging around the catering tent and getting to talk to these people. That's what's special about doing that kind of thing. When you're on stage you're just you; for me it was everything off stage that was interesting. Got to finally meet Tony Levin, who I thought was the most amazing bass player in the world. He's from New York City, played with Gabriel, played with John Lennon, all that, you know. Then I met him and he was such an arrogant arsehole I wish I'd never bothered. A tosser.

'In hindsight we made a big mistake – I think we should have done Lollapalooza. At that period of time in North America it meant you were happening, whereas we tended to think we were a bit old, that we'd been around a bit long to be associated with those kinds of bands. We thought we belonged in the other camp.'

David Fricke: 'In a way it was a shame they didn't do Lollapalooza, because I think they may have balanced the testosterone – they could have killed any of the bands on that stage. They weren't going to get wiped around by the grunge, heavy rap or any of that. But again, what do you believe in? What do you feel more aligned to? What are you more faithful to? It was a decision of the heart, not the head. And you know, you don't make business decisions by the heart, but you make decisions about your life and your art according to your heart. So everything they did was totally consistent. But not if you're in the label's office thinking, "We could have moved another tens of thousands of *this* if they had done *that*."'

Jim: 'Yeah, we went the WOMAD route, the kind of world music-y route. I suppose our politics had kind of put us into this area where we were very politically correct. Everything the band was singing about had to be run by a panel of politically correct checkers – even myself in those days. We wouldn't even bother putting it on a record if it was a bit ambiguous lyrically. When we did, it never worked. No one understood it. So we were kind of with the environment, the hessian bag, the recycled cardboard, the dye extracted from non-Amazonian plants, you know. That was the way the band went. Whereas this whole new breed of bands were just "Fuck authority, fuck political correctness, we're gonna play fuckin' loud and we're gonna throw ourselves at it and be completely committed" – and of course that was the way the youth wanted to go. I think there was a perception that maybe the album we made was very Beatles influenced. There were a lot of melotrons on it, there were *Revolver*-type guitar sounds, it was more of an old-school kind of album in that way. But it was a very honest album, and an album we wanted to make, and I'm really proud of it. But again there was this whole crossing-over of what the world wanted from the band with what the band could give the world. We couldn't give the world what the world wanted. We had in the past, but we couldn't do it again. And if I think back now I don't think we would've done it any differently.'

Nick: 'To be honest, the reason I think that album didn't happen in America was that the record company had already decided they weren't interested in Midnight Oil any more – because that's what they do. They invest, they get their money back. The people way up high in record companies in America aren't into it for the right reasons, never have been. Midnight Oil might take it personally, like, "We did things wrong, we should have done this, we should have done that", but even if they'd delivered another "Beds Are Burning" it still might not have helped.'

Gary: 'If there's anyone who comes out of it not looking good it's Donny Ienner. He sabotaged the band's international career.' While it's true that Ienner's last-minute changes damaged the launch of *Earth and Sun and Moon*, it was always going to be a risky and problematic proposition. It wasn't fashionably grunge, it wasn't a carbon copy of *Diesel* or *Blue Sky*, and the band's profile had definitely slid during the period when they stayed at home.

David Fricke: 'They didn't have the control they did in Australia. In Australia they dictated to CBS and Sony what was going to happen. They created a base and a space for themselves that was inviolable down there for a very, very long time. In America they made inroads. They had one really big record, two really major hits and a lot of love, but they simply couldn't call every shot because they couldn't control everything that happened in fifty different states – it's impossible. Maybe in a way they were doomed by honour: there was no way they could give in to the circumstances but no way they could surmount them either.'

In some ways Gary was just drawing a line in the sand that the band needed to have drawn, but how he drew it often limited the tide's ability to smooth it over and allow everyone the chance of a fresh start after difficulties. Some saw his approach as primitive, more suited to rock'n'roll's 'wild west' days, when managers like Led Zeppelin's Peter Grant literally carried a cricket bat to protect his band.

Rob is one who thinks Gary has been both the band's biggest asset and their biggest liability. 'He's our greatest asset because he's as iron-tough and barking-mad as everyone else in the industry, plus another 50 per cent, and he's worked sincerely on our behalf over a period of twenty-five years, which is almost unprecedented. An asset also because with all the crazy schemes he and the band have devised, he's the one who actually put in the hours to make them happen, while the band took the credit. But Gary has been demonised by the industry because he became known as such a prick. He's our worst liability because of an inability to let the dust of a new idea settle and be given full brainstorming before putting it into practice, and an overly cantankerous, bullying manner that alienates people, so that when we've needed help they've often quite rightly flipped the bird.'

Pete can understand why Gary might be seen as a liability, but accepts that Gary's role in the music-business environment was almost guaranteed to make him unpopular. 'Some people didn't fully see into what the band wanted to do, nor did they necessarily take a step back and see where we had been and where we were going. The band, Midnight Oil, is an ideal. In its form as five (or six) people tearing around the place trying to make it happen it's got lots of flaws, hiccups, makes lots of mistakes – but the ideal, as far as it was realised, was realised brilliantly. It was always going to fall short. Part of the ideal was to truly live the musician's life – writing the songs, performing under your own terms, and engaging the world and the business who would never normally accept you on those terms. Gary was a conduit between the ideal and the horrible reality, and he was always going to make a lot of enemies.'

Three years after weathering *Earth and Sun and Moon*, the band recorded album number nine, *Breathe*. It was shunted onto a new subsidiary label with Sony called Works and was hardly seen in American record stores, let alone the American charts. Despite some airplay for the 'Underwater' single, as far as the American music mainstream was concerned, the album, and the band, were sunk.

nine

eyes of light

When Giffo left the band they were forced to look for a replacement bass player. One of the contenders was Rick Grossman, a member of Sydney band Matt Finish (and, later, Divinyls and Hoodoo Gurus) and a friend of Rob's. Rick didn't get the job, because the band needed a singer as much as they needed a bass player, but in an acknowledgement of the strains being in a band places on relationships, Rob comments, 'I'm glad he didn't. We wouldn't be friends any more.' After the band considered a couple of other players, the angel-voiced Bones Hillman came along. He was no one's pre-existing friend and they all liked him. 'In retrospect, it worked for the best,' says Rob.

Bones was an excellent choice for the job. Apart from the quality of his singing and bass playing, and his easygoing personality, he was also tough enough to be relatively immune to the rigours of the road. He didn't fall victim to it like his two predecessors, Bear and Giffo, who were physically and psychologically drained by their experiences with the band. Neither seems to have ever fully recovered. 'Rock musician' is not a profession with a long life expectancy, and there are many reasons for that. Those bands who survive as long as the Oils no doubt each have their own recipe for longevity, but a natural interpersonal chemistry and genuine communal goodwill and respect – plus individual perspicacity – seems to have played a big part in Midnight Oil's resilience. The career has taken its toll on their friendships and, although the members all share a deep bond born of the extraordinary ride they have shared over more than twenty-five years, they don't socialise together much outside the band any more.

Connie Adolph remembers them being close despite the pressures of touring. 'Personally, they all got along great. That was very unusual. I'd worked with enough bands to see that a lot of them *don't* get along. These guys always ate together, hung out together – they always enjoyed each other's company. There was no viciousness, and I have seen that in a lot of bands! When we were touring, going to all the pubs, we were driving every day, literally in each other's pockets all the time. You'd be lucky if you had a few hours alone, but we all tended to get along. I know this sounds really corny but we'd come back from a gig and all have a cup of tea after the show. Seriously! And we'd talk. They were not your normal "Let's get drunk" kind of band. When we had nights off we'd go out. We might go and see another band play, but we'd all go together.'

The individual members occasionally needed their own space, though. Jim badly needed to go for a wander when they were making *10–1* in London. 'I always felt that we travelled so much I didn't want to travel at other times. But we were all living in a house in St John's Wood and it was pretty intense, so I went off to Ireland for a few days on my own, just travelling around and enjoying it. I remember being surprised when a woman I met said, "Hey, you look like an Irishman", or something like that. I thought, "What the fuck's this? I'm not Irish!" But I loved Ireland. I felt very much at home.'

By the time Bones joined the band there was less communal activity while on tour, but they weren't *all* going their separate ways, and they still ate together. Bones's offstage role became clearer over time, and his fifteen years in the job have left his good humour and his reputation as an ideal travelling companion undiminished. He was extremely important to the band's cohesiveness and also played a role in media responsibilities. 'Between Rob being the historian and Pete being the serious character he was, I decided to be the light relief. We'd do three days' media in New York and Pete would talk about Aboriginal politics and I'd be telling lies about racing pigeons. The last thing Midnight Oil needed was another really serious person. I'm not saying I'm superficial, but in the chemistry of things there were occasions when they needed to be reminded that they were just a rock band – that this was rock'n'roll – because there was a lot of serious shit going on, all the time. Look at the records, look at the songs!'

Staying friends over such a long period of time was always going to be hard – but staying together, and staying productive and in control, was more important. Not that they necessarily put a low value on friendship, but being effective colleagues was crucial. For the most part, when something needed doing they pulled together and differences were put aside. But they are five very distinct personalities, and inevitably there were frictions and ongoing niggles. There was a bit of stoicism, which may not have been good for personal psychological health, but as time healed most problems it was probably all for the best. 'In many ways we're just old-fashioned blokes and we suffered in silence, kept our council,' says Rob.

Rob is a fabulous drummer with a pop-music heart and finely honed linguistic skills. He writes songs you can hum but that also have lyrical resonance. He is also driven. He isn't a musician who can just sit around waiting for things to happen. It was Rob who was originally responsible for organising Jim and Bear into a band, and it was Rob who put the advertisement for a lead singer in the *Sydney Morning Herald* that attracted Pete. And he found Martin. If anyone should be given credit for creating Midnight Oil, it is Rob.

But Midnight Oil became much bigger than the dreams of any of them. And on the journey the power shifted around them in a variety of circumstances. Each had a power base of sorts. For Jim it was the studio and his musicianship; for Gary it was the business; for Rob it was his songs, his peerless drumming and his seniority; for Martin it was his silence, his reluctance to be impressed and his unswerving judgement on matters of taste and integrity and cool; for Pete it was the microphone and all that went with it. And for all of them it was the way their personalities balanced and blended and interacted with each other in the thousands of hours they spent in each other's company. The fact that they did it for so long and in such a generally good spirit spells wonders for the chemistry between them.

They are artistic but intellectual guys who were locked tight in a career where it is obvious that only the strong – and united – survive. They had a vested interest in not only thorough scrutiny of each new task before it was undertaken, but also in being in full agreement when they set about that task. Most of their differences were avoided by judiciously spending time apart. They manufactured situations to maximise their interaction in songwriting, recording and performing, and very effectively played to their strengths. As people, they were more than just civil to each other. They have been friends and colleagues, comrades and business partners, for a quarter of a century. They get on.

The recording of the band's 1996 album, *Breathe*, half of which was done in Sydney and half in the famous Kingsway Studio in New Orleans, pushed Rob's patience. Bones also had problems with the *Breathe* sessions, and both say it was their least favourite of all the studio time they have done.

Rob and Bones found the band's Canadian producer, Malcolm Burn, hard to work with, and Rob played a relatively unenthusiastic and very low-key role throughout the process. Bones: 'The album where Rob didn't sing a note! Rob's voice was not on that record. When we did the second half in New Orleans I would have been quite happy to stay at home. "Count me out of this one, guys." Malcolm came from the [Daniel] Lanois school, a "hands on" producer. We'd be in the studio and you'd say, "Just gotta go for a leak", and you'd come back and he'd be recording your part. He'd be playing drums, he'd be playing bass, he'd be playing guitar. I'd just walk in and go, "You've done it, haven't you? Let's fuckin' leave it at that, then." He was a total power freak. But maybe he suited those kinds of songs – "Time to Heal" and stuff like that. Chemistry-wise, he and I just didn't connect. I don't think Rob enjoyed it either; in fact I know he didn't, because he was gone before the sessions were finished. Left us in New Orleans and went to New Mexico. I'd never known him to do that before. It's not really obvious when you listen to the record, and for some people it's their favourite, but the actual experience of making it sucked – for me, anyway.'

However, Pete, Jim and Martin all got right into the loose and spontaneous spirit of it. Pete: 'I just thought it was so stripped-back, so organic, so non-cerebral, so feel-based. I mean, Malcolm was a total— he wasn't an easy person to work with, there's no doubt about that. I didn't *enjoy* working with him that much, but the actual idea of recording and trying to work like that I really liked. I heard the Neville Brothers every time I walked into the Darling Harbour studio. I thought, "This is right, this is worth doing."'

Jim: 'When we did *Breathe* it was just shambolic. We were all recording live and together in this one room with this weird Canadian guy who created an atmosphere of tension in a Machiavellian way that I thought really worked for the band on that album – even though I did walk out one night, and then Bones walked out the next night. On my fortieth birthday I wasn't gonna come in, because Malcolm and I had some stupid argument about something and he said, "Oh yeah, what have you geniuses got now?" But I knew why he was doing it. He was doing it to put the band on its mettle and to stop us getting too comfortable, and to question a lot of the assumptions we'd made about what works and what doesn't.

The band had taken 1995 off and Jim had a very productive twelve months. 'I did some stuff with Neil Finn in New Zealand. It was great to work with him. I felt a release from the pop prison with him, because he's very instinctive. There's a certain Irishness about the way he works that I really liked, that was very against the corporate thing Sony was turning us into. And I wrote every day, and went down to my studio and did my job as a songwriter, just recorded stuff. And I did the Fuzz Face thing as well, so yeah, it was a big year.'

Fuzz Face was a four-song recording project with Nick Launay that had the atmosphere of a hot practice session captured by happy accident – rough pop guitars, crackling amps and crashing drums, plus Nick's random effects on the sounds and Jim's Lennon-esque voice. Jim basically played all the instruments except on the track 'For Tomorrow', where acoustic guitar, tabla and tambourine were added by 'The Family Dog'. That was Martin. He had to go uncredited because of contractual restrictions with Sony that prevented more than one member of Midnight Oil playing in the same side project. Not that Martin would have minded the anonymity – he had already appeared on Bones's side project with Chris Abrahams, the Hunting Party, as Kelpie X. Much of Jim's ten-day session with Neil Finn ended up on Neil's debut solo album, *Try Whistling This*, including the co-written title track. A few months earlier Neil had tried to talk Jim into joining Crowded House in an attempt to save the band, but Jim had turned him down. He'd also turned down an offer from Silverchair to join them on the road after he finished contributing to their *Neon Ballroom* LP.

Rob recorded a new album with Ghostwriters during his year off. His contribution to *Earth and Sun* had seemed as significant as ever – 'My Country' and 'Outbreak of Love' were Rob songs, and the core elements of 'Truganini' and 'Drums of Heaven' were his, too – but he felt his songs were starting to be overlooked. He started to channel more of his material towards Ghostwriters, the part-time band he had put together during the band's first 'official' year off in 1991 with Rick Grossman (by then with Hoodoo Gurus) and Dorland Bray from Do Re Mi. Their first album had been made quickly and cheaply ('That's what I really needed at the time as an antidote to the pressures of Midnight Oil,' says Rob), and the single 'Someone's Singing New York, New York' had been a substantial success with plenty of commercial radio airplay. The album had some other excellent songs, particularly 'World Is Almost at Peace', which you can't help but wonder how it may have sounded as an Oils song.

The name 'Ghostwriters' reflected something of Rob's frustration at writing songs that were primarily sung by someone else. He was also interested in seeing how his songs would develop outside the Midnight Oil context. Increasingly he was tending towards more personal writing and songs that were therefore more suited to Ghostwriters. Those songs became unavailable to the Oils. Rob: 'What I would do to be scrupulously fair is play an early version of the song to the band, or at least to Jim, and if they or he really responded to the song or part of the song, I would set it aside. That doesn't mean that the Ghosties was full of secondary material or rejects or whatever. Often I think that the choice of the stuff at hand depended on whether it was already too "worked up" so the band didn't feel like they could get enough "Midnight Oil" into it, or whether it was too personal. There was a whole lot of material that was clearly not designed for Pete to sing. It's easier when you're writing an "anthem" to see it as a Midnight Oil song, but when it became darkly personal stuff I would think, "Well, this is not necessarily something that anyone else can relate to." So as a result, when it came time to make the second Ghosties album, *Second Skin*, it was full of really dark, personal stuff. I can jokingly refer to it now as my midlife-crisis album. It cost a bomb. I became obsessed with the recording of it and even went to London to get Warne Livesey to mix it – which he did beautifully. I think I was keen to get hold of something where the songs would be recorded exactly as in my head. It was a learning process and a challenge and I got a whole lot of songs off my chest, which all songwriters have to do. It's bad if the songs just sit there, if you don't get them out into the public domain.'

Rob's relatively small contribution of songs for *Breathe* was supplemented by Jim's almost endless supply. Jim: 'Rob had Ghostwriters, and it had taken away quite a lot of the songs we would normally have had. But there were some that we all had, and we just barrelled into *Breathe*. It was the Oils trying to be anti-corporate, trying to be themselves, and I had a lot of songs written for that.' The drumming on the album was always going to be low-key, so they met the challenge of changed circumstances and found yet another new way of making a record.

Pete was being drawn to his other responsibilities, particularly his second term as president of the ACF. Jim says he felt a shift in band relations as their public acclaim stalled. '"Hey, you've sold ten million albums, great – you know, here's an award", blah blah blah blah. There were awards coming left, right and centre. But I felt very unhappy because, well, Pete was the front guy but Rob sensed there was change in the wind, so Rob was kinda trying harder to be the front guy as well and competing with Pete.' Over the years there had been occasional tension and plenty of disagreement between Rob and Gary, and Rob and Pete, but the *Breathe* sessions marked an unprecedented low point in band relations. The heart of Rob's frustration seemed to be Pete and Gary's tendency to work things out between the two of them and then present the band with a united proposition. Gary and Pete were frequently the first to discuss issues, and once Gary got started it was hard to stop him. Inevitably their debates involved hours or days of arguing and thrashing an issue out, often over the phone, and the rest of the band felt removed from that part of the process to a greater or lesser extent.

'The first thing that breaks bands up is money,' says Jim. 'The second thing is recognition, or too much recognition for one person and not enough for another. I think there was also a bit of a jostling for who was running the show at that stage. Pete was always gonna win, because he was the singer. I remember an interview Rob and Pete did for MTV when we were in Boston doing Earth Day. They disagreed with each other on camera and Rob stormed off, or Pete stormed off – I can't remember which one – and they came downstairs, and oh fuck!'

Rob: 'The essence of the argument was I became infuriated when Pete contradicted me repeatedly in front of the camera. I think it became obvious to everyone who was watching that I was really pissed off at what was happening. Some of us wear our hearts on our sleeves. Some of us don't keep our political cool as well as others.'

That sort of public discord between band members was extremely unusual. Pete can remember the occasion but not who walked out. 'Maybe it's exceptional because it happened. I can't remember the exact sense of it, but I suspect he would have walked out. Maybe I'm wrong about that, but it's not like me. We did the show and came back happy. The Kinks blew us off stage totally – absolutely slaughtered us! They came on and played "Lola", "You Really Got Me", "All Day and All of the Night" and about five others at about 138 bpm, jumping up and down with their skinny legs, and the place went wild.'

Jim: 'Bands always evolve anyway, and someone might be the leader at the start and later gets dispossessed and something else happens, someone else joins – it's a very delicate balance. When Bear left the band the balance changed and had to readjust itself. Suddenly there was no one to deride! And I actually remember feeling a bit derided in Bear's place – just coz I'm a sensitive prick – and having words with everyone about it. Then Giffo joined and it all changed again. Some people are more active at certain times, and some people might be having problems at home and be feeling a little bit left out or whatever. It's inevitable. There are always Indians and chiefs, you know. I've always felt like an Indian. I'm quite happy to be one, really. It's fine. I don't mind being an Indian, as long as someone is doing it.'

Gary was doing a good deal of 'it' – making the difficult business decisions – and a good deal of the deriding as well. He saw his role as that of a bulldozer. 'I never taught them anything or told them what to say. I just ran over them with a bulldozer – just rode over the individual and their selfish way!'

The band found Gary extremely trying at the best of times, but they especially hated him going on the road with them.

He would go backstage and inevitably make them angry and jacked-off after shows with his criticisms. After one show in Newcastle he didn't even hang around; he just left a note pinned to their dressing-room wall. The members of Silverchair, who lived locally and were at the gig, were the first backstage to see 'You guys sucked' scrawled on one sheet of paper, and a list of the reasons why on another. When the band came stumbling into the room a minute later, exhausted, they barely noticed it, and when it was pointed out to them they just shrugged their shoulders. They all seemed quite relieved that Gary hadn't waited. Bones thought it was hilarious: 'I wish I'd kept it.'

Even after the success of the Exxon gig, Gary gave the band a pasting for cutting things so fine. Chris Moss: 'When they arrived they literally ran up the stairs onto the stage and started playing. After it was over they came down off the stage and there was a van at the side for them to go into because of the crowd that was all around. So they all went into the van, with Gary in last. He slammed the door behind him, and the van started to rock like crazy, like a WWF wrestling match was going on. You could hear Gary screaming and going completely nuts, with the guys just taking it as he was tearing them apart. "Where were you? Why weren't you fuckin' down there? You should have been there! Fuckin' why weren't you across this?" He just launched into them. It was hilarious, very funny.'

Jim: 'Yeah, he screamed at the band after that performance. After he finished we just jumped outta the van and all met round the corner at the coffee shop, had a laugh about it and how we weren't responsible – and we weren't. We didn't care. I suppose no one had woken us up. Maybe we should have set our own alarm clocks. Sorry, Gary.'

Gary says that for a time he resented Pete's authority and saw him as an impediment to the band's progress. 'They were a potent, entertaining rock act. They needed to play the game. I thought Pete was an obstacle. He always reacted against the role of performer/entertainer, of doing the showbiz things.' But Pete was determined not to get drawn into the superficial and disposable elements of the music business and somehow persuaded Gary of the bigger picture. 'He imposed a regime that demanded that I become a thinker, from a cosmic ranter! His scrutiny saw through any falsehood, deception or second-rate activity, challenged me to be better than I am.'

In turn, Gary says, he and the rest of the Oils challenged Pete to be 'more disciplined and accountable, not quite so free range. Garrett needed it. He was a wild tree that needed to be cut and culled. It refined him. His high-principled decision-making became honed because the bulldozer kept going over him, making him justify everything.'

Gary's analysis of Rob and Pete's relationship is provocative and speculative, but worth knowing for its inevitable grains of truth. 'Rob resents Pete because Pete is not negotiable, like the Calvinists – for him life unfolds almost fatalistically. Pete had a sense of history right from the beginning, a sense of destiny. He conscientiously deals with principles, whereas I'm the time-and-motion process working at the coal face of now.'

(Gary applied his bulldozer metaphor to a project for which he bought a valley of former rainforest near Noosa that had become a rundown dairy. 'It was full of weeds and thorns and rubbish and barbed wire. But I could see something that others couldn't: what would grow back after the bulldozer. There was always a pristine valley there but it needed the affliction of the bulldozer.' Unfortunately the financial institutions Gary needed to convince about all this potential couldn't see the picture like he did, and his plan for an international golf course in his restored pristine valley never eventuated. He unfortunately not only lost all his money, but had to persuade the band to buy out his share of Midnight Oil to allow him to survive the disaster financially.)

Gary was not only a bulldozer. Jim: 'He was like the dog that guarded the band, the barking dog. Gary would bite people on the leg, he'd drive people away if he thought they were trying to suck up to the band or feed the band a line that was in *their* best interests. He could smell 'em. As a result, he put up this big fence around us and I think that isolation was good for the creativity of the band.'

Rob says Gary's motivation, above all, was for the band to survive. 'When the band was dysfunctional, for whatever reason, he would make long phone calls to individuals to try and sort it out. Sometimes the calls were conciliatory, rational. Sometimes they were browbeating and bullying. Sometimes they were open, heartfelt. They were *always* longwinded.'

In his international job with Sony, John Watson was an observer of Gary's techniques. 'People weren't allowed into the Oils. No one has ever really been allowed into the Oils. Some people were allowed into the room *next to* the Oils. The effect was that in every country you can count on one hand the number of people who were let into that room. Mossy was that guy in Australia, Mason was clearly that guy in America. By that kind of "*You* get a gold star; everyone else has to wait outside" approach, you had this little cadre of people who would take a bullet for the band.'

However, at regular intervals Gary's manner became too much even for the band, and there was talk about whether they would be better off without him. In the early '90s, about the *Earth and Sun and Moon* period, there was a concerted move to oust him. Ironically the band discussed it at a gathering that Gary had organised at a motel in the Blue Mountains for the band to work out some problems. He wasn't there himself.

Rob: 'I'd have to say Gary was normally entirely genuine in trying to keep the band from coming apart. The sermon on the mount [the Blue Mountains experience] was an example. He told us, "Go up there, get away from distractions, phones, wives, girls, concubines, whatever. Go and sort it out." We were the only people at the motel. It was like Gary had hired the whole joint. The actual experience wasn't that unpleasant. It was foggy outside, so you felt like if you went out there you'd get lost somewhere in the mountains forever and they'd find you years later, a skeleton on a mountainside. So we tended to remain inside and keep eating. I still laugh when I drive past the place at how well they fed us. They served this heart-stopping breakfast, then about an hour and a half later morning tea in the courtyard, and then this gelatinous lunch, followed by afternoon tea, which was Devonshire tea with scones and other carbohydrates, topped off in the evening by a fatted calf or a suckling pig. We just lay around groaning.'

Unlike Rob, Jim hadn't made up his mind about the future of Gary. He doesn't remember the eating, but he does remember the outcome of the gathering. 'The only thing to come out of it was to sack Gary. Rob and Martin definitely didn't want him as manager, but I must admit I fell into both camps. When we came back and told him, Gary complained bitterly and demanded a meeting with us. He called us on it and said we were gutless and bullied and cajoled us. We weren't going to have him back, but we couldn't find anyone else! No one could find an alternative, or no one was *prepared to* find an alternative. It was always, "Well, Pete's got to be happy with whoever it is." And Pete was only ever happy with Gary, coz he knew him and they could control each other. But Gary had principles, and still does, really, really strong principles, and he would not sell this band out to anybody. He loves this band, completely adores it. That in itself is enough for me to be very loyal to Gary. He and Peter always had a bond, and I think Peter only lost confidence in Gary towards the very, very end, because he was just worn out from the confrontations – simple as that. That's when it all fell apart. Gary, by the time Peter left, didn't trust the band's instincts at all, I don't think. He thought we didn't know what we were doing. And maybe he was right in terms of the marketplace. Maybe we weren't able to be cutting edge any more. We were just the Oils.'

Gary is aware that the band all criticise his 'bedside manner', but says the kind of relationship he has with them makes it hard to be friends. 'My responsibility is in terms of management and the band's career. I'm not a personal manager. Pete was the personal manager – that is, what was important to the band as people.'

Jim struggles to illustrate Gary's heart of gold. 'I can't think of a time when he's been nice to us. But instead of being nice, he is honest. He will quite often be confrontational – his style gets him into trouble – but the content is always worth hearing. His judgements, though, are quite often wrong! He has a love for the band, but always wanted to keep this idealised version of it. Out there in the real world Gary is incredibly confrontational. When he had that meeting with somebody at Sony in the US and was asked to get his penis out on the table – "We want to see how big you really are" – that's the sort of adversarial environment he works in.

'I mean, Gary can breathe into a dog's mouth to get it to obey him! He's a real Old Testament prophet. There's a famous argument he had with Pete when we did the Black Fella White Fella tour out in the desert, at Uluru first thing in the morning, about something to do with which road to take. They were just standing there slagging each other off in the middle of nowhere. Janet Hawley, who wrote an *Age* article about the tour, called it "a stag fight in the desert". That kind of stuff happened every day. Peter, to his credit, could kind of corral Gary and get him to be effective. It was a good combination, because Gary was really wild and would sort of call Peter if he was being a bit lofty or pretentious or arty or whatever. So they had a good relationship like that. Gary is very tough, and so passionate about the band it almost killed him!'

Jim's reference to Gary breathing into a dog's mouth is something I witnessed when Gary visited me unexpectedly one day. We were in the backyard when a nasty-looking dog started hanging around. Gary said he'd deal with it and confidently grabbed the dog firmly by the snout with both hands. He held it tight until the dog stopped struggling, then took a deep breath, prised open the dog's mouth and exhaled his lungful of air into it. He then held the dog's snout shut and shook it hard, all the while looking fiercely into the dog's eyes and growling. He repeated the procedure two or three times before finally shaking the dog hard, throwing it roughly away and turning his back. It came bouncing up to him wagging its tail, and a couple of minutes later was curled up at his feet as we finished our cup of tea. Not quite the horse whisperer, but pretty effective nonetheless! I don't know how often he did this, but news of his talent leaked to the press and in a *Rolling Stone* article about the band it was implied that this was also the way Gary dealt with people in the music industry.

Meanwhile, the *Breathe* sessions, with or without Rob's wholehearted contribution, went ahead at the freezing studio in Sydney's Darling Harbour – a rehearsal room with Jim's home studio installed – and then in the steamy heat of New Orleans at Daniel Lanois' Kingsway Studio on the edge of the French Quarter. Lanois had originally been expected to produce the new record, but scheduling problems resulted in his assistant Malcolm Burn taking the job as producer and engineer. Malcolm had recently worked with Lanois on Bob Dylan's *Oh Mercy* album and the Neville Brothers' *Yellow Moon*. He'd also done Iggy Pop and Emmylou Harris on his own.

The studio sessions, as usual, were a very collective exercise – with Malcolm well and truly in the mix and Rob well and truly not – and the collective writing credit seems more likely to have been an expression of solidarity in divided times. They did a lot of instrument swapping during the recording. This was something they had often done before in an effort to approach a song differently, but with a producer like Malcolm at the helm, those different combinations of players and instruments often ended up as the final take.

Except for one song of Rob's all the tracks were originally Jim's, with Pete by necessity increasing his contribution. Pete and Jim were at the core of the songs. As there are no individual songwriting credits on the album (all the songs are credited 'Words and music Midnight Oil'), Pete's thumbnail outline of the songs is revealing. '"Underwater" is a continuation of "Koala Sprint" and "Surfing with a Spoon" and those sorts of songs, and so is "Surf's Up Tonight" – that's Jim's little hook and chorus and I wrote the verses sitting on the floor of Darling Harbour. "Common Ground" is classically where I was at the time and where I thought we were as a band. "Time to Heal" – we did that one together, about reconciliation. "Sins of Omission" we did over in New Orleans. It's about the fact that you can keep going even though there are things you regret and find difficult. That was one Jim and I did together. The boys only ever played it in the studio really. Malcolm's playing bass on that; he played on quite a few things! "One Too Many Times" is a great little song of Jim's. "Star of Hope" – one of Jim's. "In the Rain" – live, in New Orleans; that's my song about hurt. "Bring on the Change" – that's Jimmy with a few little bits here and there. It's his great wild rocker. "Home" is the one that talks about his own state. "E-Beat" – that's my greenie song with Jim giving me the intro lines; we did that one together. "Barest Degree" is one of Rob's.'

'Underwater' is a particularly strong song. It is driven by a relentless tidal rhythm from Bones (and Malcolm) on bass, and features some beautiful coastal imagery in the lyrics. In 'Surf's Up Tonight' Pete identifies the essence of his love for the surfing life in the lyrics 'You get wet/It's free/You get high/You're alive'.

If 'Common Ground' is about the state of the band's career at the time, then the quandary is clearly laid out:

Oh the wrecking fields are a terrible place
With a sulphurous smell and a frightening pace
And the hook goes in early and the critic is king
And it's hard to stay human and stand in the ring

On the sparse 'In the Rain', Bones plays Clavinet, Jim plays marching drums and Rob plays nothing – he had gone to bed early that night. The lyrics deal with hurt caused to others through careless words, and the song sounds heartfelt and confessional. One of only two tracks on the album where everyone is playing their designated instrument is the relatively underappreciated 'Bring on the Change', one of the band's all-time great 'rockers'. Restraint is its hallmark, and it's the gradual build in each successive chorus that makes it such a killer.

In almost total contrast is 'Home'. On this most gentle of songs Emmylou Harris joins Pete on vocals, to stunning effect. Martin plays some sympathetic mandolin, Jim plays bass and electric guitar, and Bones and Malcolm play acoustic guitar. Malcolm also plays tambourine. 'Home' is one of the most personal pieces in the band's entire career, with Jim's lyrics relating to his adoption and his search for his birth mother. Pete: 'Even though we'd worked together and written together for two and a half lifetimes plus, still, it's a real trusting thing for someone to give you a song like that to sing. I was very touched to sing it and very honoured. Then when Emmylou came in, it really made it into something.'

Jim: 'That was fantastic. She was the most lovely person, who just sat in the corner singing away. And her voice was a beautiful voice, with these cracks in it, just gorgeous, like an old leather book. Pete did a vocal, and then Emmylou came in and sang around it. Pete was in the studio when that happened and helped her with it, him and Malcolm. The lyrics were all kind of written already.'

There is a place I was born
It is a place I've never seen
Don't even know where it is
Don't even know my name
Where is home? Where is my home?
I'm searching far and wide

It's a bastard song
It is a feeling that everything's wrong
But we are alive, we that have wings
We have devices can do anything
I say where is home? Where is my home?
I hear my spirit cry

If you're out of transmission, way out on the road
If you're out of commission I can give you the code
Darkness is coming and it's in your command
Time to be moving, time

There is a town that I was born
Now there's a place I've got to call home
Where is home?
I hear my spirit cry
It's in the clear blue sky

A few years later, Jim picked me up one evening to travel to Tempe in Sydney's southern suburbs. He had agreed to do a gig with Neil Murray to play some songs from Neil's new album, *Going the Distance*, which Jim had helped record a month or so earlier. On the way there, travelling under Sydney Harbour and then on through the other endless tunnels that take traffic south below the city, Jim told me he had met his mother that afternoon, for the first time.

He said he had started the search a few years earlier for the woman who had given him up for adoption, but his first success had been painful. The day before our trip to Tempe, he had found his father in a Canberra nursing home, suffering from dementia. Jim's father had spoken a little and looked at Jim's photos, but had been unable to help with the whereabouts of Jim's mother, his ex-wife. As Jim was departing, a guy similar in age to him arrived to visit the sick man. At first incredulous about Jim's existence, his younger brother after a time embraced the truth, saying, 'I suppose you'd like to meet your other brothers and sisters? There are five of us – six, now.'

That meeting took place later that afternoon, when Jim discovered four of his new siblings and their partners. One of his new sisters looked so like his own daughter he was overcome. It was strange and exciting for all of them. Some of his new extended family had attended Midnight Oil shows and had the band's records. None had a musical streak, but Jim wondered what may have come out 'if they had felt a little bit lost as a kid', as he had. He discovered that afternoon in Canberra that only six months after he had been adopted out his natural mother and father had married, and then proceeded to have the first of five more children before divorcing.

'Would you like to meet Mum?' Jim's siblings asked. 'She lives in Goulburn.'

Jim followed nervously in his car the next day at a discreet distance behind his brothers and sisters, waiting on a telephone call from them to let him know if his mum was OK about the meeting. She was. As he pulled up outside the little house in Goulburn and stepped out of the car he saw his birth mother for the first time, standing on the front step. He walked up the path in a nervous but blissful trance buoyed by expectation and a sense of mystery, and then looked into her eyes. 'She looked like an angel,' he says. During their reunion his mother said she'd thought of him every day of her life, and cried for him on each and every birthday. He was a secret she had not shared with her other children, or with her second husband. She had been pregnant and unmarried and certainly hadn't shared the news of her illicit pregnancy with her mother – the fear of her family's reaction, and that of the wider Irish Catholic community in their small New South Wales country town, was what had forced her to make the decision to give Jim up for adoption in the first place.

As we pulled into the car park of the Harp hotel in Tempe Jim said he wasn't going to tell Neil his news, at least not before the show. I can only imagine how he felt as he played his guitar and little keyboard and ukulele during the show. I couldn't see his eyes, but I could hear his music. The gentle opening bars from one of Neil's new songs made me take a deep breath, and as Neil sang, before I knew it the tears were running down my face.

I saw you today
Out on a hill

You were with your mother
Time stood still
I was riding by
You didn't see me
I saw your hair
Move with the breeze

Circumstances
Keep us apart
Circumstances
Can be hard
Circumstances
Against our will
But I want you to know
I love you still

Neil was singing about his young daughter, but the song's wording was uncanny. Every note and nuance of his and Jim's performance seemed imbued with the universal truth of their individual stories of separation and pain.

Jim loves the mother who brought him up very much, and he still has a studio at her house. But his need to know about himself, to answer questions that most of us take for granted, was something he had to pursue, and his adoptive mum supported him in that. He found out that his heritage was Irish, and now he knew his home and his name. He remembered the woman in Ireland who had insisted he was an Irishman, and how brightly the musical spirit had burned when he was playing loose with Neil Finn. And a whole lot of other things made sense as well.

Jim, Rob and Pete all threatened to leave the band at various times through their career. Gary says he was supportive whenever Pete declared he was going – which, according to Gary, was every second year. He remembers once getting a call from Pete saying he felt too old for it all. Gary asked him, 'When you get up on stage to perform, are you wanting to give to the audience, or wanting to get something from them?'

'Good question,' said Pete, and, after a pause, 'Something to give.' He stayed.

Rob remembers Pete very nearly going in 1993. 'It was at the end of a show in Ludwigshafen on a miserable German tour, after a year of touring. Overcast skies, and this horrible racist bus driver. And Pete said, "I'm out. I want to make a statement." We got back from Europe and he was still adamant. Back and forward it went for a while. In his proposed statement the suggestion was that the band were at a creative brick wall and we'd all decided mutually to call it quits. I said, "I'm not in it, mate." So it stalled for a while, long enough for Pete to change his mind. It wasn't just him, though. Other people suggested exits, probably Pete more than the rest. I think it normally happened after long bouts of touring when everyone was completely pissed off and we were at our lowest ebb, in spite of all the big gains we may have made. But it also happened during problematic albums.'

For Jim it was while trying to get the album after *Breathe*, *Redneck Wonderland*, off the ground. There was pressure outside and inside the band to do a career compilation album instead, to be called *20,000 Watt RSL*, and although Jim was not alone in not liking the idea, he was outvoted, and took the defeat hard. 'I left about when *20,000 Watt* was released, late

'97. I was really disappointed that Sony rejected the first version of *Redneck*, and maybe more disappointed that Gary and Pete seemed all for the alternative – the "greatest hits" option. I felt we were going to become more of a nostalgia band if we released a greatest hits, which I think we did become in the last few years precisely because of it. I felt that the band had always been a creative force, breaking down frontiers with every album, blazing away into new areas. In my mind we were on an artistic trajectory untouched by any other Australian band, but something died after that for me.'

The *20,000 Watt RSL* collection (named after the power requirements for a potential RSL club venue) was released with two brand new songs, 'What Goes On' and 'Black Skin White Heart'. Predictably it went straight to the top of the local charts, and thankfully that success facilitated the release of *Redneck Wonderland* six months later in early 1998. Jim was back on board by then and determined that the band should be seen as more contemporary-sounding – a band that could engage the challenge of the new music as well as respond to the alarming politics of the time. Pauline Hanson was leading an emergence of extreme right-wing politics in Australia, which seemed part of a global phenomenon. The band felt angry about the state of things, but the new sounds, incorporating noise and mechanised beats, suited their mood. Rob committed to the project and, with the band all fully contributing, they began work with the most happening young producer of the time, a guy known as Magoo.

Rob: 'We were starting to think of rock – R-O-C-K – as being a bit of a joke, but what we learnt with Magoo was that when he said, "You guys rock" there wasn't a scrap of irony. He meant it as a great compliment, in the same way he did when he spoke about the other bands he was producing, like Regurgitator and Grinspoon. It was just great working with him – once again a combination of an inspired producer/engineer, great studio [Sing Sing in Melbourne], a band hungry to re-invent, and lots of strong songs. There's nothing polite about the performances on that album. It's very uncompromising and dense. To listen to it from go to whoa is quite a mind fuck – it's not an easy-listening experience, nor was it conceived to be. I think that "Redneck Wonderland" the song, Jim's song, is one of the most completely realised pieces of music we made in the nineties – it stands up with anything from the entire catalogue.'

The production of that song, and quite a bit of remixing and rerecording of others, was done by Warne Livesey. Rob: 'He came in near the end, when we weren't sure we were getting the mixes right, and we actually did some rerecording.'

Warne: 'I thought a lot of what they had got with Magoo was very, very creative, very inventive. And there was bags and bags of stuff on tape and you'd listen and go, "My God, what the hell is that? That's incredible – I've never heard anything like that." But it was almost as if there was too much of it, as if it kind of lacked a bit of focus, and that's why they wanted someone else to come in and try to bring a bit of perspective to that way of working. To me, that's the album that's most affected by the grunge thing and by the more industrial stuff. And also, because *Breathe* was quite an understated sort of record, it was like, "We've done that now. Let's get back to being what we are, which is more of a rock band, and challenging the audience a bit more", I guess.'

Rob: 'It had technology, it had strings, good musicianship, interesting arrangements, provocative lyrics, some furious riffs and drumming, and harmony singing. Harmony singing! As well!'

Bones wasn't quite convinced the style of the album suited them. 'It was an aggressive little thing, heavily distorted. Things like "Blot" – whoa! About that time we were farting around a bit more with drum loops. That's what was happening with popular music at the time. Once again I don't think it was a successful amalgamation, technology and us. We were bringing in lots of loops and all these things were firing off left, right and centre, and only some of them worked. "Redneck" the song worked. But us being dictated to by machines – nah. We speed up and we slow down and we rise and we fall, and we feel the power. But this click, click, click was like having a little Nazi inside your head and you couldn't even move coz it was a fascist time-keeping device – which is fantastic for someone because they can put it into a computer. Everything is the same tempo and they can splice it back together. It works wonders for that. But for a band like Midnight Oil, I found it quite difficult to adjust to.'

Jim: '*Redneck* was like a reaction to what was going on in the world, an answer to it. "Hey, we're not gonna go down quietly here. We're gonna come back fighting, and this is it." I remember thinking at certain times it was just a whole bunch of yelling and noise. But then, well, what's wrong with that? That's what great music is. There was a feeling in the band that after *Breathe*, which was a bit of a dud sales-wise, we'd taken the wrong tack. I kinda felt it was important we'd gone down that road, but in terms of our career, you know, you only get so many chances. So I was pretty keen with *Redneck* to get onto it, to try and help with a new direction for the band — a more energetic sort of one that was more vital. I felt the band were really up against the wall then, because we had something to prove. And I think it got Rob back into the band again, coz after *Breathe* he was pretty well gone in spirit, I felt. Parts of *Redneck* were really a lot of fun to make, but my dad was dying at the time, so I was— you know.'

All tracks were again simply credited to 'Midnight Oil', but this time Rob had much more studio input than in the *Breathe* recordings. The album already had a title, from some graffiti seen during rehearsals scrawled on a wall in the middle of a rough map of Australia near the Sing Sing studios. The title track was only arrived at the last minute, when Jim delivered a song that encapsulated the mood and feel of the whole session.

I don't want to run, I don't want to stay
Cos everything that's near and dear is old and in the way
Emergency has gone, apathy rolling on
Time to take a stand
Redneck wonderland

Got you in my sights, spotlit by the fence
If it's love you're faking it's just common sense
Brick and tile for miles, rolling in the aisles
Rifle in my hand
Redneck wonderland

Well, the streets are clean, nothing gets away
I can see the beauty treatment draining from your face

It is vision free, it's poor bugger me
Something less than grand
Redneck wonderland

Martin continued to play a crucial role in all the songs and, as usual, was up for the challenge of the new direction. The full-sounding style allowed plenty of room for his guitar vitriolics and dark aggression. Martin has 'a riff and a lick for every occasion', Gary says, and he sounds brilliant on this album – not that you can always pick out his playing, but you can sense him. Gary has a colourful description of Martin's overall role in the band: 'Martin is like slow-release fertiliser, those white nitrogen balls on the surface beneath a plant. Every day you look and the balls haven't moved. Is the plant getting any benefit from them? Nothing seems to be happening. Then they're gone, and the plant is greener, bigger. It's that edge, that toxicity, which causes great growth, but taken in one mouthful you'd spit it out. When Martin says something, it's like acid. It's very potent. In band meetings there'd be two hours of silence, then he'd say something like, "But—" He puts the "but" into everything.'

In Melbourne during their very early days, the band were staying at the Majestic Hotel in one huge room with a partition down the middle that had windows with no glass. Rob, Jim and Bear were asleep on one side and on the other Pete, Gary and Martin were supposed to be sleeping as well. But Pete and Gary were disagreeing with each other over some aspect of the music industry. Martin spoke up whenever there was a pause, saying something insulting and provocative about the pathetic level of debate. Gary suspects Martin was having half-hour naps and not even following the conversation, just waking up, tossing in a toxic barb, then going back to sleep. 'He doesn't engage. He just talks and moves on. He kept us up till sunrise, and we had a gig the next day at the Crystal Ballroom.'

Martin didn't submit to a formal interview for this book. He's never done an interview about the band, and why would he start now? The time is not right. The story isn't over. 'Pete's just left the band,' he told me. Martin probably stayed most true to Midnight Oil's essence by rejecting my offer to be part of this fundamentally parasitic and exploitative project (my words, not his!), reflecting his unwavering determination to let the band's music do the talking.

In the 'punk' days Martin was the only one who looked the part. It helped that he effortlessly dispensed gunfire guitar from his Stratocaster, and that an expressionless face and a cigarette wedged in his guitar's machine head were his only affectations. He got on his toes occasionally and moved about the stage just enough to avoid being knocked over by Pete, but basically he and Jim were Pete's dark, stationary bookends. Martin was involved, very involved, but always kept something back. He smiled at his bandmates, but rarely smiled at the crowd. His only engagement with them was through his playing.

Martin is hard core in most things to do with the band, and usually right on the money with his big-picture observations. It was Martin who first decided to cover all brand labels on the band's stage gear with gaffer tape. Amplifiers, drums, speakers and shoes, anything with a brand – except guitars. What you saw during a show had to be all Midnight Oil. No free commercials. His respected role as honest broker when

Pete and Rob are both extremely physical performers and worked up quite a sweat during every show, such as this one during the *Red Sails in the Sunset* tour of 1984 *(Patrick Jones)*

Jim, Giffo, Martin, Pete and Rob 'back of Bourke' in 1987 while making the 'Beds Are Burning' film clip *(Ken Duncan/CBS Records)*

Charlie McMahon's hook is the result of a teenage explosives accident. His didj reflects his contact with and respect for Aboriginal communities *(Adrienne Overall)*

Larry Jordan, who also filmed the Exxon show, captures Pete for the 'King of the Mountain' clip near Los Angeles in 1990 *(Jim Moginie)*

The band's first publicity shot, in the garage at Rob's Albert Avenue address in Chatswood, 1977 (from top: Rob, Jim, Martin, Bear, with Pete down low)

Place Without a Postcard gold-record celebrations backstage at the Tivoli in Sydney in 1981 with (from left) Connie Adolph, Paul Russell (CBS), Giffo, Pete, Martin, Rob and Jim, with Zev Eizik at the front

In Verdun, France in 1990 for the filming of the 'Forgotten Years' clip amid the hundreds of thousands of First World War graves. Bones is on bass, second from right *(Youri Lenquette/Sony)*

About 5 a.m. in the Devil's Coachhouse in New South Wales's Jenolan Caves, 1982, attempting to create an eye-catching publicity photograph between takes for the 'Read About It' film clip *(Adrienne Overall)*

Presenting Gary Morris, the band's 'sixth member' in 1983 (from left, Jim, Pete, Gary, Rob, Martin, Giffo)

Long-serving crew member Michael Lippold in his pin-up pose *(Adrienne Overall)*

At Megaphon Studios in 1993 making the *Earth and Sun and Moon* album. Everyone could play guitar, even Pete *(Mark Lang/Sony)*

The insides of hotel rooms look pretty much the same all over the world. Here Jim tries out his new Gretch Country Club guitar in Cannes, France in 1993 *(Jim Moginie)*

Bands spend most of their time on tour 'in transit'. Rob waits somewhere in the USA, 1983 *(Adrienne Overall)*

It's just another no-frills dressing room for the band, deserted while they're on stage *(Adrienne Overall)*

Plastic cups were better than bottles or cans, but the floor *après gig* was always a sticky mess of discarded clothing and footwear, and spilt beer (Adrienne Overall)

it comes to judging new songs is invaluable, but has come at the cost to him of not really being able to submit his own songs. He may be relieved to be out of the competitive fray, he may have given up writing in frustration at the quality and number of songs being written by Jim and Rob, or he may have consciously decided just to contribute licks and riffs on every possible occasion – probably all of those are true. He may harbour some frustrations about songs he's never submitted to the band, but has to be credited for much of their musical snarl and ongoing non-compliance.

Bones felt the band's profile and engagement ebb and flow. 'With the Oils we used to have periods of time when we would gel with each other and other times when we would gel with the outside world as well, radio or youth culture or whatever. And there were other times when we didn't gel with them but were internally OK. We just kept going. It's like hitchhiking: if you get a ride you get a ride, but if you're prepared to walk, well, you walk.'

Band meetings were often incredibly difficult. They were confrontational, and Gary was difficult to make accountable. Bones was more than happy for Pete to bear the brunt of relations with Gary. 'Gary's a hard man to keep in check – very enthusiastic, very passionate, just goes at a million miles an hour with his brain and his mouth at the same time. Pete was like a really good sieve. There might be 8000 bits of shit, but there might be fifteen really good ideas as well. It was a matter of getting through it. Pete did that, which meant the rest of us didn't have to deal with Gary.'

•

Pete's patient side was not often seen in the early days. His reckless stage show in part reflected his free-ranging lifestyle. But when he started doing regular tai chi exercises in the early eighties he calmed down marginally and often had the air of a Buddhist about him. The tai chi reflected his love of nature and simple pleasures and his frugal lifestyle. On stage, even his wild, abstract dancing seemed influenced by the daily tai chi routine.

When the band went to Tokyo in 1984, at the start of Pete's serious political responsibilities at home, he seemed in search of spiritual or moral clarification. Giffo remembers the rooms of the President Hotel where they were staying. 'He had the Bible on one bedside table and Buddha on the other, and I think he was having a crack at both of them and trying to figure out which way he was going to go. I think he got all caught up with what it was to be a politician.'

During the recording of *Red Sails* Pete would often go to another room or to the top of the Aoyama studio building, where the big turbine air-conditioning units were, and meditate. The top of this six- or seven-storey building was all very industrial and theoretically out of bounds, but there was a feeling like you were overlooking Tokyo. Pete did quite a bit of sitting up there. 'By the time we got to Japan there's no doubt my political antennae and responses to what was going on were becoming more acute, and I was also wanting to explore fully a deeper and more spiritual basis for things rather than just how many shows we were doing or whether we were still selling out Selinas or wherever – in other words, life outside the music industry. I actually look back on the period in Japan as a really important time for me and a period I got a great deal from.'

But when he returned from Tokyo there was no real change in Pete's behaviour or his personality. He was a Christian, he said, but not born again, just reawakened. His spiritual approach and Biblical interpretations vary greatly from Gary's. After I moderately blasphemed in the band's office one day Gary rebuked me and started to explain why I wouldn't go to heaven. Only by accepting Jesus Christ as lord and saviour could anyone make it to heaven, he said. My protestations about Buddhists, pre-Christian peoples and good people everywhere made no headway. But then Pete joined in, and before long I was way out of my depth as he and Gary began quoting chapter and verse back and forth. It was very educational, but the clincher, I thought, was Pete's Biblical paraphrasing: 'The person who does good in my name shall come to heaven and sit at my left hand, but the person who does good without even knowing of me shall come and sit at my right hand.'

For me that seemed to indicate a very inclusive take on religion, where not everything in life was motivated by reward and judged by dogma. These days, people who embrace a more inclusive approach to Christianity find comfort in the revelations of the unearthed Gnostic documents, which describe earlier, more feminist and personal interpretations of Christian philosophy than those in the conventional version of the Bible. The so-called lost gospel of Thomas, which encompasses enough diversity to allow non-Christians to find God too, is particularly important. Thomas's interpretations were rejected by the church's revisionists and he was marginalised as 'doubting' Thomas in orthodox mythology. Arguably, and perhaps unfortunately, 'doubting' could be seen as almost as important a quality as 'believing' at this time in our history.

Whatever Pete's brand of Christianity, he doesn't flash it around, nor did he let it intrude into band lyrics. According to Rob, the religious references in the band's lyrics weren't written by Pete. 'All of those were written by Jim. There may have been some lyrics embellished later on, but that's the amazing thing. With religion, Jim always had a wonderful way of twisting it in all its variety of magic, mystery and inconsistencies. In "I'm the Cure" (from *Bird Noises*), he wrote: "God is hiding in this teacup/Kilopascals in my finger". These were the kind of ambiguous lyrics I always felt we had to have but increasingly, unfortunately, they were edited out as perhaps other band members became a bit too sanctimonious and serious. To Pete's credit, he was always determined to keep church and state separate, never made a big deal out of it. But at the same time it became an integral part of everything we did – more, perhaps, than he was aware. We'd tread softly around Pete sometimes for fear that some of our blunt secular comments might hurt him – in retrospect, totally unnecessarily. But at the same time it gives you an idea of the measure of respect in the band for each other's sensibilities.'

In 1984, after a show at the London Forum, a fan reviewed the concert. An extract: 'Speaking of Peter, he was obviously in a touchy-feely mood. He hugged Bones at a line in "Renaissance Man" about "new-won friends" and reached out to him during both "Forgotten Years" and, understandably, "In the Valley". Peter also hugged Martin at a point in his patter where he spoke about those who have been here forever, and leaned on him during his talk about companies before "Blue Sky" – maybe a setup for the killer full-spotlight solo Martin took during this song. So why can Peter get away with going to his knees repeatedly during the course of the show and crossing himself during "Sell My Soul" without either looking fake or foolish or getting pilloried for it?'

Maybe it's because those iconic religious gestures have been so widely adopted in pop music that most observers didn't give Pete's occasional variations a second look. Going to your knees has long been a popular declaratory position in many branches of the arts and, although he certainly went to ground regularly, Pete didn't spend that much time in the position. When he did kneel, it's true that he often held the microphone with both hands, but to my mind this conveyed pleading for reason as much as it did praying for help.

'Say Your Prayers' appears on *The Real Thing*, the band's 2000 follow-up album to *Redneck Wonderland*. The song was originally recorded for an East Timor benefit album, *Liberdade*, but wasn't a religious song. 'I got a cure for compassion fatigue/Spend a week with the Timorese,' wrote Jim. 'Say your prayers for the future/Say your prayers for the past'. It was one of only three new songs included on *The Real Thing* album, and those tracks, plus the title song, should really have been released as a fabulous EP like *Bird Noises* and *Species Deceases*. However, due mainly to the band's need to fulfil their contractual obligations with Sony, the new songs went onto an album where they were supplemented by some 'live and unplugged' recordings of older material and a cover version of Russell Morris's sixties hit 'The Real Thing'.

The inclusion of those live recordings rather than all new material was a source of more band disagreement, but the four new songs were all strong, particularly 'The Last of the Diggers' and 'Say Your Prayers'. The version of 'The Real Thing' was also pretty good – a spirited revisiting of the iconic original – but, as Rob points out, 'As a rule, when our band has attempted cover versions, particularly of seminal songs like Lennon's classic "Instant Karma" and even "The Real Thing", I don't think we've come close to adding enough to the originals to make them stand up as "Midnight Oil" tracks. In the case of "Pub with No Beer" [recorded for a 1998 Slim Dusty tribute album] we had a sense of ownership, if you like, because the version was so different to the original and had enough of Midnight Oil in it. When you do a cover version, the best thing while you're recording it is to assume that you wrote it. "This is the way we would do it". I think in the case of "Pub with No Beer", it's quite a neat version and Pete's vocal delivery, being so Australian, is really quite strong.'

Circumstances at the time of the release of *The Real Thing* were not good for the band. Their profile was stagnant, radio-station support for the new material was negligible and there was a lack of cohesion and direction in the band. They were still able to create great music, but, according to many voices inside and out of the band, some wrong decisions were being made. It was another point when things became too much for Jim to tolerate. 'I left again when we were doing the extra tracks for *The Real Thing* – again, a regurgitation of "golden" material, this time acoustic and some of it dodgy. I had written a whole swag of new songs that were met with muted reactions. I remember an afternoon at Bones's playing them and feeling like the band weren't getting it. Everything had turned around. It was as if "appease Sony" was the mantra. We did "Say Your Prayers" around this time, which was good, and "Last of the Diggers" was good too, but Sony had Gary in a fever about doing cover versions. And so "The Real Thing" was suggested by Gary's wife, Amanda. In retrospect we were on a downhill run and no one had any other good ideas, so we just did it. It was hard standing up to Gary and Pete when they agreed – which they almost always did, as they were in constant touch. So the lack of spine from the band, who were too tired to argue with Gary, plus the regurgitation of more old stuff, plus this feeling of the power slipping away, was an unhappy situation for me and probably why I went, over Christmas '99. It seemed Gary hated anything new we did at that time. He always wanted *Species Deceases* all over again, God bless him.'

After the heady Olympic finish to 2000, the following year was low key. In March 2001 the Oils played a surprise set on a little outdoor stage in front of 200 local supporters of a campaign to keep the Manly Reservoir clean. A little later a 'Power and Passion' postage stamp was released as part of a series honouring various Australian bands. Then there was a portrait of the band, *Nothing's as Precious as a Hole in the Ground* – using mangrove bark pigment, watercolour and gouache on vellum – by eX de Medici. The work has its origins in the artist's background in tattooing, and hangs in the National Portrait Gallery in Canberra.

There was also a plan for an enormous tour of America named 'The Great Australian Bite' with INXS (and at one stage Men At Work as well). From the start there were serious misgivings inside the Oils that they were being pigeonholed as a 'great Aussie band of the eighties', but Gary kept things rolling. As the project advanced, the band grew increasingly hostile to the idea, and there was a general sense of relief when a managerial clash over billing resulted in the plug being pulled at the last minute. But was this another missed opportunity?

Midnight Oil may have seemed to be down, at least relative to their former success, but they were still in the ring. The band knew that Pete's urges to move on to other things were getting stronger, but there was no telling what a hugely successful album on the scale of *Diesel* or *Blue Sky Mining* might do to his resolve. There was a general feeling that even if Pete did increasingly stray into other opportunities, the band could still continue as a recording and touring entity, albeit on a more modest and irregular scale. So, with the whole band again completely committed, they started work on songs for *Capricornia*. It was to be their eleventh studio LP, and their final release with Pete.

Jim had heaps of songs and he called Rob and Martin over to hear their ideas and play around with some of the new material. These sessions then became rehearsal sessions with Bones. Then Pete was given Jim's and Rob's lyrics to play with and learn, and soon he started to attend rehearsals as well. It was a confident start, and the songs advanced well. When the writing was complete they headed to the famous old wood-panelled Festival Studios in Sydney, where 'the wild one', Johnny O'Keefe, recorded and where a great deal of other Australian music history has been committed to tape. Warne Livesey arrived to oversee proceedings, the songs were sounding great and spirits were up. They put their heads down and worked together for six weeks to make the new songs ring and hum. If anything had to be rewritten, like 'Kiss That Girl', it was done on the spot and in a generous and collective spirit.

Capricornia started life in Jim's head as a musical interpretation of the relatively dark Xavier Herbert novel of the same name – part soundscape, part concept album – but the urge from the others to play to the band's strengths with pop hooks, rock'n'roll guitars and accessible, contemporary lyrics left some of Jim's more radical ideas, if not his melodies, behind. They were making a record that was full of all the things they were renowned for: inventive sounds, provocative poetic lyrics, kick-arse guitars, and a classic Pete scream on the album's single. Warne: '*Capricornia* very much got back to some of the aesthetics and priorities that *Diesel* had. And in a lot of ways, actually, it's probably – for me, anyway – the best album out of all of them. The writing is fantastic, the energy is great and the playing is the best they've ever done. The album is chock-a-block full of catchy songs, and it's got a fantastic spirit to it. I remember it really, really fondly – it's one of the most fun albums I've ever worked on.'

But there was a sense of it all being a bit late and a bit ill timed – including the fact that the subsequent tour took the band to the USA within weeks of the World Trade Center towers being hit in September 2001. In the wake of the devastating attacks, the band compiled a set list to reflect their collective mood, adjusted their rhetoric and travelled in a spirit of concerned optimism, determined not to be terrorised into cancelling the tour or getting distracted from their plans.

Being in America at that time was being part of history. The whole country was in major shock, and for months the Stars and Stripes was flying by every doorway and on every car. There was a confused air of solidarity and suspicion, of a commitment to basic humanitarian values and a vengeful disregard for them. There was continuous TV coverage of the event and its consequences, and weeks and weeks of funerals in New York. And all the while the smoke and the smell of the attacks hung around the downtown location. The band were there in the thick of it, and as always their message was clear: the things that unite us as people are much bigger and more universal than those that divide us.

Although it was a thoroughly surreal experience, the tour was an outstanding success. The fans from years past had stayed true, the venues were full and there was a sense that the things the fans and band shared were even more precious than before. The band's touring patterns had been erratic, but the legend of their live shows was undiminished.

But great shows are not enough without the support of a major record company or major radio airplay. The music business is big business, and the odds are stacked against the smaller players — which Midnight Oil now were. The new album was released in the US through Mason Munoz's small, independent Liquid 8 label, and while it had major distribution through BMG, the only way to get people into the shops was via radio airplay. And that was where the story stopped. One company, Clear Channel, owns over 1000 radio stations and two-thirds of the concert venues in America. They are a very powerful organisation in the entertainment business and, understandably, tend to focus on acts from which they think they can get the biggest return for the least effort. For them, an act like Midnight Oil was a long shot, and 'Golden Age', the new single, didn't fit the list of acceptable criteria. For a start, it had a scream in it.

Mason couldn't believe the reaction from some decision-makers at key radio stations. 'I remember KGFR in Austin, Texas, one of the really cool markets, giving me a flat answer: "We'll never play this song. We can't deal with the scream." I said, "You're kidding. It's the pay-off. How can you *not* play that?"'

David Fricke: 'The audience wasn't resistant to it – the audience hadn't *heard* it yet! This was all about micromanaged radio, and I'm sure you've got a version of that in Australia. Everybody's got it, because as the world gets smaller with communications, controlling them becomes much more important. So they play an eight-second lick from a song over the phone to people as part of focus research and ask, "Does this turn you on or turn you off?" There's not enough there to care! The fact that somebody thought that Peter was screaming a bit, well, it's absurd, it's horrifying and it makes absolutely no sense.'

'Golden Age' is a classic combination: enough grunt to be rock, yet catchy and uplifting enough to be pop. There is beautiful, chiming twelve-string guitar and a provocative lyric exploring the conflicting modern attractions of bushwalking and surfing the Internet, plus it's all driven home with the erupting impromptu scream Pete delivered in the studio one night for the final chorus. It had everything a great song needs, except luck and airplay. But that's the business – and the band had been in the ring long enough to know how these things worked. They were disappointed, but not surprised, and returned to Australia to begin the local leg of the *Capricornia* tour.

The lack of success of the single, after an initial surge into the charts when the most faithful fans bought it, meant a lot more than poor sales figures. It meant the end of the band – or at least the end of the band as we know it. Even if the figures from America had been spectacular, at 'Beds Are Burning' level, Pete says that would only have prolonged the final tour, not changed his mind to finish. One night in Adelaide he told the rest of the guys of his firm intention to leave when the tour was completed. It didn't really sink in. They couldn't decide how to deal publicly with his decision. To just announce that these were Pete's last shows, mid-tour, seemed awkward and anticlimactic. A proper end to their playing days together should be devised. But these things take time, and they didn't have enough right then, so the tour continued with only the band members and a handful of others aware of the situation. Some of the band secretly harboured hopes of a last-minute change of heart from Pete, but mainly it was a case of if and how they would continue after his departure.

When the band came to the front of the stage at their second Tweed Heads show and put their arms around each other for a final theatrical bow at the end of the tour, not even the crew, let alone the audience, knew it was all over. Backstage the band members kept things light, laughing over an end-of-tour prank by the crew – a pair of Pete's giant underpants had been lowered from the ceiling during their last song.

It was a very rock'n'roll end to an illustrious rock'n'roll career. In many ways, for the band to do their final show to a full house at a beachside venue without a whole lot of bells and whistles was quite fitting. It was a moving show for everyone, in or out of the know. The atmosphere on stage was extraordinary. My son managed to see his first full Midnight Oil show that night. It was his eleventh birthday, the 22nd of November, 2002, St Cecilia's Day – twenty-nine years exactly since Pete had joined the band.

•

Ten days later, my modem squealed and in a matter of seconds a new front page to the band's official web site hit cyberspace with a statement about Pete's departure:

December 2nd 2002
Pete has resolved to call it a day with Midnight Oil, resigning from the band to take up challenges outside music.

'The last 25 years have been incredibly fulfilling for me, and I leave with the greatest respect for the whole of Midnight Oil. The band has brought a lot of pleasure and meaning to people's lives, including my own. Who could ask for more? But it is time for me to move on and immerse myself in those things which are of deep concern to me and which I have been unable to fully apply myself to up to now.'

The band wishes Pete all the best for the future and reinforces the respect, good intentions and values we mutually share. Jim, Rob, Martin & Bones plan to continue making music together in another guise at some point down the track.

We've had a unique relationship and special chemistry for many years, one too good to lose. We want to thank our families, all fans worldwide, our crew and the Office team for their enormous support over the years. It's been a great ride together. Many, many thanks.
(Signed) Peter Garrett, Bones Hillman, Rob Hirst, Jim Moginie, Martin Rotsey and Gary Morris

The message went up at about 11.30 on Monday night in Australia – mid-afternoon in Europe and early morning in the USA on the same date. It was a simple, grassroots way of breaking the news and all the more effective for that. Within a few minutes the fans started to find out, and by breakfast on the Tuesday all the local radio stations had heard the story – some from their international bureaus – and were playing Oils songs and airing reactions from 'experts'. The TV stations picked it up by mid-morning and their evening news programs were full of the band's clips and footage from the Exxon gig. The newspapers, which normally set the agenda for the other media, had to wait until the following day, Wednesday, for their turn. Their tributes were fulsome and expansive and most stories included speculation about Pete's plans and the future of the remaining band members.

But, apart from the brief statement on the web site, the band were silent. After the announcement had gone up, the Powderworkers fan site had been deluged with words from shocked and stunned readers and for weeks was awash with despair and disbelief. Eventually came acceptance – there was no doubting the fact that Pete had left the band, and change had to be embraced by everyone.

Midnight Oil often drew on iconic aspects of the Australian landscape for their songs, and in 'Golden Age' the jacaranda tree in Jim's backyard took a significant role. When in season, the jacaranda is a gorgeous purple-flowered tree. Such is the inspiring nature of its display that jacaranda festivals occur in many country towns around Australia as people celebrate its colourful indication of seasonal change.

But the jacaranda is not a native Australian tree. Like much of the population of this country, its roots are elsewhere. It thrives and contributes colour and worldliness and variety, and has become 'part of the scenery' in the populated areas of our astonishing brown land. Inevitably the jacaranda shares its spaces with the unique indigenous environment of Australia. Rows of simple wooden houses scattered along dusty streets are shaded by the grand but understated green-and-grey stands of local eucalypts as well as the purple splashes of the immigrant jacaranda. We need to welcome strangers, particularly those in difficulties. We need to embrace change, understand ourselves and the original Australians, respect the environment and be prepared to bend with it, and let go the apron strings of the British monarchy. Only then will Australia move on and grow up. And only then can we realistically anticipate any sort of golden age for us all.

I can see a purple patch of jacaranda
Framed in eucalypt from this wooden-floored verandah
Heading past the watermark
Heading for the hills
Heading for the edge of time
Heading for the thrills of the golden aaaaaaaaaaaaage

Pete: 'Before the *Capricornia* album was done, yeah, I knew in my head it would be the last record we'd make together. The writing was on the wall. You didn't have to be particularly sensitive to figure out that we were on a path that way in terms of sales. We were barely selling enough records to keep ourselves alive, we weren't getting airplay, and we weren't getting a huge amount of interest in what we were doing. On one level it didn't matter what the world thought: if we felt good about it that was fine by me. But it was very clear, I think to everybody but particularly to me and Gary, that there was nowhere else to go. We could go to a cottage industry sort of format and continue just to do it at our level, but that would have been very different to the Midnight Oil of the previous thirty years. So for me it was very clear, and in fact I said that to them. Not in an ultimatum sense – it was more like, "Well, look, guys, this is kind of it – end of contract, again, and the books don't balance any more. There's a lot of demands on my time and I'm really keen to be working proactively. We're not going to go back on the road again. We can't *afford* to go back on the road again overseas, and we can hardly go around the block again here. So?" For me it was never about leaving the band. It was always about finding the opportunities and the space to do the other things that were calling me – loudly. And unfortunately, that eventually necessitated me leaving because the band wouldn't stop! I *had* to leave it! If we had all agreed and stopped, then, well, that would have been just as fine for me, but we didn't. And you saw the statement: the others still harbour some kind of indefinable desire to continue.'

Midnight Oil won't ever burn quite the same again – but they may still burn. Meanwhile, there are always the recordings and, if you were lucky enough, memories of just about the best live band on the planet.

epilogue

as big as U2

So why didn't the band transcend to superstardom? Was it because they didn't want to, or because they couldn't? Was it missed opportunities? Was it bad luck, bad management, diminishing music relevance or even cowardice? All these reasons have been espoused, and many people genuinely believe that the band could or should have been 'as big as U2'. The equivalent phrase in past decades may have been 'as big as Elvis' or 'as big as the Beatles', but since the early nineties 'as big as U2' has been shorthand for being at the high-water mark in global music success and influence.

People I spoke to, both officially and unofficially, for this book who used the phrase were indicating that they felt the band failed to realise its full potential. Such a view is a matter for discussion that goes beyond 'fans' of the band to observers of the music industry in general. There is broad interest in the often perplexing machinations of how bands do or don't 'make it' in the entirely unpredictable world of modern music. It's a world at the pointy end of capitalism, where quality is not always the major criterion, and a ruthless, bloody game that arguably even the winners lose.

Of course, there are many who simply found the band's politics, or Pete's voice, or their defiant attitude, too much. Plenty of people have found their musical tastes satisfactorily served elsewhere. But it is hard to ignore the fact that at one stage in their career Midnight Oil shared the same status and sales and stages as REM and U2 all around the world. They also shared similar political viewpoints with these bands and made an effort to get to know each other as people.

John Watson, who worked at Sony during the early nineties and is now the manager of Silverchair, says, 'The fact that they weren't as big as they could have been probably doesn't matter that much really, but the fan in you wants to see that band get their just rewards. Midnight Oil were the kings of alternative music in the same way as REM and U2 were. And they were positioned to have that same crossover appeal, with their credibility intact. By 1994 everybody knew the alternative music scene was where it was at. Yet the weird thing was that in 1993 the whole world turned left and bands like REM and U2, who had always been to the left in the eighties, all of a sudden woke up one morning and the world was on their doorstep. They kept travelling in a straight line. At that exact moment Midnight Oil turned right. Why they turned right I've got absolutely no idea.'

Michael Lippold: 'I was just a roadie. I wanted to get out there amongst it and I wanted to work for an Australian band and go and sell Australian rock'n'roll to the world – and kill it! And I'd dropped into an outfit, through pure arse, that I thought was more than capable. I'd dropped into an A grade football side and I thought, "This is the band that can do it –

they can go all the places other Australian bands haven't been able to go. This band can, and will, do it." But they didn't – and it was their fault. They chose not to. They could have marched through. They could have been huge. It was an unconscious fear.

'They're perfectionists, they were a band's band, but they were cowards. One thing that drove them was that they were scared of failure. I think it drove them and it stopped them as well. It stunted them. I really believe they could have been as big as U2, I have no doubt. They just wanted to have too much control over things. Sometimes I look at the things we could have done around the world and I think, "Was it really because they wanted control, or were they too scared to fail?" And I don't mean that in a bad way, or that they thought that consciously, I just think it did hold them back. I think they hid behind "We don't want to be stars".'

Bones: 'We didn't play the game. We had the opportunity, we were there, we were poised. But when we had our highest peak in the United States we took a year off touring! We sat round for months debating whether we should relocate ourselves to the northern hemisphere, base ourselves out of there, whether it be Europe or America, which would enable us to tour more frequently. We chose staying in Australia – this is where we live. So you come back here and it removes you. "Out of sight, out of mind." U2 embraced America; we barely put up with it. We'd just go and do our bit and leave. We didn't fit into that limousine–fan-scene–celebrity thing. It wasn't our thing. And I don't think anyone has any regrets. Maybe if we had gone to that next level we wouldn't have lasted as long as we did anyway. Just the way it worked out was fine.

To go the whole hog you've got to sell your soul. You are consumed by it. As it was it was consuming – and I gave up trying to plan my life years ago. Every time I planned to do anything as an individual it clashed with something we did as an enterprise. I just stopped. You realise that it's bigger than you. I fitted into *it*.'

Eventually, the pull of their families and the need to have 'normal' lives led the band to step back from the front line of international music. The dual responsibilities of family and career proved incompatible, and the tyranny of distance prevented the closeness that all the band members wanted with their children. The logistical problems were clear to all. Rob: 'The job was made harder by us living in Australia. It was made more difficult because when we went away we *really* went away – there were greater distances, greater homesickness, the tours became longer because we couldn't afford to be dashing back and forward. On various occasions there were opportunities or suggestions to go and live in the northern hemisphere somewhere and set up base – all our families out of Australia, kids in schools, big operation and change – so that we could respond to opportunities there and be part of the musical community that was, between Europe and the States, the most vibrant in the world. We always felt we were swimming in another sea there, which was one of the reasons that we wanted to go and tour and play in Europe and the States and record in England or Japan or whatever – to swim back into the mainstream current, breathe new life into the band. Bands in Australia, even the best ones, become stale, and we didn't want that to happen. But it doesn't matter what hemisphere you come from, it takes its toll over an impossible period like a quarter of a century, to maintain that peak of your form.'

Rhonda Markowitz: 'There are many times when they can be their own worst enemies. There is absolutely nothing wrong with making your own decisions and not being someone else's puppet, but you can take that to a degree where you're so paranoid about everybody coming at you that you think everybody is out to get you or to use you, when frankly all they could be trying to do is getting to know you or help you because they like what you represent or what you do. I think the band's wariness has hurt them, but having said that, it's entirely their right. They are all strong-willed people, they have discipline and they have integrity, and they had a very specific goal in mind that they all, in harness, worked towards. And you got the feeling that payday is all very good and well and nice, and they have families to support and so on, but these guys were going to be out there doing it no matter what. Whether they got paid or not, they were on a mission – a mission from God, the Blues Brothers might say. And that is very different from "I want to be a rock star and get laid and wear fancy clothes". You got the sense that they had something to say. They'd thought about it, they'd honed it, they made it as "hooky" and pleasant as possible, or as confrontational as possible, or as unignorable as possible, and by God you were going to hear it! And whether they got paid or not wasn't the issue. And that, I think, was what made them different from other rock bands.'

Chris Moss: 'There are career choices that are made as a band, and if they wanted to step onto the U2 treadmill they could probably be as big as U2, but of course they wouldn't be Midnight Oil. Not that I think U2 are victims of the system – they have chosen to exploit it and feel very comfortable with that, doing it their own way for the reasons and in the manner they do it. Midnight Oil had those choices in front of them as well. All of those opportunities were there. They chose not to participate for moral, business, music, family reasons – for whatever reason. It's a multiple choice. They had a different multiple choice to a band like U2. But creatively, musically, impact on people's lives, they have as big a footprint as U2 will ever have. Are they U2? No. Are they involved in a conversation alongside an act as large as U2? Yes, they are. The sheer fact that those two names are spoken of alongside each other says that they are equally as powerful – maybe not equally as successful, but equally as powerful.'

Mason Munoz: 'When *Capricornia* came out I wanted them to do *Good Morning America* and Gary said to me, "No. You have to ask yourself, would REM do it? Would U2 do it?" I said, "Gary, I saw a picture of Bono on the front page of the *New York Times* with George Bush last week! They played half-time at the Superbowl! The only reason U2 might not do *Good Morning America* is that it's not big enough. I saw REM on *Good Morning America* just last week, in the Rockefeller Center." I can't think of any other band who would turn down these things. Those guys! And people here know that. I mean, some people resent them for it and don't respect them for it, but other people are like "Wow. They walked the walk." Incredibly cool.'

But what about the other rejected opportunities: not touring America with the Who, not performing at the Grammys, knocking back Lollapalooza? John Watson: 'You never know about the road not taken, but the great pity for me of it is that they were the band of their generation in Australia and they could have been the band of their generation around the world. The number of barriers they broke down ten or twelve years before other acts broke down the same sorts of barriers overseas! If you think about what became the dominant paradigm of the alternative movement, the thing everyone was doing in the nineties – bands like Pearl Jam, Nirvana, Red Hot Chili Peppers, "We don't take corporate sponsorship, it's all about playing live, we've got a political conscience, it's all about the music". If ever there was a band who should have been shoulder to shoulder with those acts and making exactly the same kind of difference around the globe that they made here in Australia, it's Midnight Oil.'

Gary says the band members chose their families over their international career. 'The band consciously made that decision and paid a price for their families, and they're to be admired for that. And I support them in that decision. It was a grand decision and I fully understand it. As a professional manager, as a strategist, it was disastrous. But I hold no resentment towards the band because of it. We've always made decisions based upon what was important to us, not what was important to the business or anything else.'

Pete: 'Maybe we were never going to be any bigger than we were, I mean, I don't think we should necessarily have any false ideas about that . . . I think we didn't have sufficient capacity within ourselves, and it may have been different things in different people: it may have been ability and judgement, it may have been resourcefulness, creativity, determination, chutzpah, luck, psychological temperaments. I don't know what it was, and I haven't spent a lot of time analysing, but whatever "it" was, we didn't have it to the level that was necessary.'

A career in music is like a ride on a wave – if you're lucky. It's often impossibly difficult to get out through the breakers to start with, and once you're out there it can be a while, sometimes a very long while, before conditions are good and a wave comes along, and then you have to catch it. Midnight Oil paddled out on a home-made board that they were determined to ride in their own distinctive way. They faced the open sea, turned the board around at the first opportunity and started to paddle. They felt the irresistible swell of the ocean squeezing into the beach's shallows lift and accelerate them, and after more frantic paddling they sprang to their feet.

It was a great ride, and whether they fell off, jumped off or were pushed, they had already hung ten inside the green room and come out the other side. The ride had already exceeded their wildest dreams. You could paddle out and try for another ride, but the ride was so long (twenty-six years), so brilliant (hundreds of songs written and millions of records sold) and so exhausting (over 2000 live performances). Do you really try for another ride of a lifetime?

Pete and Bones have now both officially left the band – Pete to pursue his political ambitions through the Australian Labor Party in the seat of Kingsford Smith, and Bones to marry his girlfriend of several years standing, in Las Vegas with an Elvis impersonator as celebrant (to the tune of 'Suspicious Minds' and 'In the Ghetto'!), and then relocating to New Zealand. Rob and Jim and Martin, however, are still members of

Midnight Oil and have written, rehearsed and recorded new material.

So there may or may not be another CD before the distinctive Midnight Oil board is finally pulled onto the beach, strapped to the top of the car and relegated to the corner of someone's garage. There remains only the vexed question of whether anything will be capable of enticing the five of them together again for some sort of reunion ride. The water will need to be clean and the surf will need to be big.

discography

All dates and track listings are for Australian releases.

Midnight Oil – Released November 1978
Produced by Keith Walker and Midnight Oil/Recorded at Alberts, Sydney
Track listing
Powderworks (Hirst/Moginie/Rotsey/James)
Head Over Heels (Hirst/Rotsey/Moginie)
Dust (Moginie/Garrett/Hirst)
Used and Abused (Hirst/Moginie)
Surfing with a Spoon (Hirst/Moginie/Rotsey/Garrett)
Run by Night (Moginie/Hirst/Rotsey)
Nothing Lost, Nothing Gained (Moginie)

Head Injuries – Released October 1979
Produced by Les Karski/Recorded at Trafalgar, Sydney
Track listing
Cold Cold Change (Hirst/Moginie)
Section 5 (Bus to Bondi) (Rotsey/Hirst/Garrett/Moginie)
Naked Flame (Rotsey/Hirst/Moginie)

Back on the Borderline (James/Garrett/Hirst)
Koala Sprint (Garrett/Moginie/Rotsey)
No Reaction (Hirst/Moginie/Rotsey)
Stand in Line (Moginie/Hirst/Rotsey/Garrett)
Profiteers (Hirst/Moginie/Rotsey)
Is It Now? (Moginie/Garrett)

Bird Noises (EP) – Released November 1980
Produced by Les Karski/Recorded at Music Farm, Byron Bay
Track listing
No Time for Games (Hirst/Moginie)
Knife's Edge (Garrett/Rotsey/Moginie)
Wedding Cake Island (Rotsey/Moginie)
I'm the Cure (Moginie)

Place Without a Postcard – Released November 1981
Produced by Glyn Johns/Recorded at Glyn's Farm, Surrey, UK
Track listing
Don't Wanna Be the One (Hirst/Garrett/Rotsey/Moginie)
Brave Faces (Moginie/Garrett)
Armistice Day (Hirst/Moginie/Rotsey)
Someone Else to Blame (Hirst/Moginie/Gifford)
Basement Flat (Rotsey/Garrett/Moginie)
Written in the Heart (Hirst/Moginie/Rotsey)
Burnie (Moginie/Garrett)
Quinella Holiday (Garrett/Moginie)
Loves on Sale (Garrett/Rotsey)
If Ned Kelly Was King (Moginie/Garrett)
Lucky Country (Moginie/Garrett/Rotsey/Hirst)

10,9,8,7,6,5,4,3,2,1 – Released November 1982
Produced by Nick Launay and Midnight Oil/Recorded at Town House, London

Track listing
Outside World (Moginie)
Only the Strong (Hirst/Moginie)
Short Memory (Hirst/Moginie/Garrett)
Read About It (Hirst/Moginie/Garrett)
Scream in Blue (Rotsey/Moginie/Garrett)
US Forces (Moginie/Garrett)
Power and the Passion (Hirst/Moginie/Garrett)
Maralinga (Moginie/Garrett)
Tin Legs and Tin Mines (Rotsey/Moginie/Garrett)
Somebody's Trying to Tell Me Something (Hirst/Rotsey/Moginie/Gifford/Garrett)

Red Sails in the Sunset – Released October 1984
Produced by Nick Launay and Midnight Oil/Recorded at Victor Aoyama, Tokyo

Track listing
When the Generals Talk (Hirst/Moginie/Garrett)
Best of Both Worlds (Hirst/Moginie)
Sleep (Moginie/Hirst/Garrett)
Minutes to Midnight (Moginie/Garrett)
Jimmy Sharman's Boxers (Hirst/Moginie)
Bakerman (Hirst)
Who Can Stand in the Way (Moginie/Garrett)
Kosciuszko (Hirst/Moginie)
Helps Me Helps You (Hirst/Moginie)
Harrisburg (Moginie/Kevans)
Bells and Horns in the Back of Beyond (Midnight Oil)
Shipyards of New Zealand (Moginie/Garrett)

Species Deceases (EP) – Released December 1985
Produced by Midnight Oil and François Kevorkian/Recorded at Paradise, Sydney
- *Track listing*
- Progress (Garrett/Moginie)
- Hercules (Garrett/Hirst/Moginie)
- Blossom and Blood (Hirst/Moginie)
- Pictures (Midnight Oil)

Diesel and Dust – Released August 1987
Produced by Warne Livesey and Midnight Oil/Recorded at Alberts, Sydney
- *Track listing*
- Beds Are Burning (Midnight Oil)
- Put Down That Weapon (Midnight Oil)
- Dreamworld (Midnight Oil)
- Arctic World (Midnight Oil)
- Warakurna (Midnight Oil)
- The Dead Heart (Midnight Oil)
- Whoa (Midnight Oil)
- Bullroarer (Midnight Oil)
- Sell My Soul (Midnight Oil)
- Sometimes (Midnight Oil)
- Gunbarrel Highway (Midnight Oil)

Blue Sky Mining – Released March 1990
Produced by Warne Livesey and Midnight Oil/Recorded at Rhinoceros, Sydney
- *Track listing*
- Blue Sky Mine (Midnight Oil)
- Stars of Warburton (Moginie/Garrett)
- Bedlam Bridge (Hirst)
- Forgotten Years (Hirst/Moginie)
- Mountains of Burma (Hirst)

King of the Mountain (Hirst/Moginie)
River Runs Red (Hirst/Moginie)
Shakers and Movers (Moginie/Garrett)
One Country (Moginie/Garrett)
Antarctica (Moginie/Hirst/Rotsey/Garrett)

Scream In Blue – Released May 1992
Produced by Midnight Oil and Keith Walker/Recorded at various locations
Track listing
Scream in Blue (as credited, *10–1*)
Read About It (as credited, *10–1*)
Dreamworld (as credited, *Diesel and Dust*)
Brave Faces (as credited, *Place Without a Postcard*)
Only the Strong (as credited, *10–1*)
Stars of Warburton (as credited, *Blue Sky Mining*)
Progress (as credited, *Species Deceases*)
Beds Are Burning (as credited, *Diesel and Dust*)
Sell My Soul (as credited, *Diesel and Dust*)
Sometimes (as credited, *Diesel and Dust*)
Hercules (as credited, *Species Deceases*)
Powderworks (as credited, *Midnight Oil*)

Earth and Sun and Moon – Released February 1993
Produced by Nick Launay and Midnight Oil/Recorded at Megaphon, Sydney
Track listing
Feeding Frenzy (Garrett/Moginie)
My Country (Hirst)
Renaissance Man (Moginie/Garrett/Rotsey)
Earth and Sun and Moon (Moginie)
Truganini (Hirst/Moginie)
Bushfire (Moginie/Garrett)
Drums of Heaven (Hirst/Moginie/Garrett)

Outbreak of Love (Hirst)
In the Valley (Moginie/Garrett/Hirst)
Tell Me the Truth (Moginie/Garrett)
Now or Never Land (Moginie/Garrett)

Breathe – Released October 1996
Produced by Malcolm Burn and Midnight Oil/Recorded at Darling Harbour, Sydney and Kingsway, New Orleans, USA
Track listing
Underwater (Midnight Oil)
Surf's Up Tonight (Midnight Oil)
Common Ground (Midnight Oil)
Time to Heal (Midnight Oil)
Sins of Omission (Midnight Oil)
One Too Many Times (Midnight Oil)
Star of Hope (Midnight Oil)
In the Rain (Midnight Oil)
Bring on the Change (Midnight Oil)
Home (Midnight Oil)
E-Beat (Midnight Oil)
Barest Degree (Midnight Oil)

20,000 Watt RSL – Released September 1997
Various producers, as previously credited/Recorded at various locations
Track listing
What Goes On (Midnight Oil)
Power and the Passion (as credited, *10–1*)
Dreamworld (as credited, *Diesel and Dust*)
White Skin Black Heart (Midnight Oil)
Kosciuszko (as credited, *Red Sails in the Sunset*)
The Dead Heart (as credited, *Diesel and Dust*)
Blue Sky Mine (as credited, *Blue Sky Mining*)

US Forces (as credited, *10–1*)
Beds Are Burning (as credited, *Diesel and Dust*)
One Country (as credited, *Blue Sky Mining*)
Best of Both Worlds (as credited, *Red Sails in the Sunset*)
Truganini (as credited, *Earth and Sun and Moon*)
King of the Mountain (as credited, *Blue Sky Mining*)
Hercules (as credited, *Species Deceases*)
Surf's Up Tonight (as credited, *Breathe*)
Back on the Borderline (as credited, *Head Injuries*)
Don't Wanna Be the One (as credited, *Place Without a Postcard*)
Forgotten Years (as credited, *Blue Sky Mining*)

Redneck Wonderland – Released January 1998
Produced by Magoo, Warne Livesey and Midnight Oil/Recorded at Sing Sing, Melbourne and Electric Avenue, Sydney

Track listing
Redneck Wonderland (Midnight Oil)
Concrete (Midnight Oil)
Cemetery in My Mind (Midnight Oil)
Comfortable Place on the Couch (Midnight Oil)
Safety Chain Blues (Midnight Oil)
Return to Sender (Midnight Oil)
Blot (Midnight Oil)
The Great Gibber Plain (Midnight Oil)
Seeing Is Believing (Midnight Oil)
White Skin Black Heart (Midnight Oil)
What Goes On (Midnight Oil)
Drop in the Ocean (Midnight Oil)

The Real Thing – Released July 2000
Studio producers: Midnight Oil and Daniel Denholm/Recorded at Festival, Sydney, Metro Theatre, Sydney and Sony Studios, New York

Track listing
The Real Thing (J. Young)
Say Your Prayers (Moginie)
Spirit of the Age (Moginie/Garrett)
Feeding Frenzy (as credited, *Earth and Sun and Moon*)
Tell Me the Truth (as credited, *Earth and Sun and Moon*)
The Dead Heart (as credited, *Diesel and Dust*)
Tin Legs and Tin Mines (as credited, *10–1*)
Short Memory (as credited, *10–1*)
In the Valley (as credited, *Earth and Sun and Moon*)
Blue Sky Mine (as credited, *Blue Sky Mining*)
US Forces (as credited, *10–1*)
Warakurna (as credited, *Diesel and Dust*)
Truganini (as credited, *Earth and Sun and Moon*)
The Last of the Diggers (Hirst)

Capricornia – Released February 2002
Produced by Warne Livesey and Midnight Oil/Recorded at Festival, Sydney
Track listing
Golden Age (Moginie/Hirst/Garrett)
Too Much Sunshine (Moginie)
Capricornia (Moginie/Hirst)
Luritja Way (Moginie/Hirst)
Tone Poem (Moginie/Garrett)
A Crocodile Cries (Midnight Oil)
Mosquito March (Moginie/Garrett)
Been Away Too Long (Moginie/Garrett)
Under the Overpass (Moginie/Hirst)
World that I See (Moginie/Hirst)
Poets and Slaves (Moginie)

references

Apter, Jeff, *Tomorrow Never Knows: The Silverchair Story*, Coulomb Communications, Port Melbourne, 2003.

Best of Both Worlds, DVD (shows at Goat Island 1985 and Capitol Theatre 1982), filmed by Mark Fitzgerald and Dave Bradbury, restored by Justin Heitman, sound by Keith Walker and Jim Moginie, Australian Broadcasting Corporation, 2004.

Black Fella White Fella: Midnight Oil, video (documentary of tour with Warumpi Band through Central Australia), produced by Rob Stewart, Des Horne and Midnight Oil, Sony, 1987.

Bowman, David, *Fa Fa Fa Fa Fa Fa: The Adventures of Talking Heads in the 20th Century*, Bloomsbury, London, 2001.

Fisher, Gillian, *Half-Life: The NDP: Peace, Protest and Party Politics*, State Library of NSW Press, 1995.

Hirst, Rob, *Willie's Bar & Grill: A Rock'n'Roll Tour of America in the Age of Terror*, Pan Macmillan, Sydney, 2003.

McMillan, Andrew, *Strict Rules*, Hodder and Stoughton, Sydney, 1988.

Midnight Oil: Black Rain Falls, video (New York Exxon protest performance documentary), produced by Larry Jordan and John Diaz, CBS, 1990.

REFERENCES

Midnight Oil: 20,000 Watt RSL: The Midnight Oil Collection, video (collection of videos and live performances and interviews), produced by Stephanie Lewis, Sony, 1997.

Murray, Neil, *Sing for Me, Countryman*, Sceptre, Rydalmere, NSW, 1993.

Watson, Don, *Recollections of a Bleeding Heart: A Portrait of Paul Keating PM*, Knopf, Milsons Point, NSW, 2002.

Zappa, Frank, with Occhiogrosso, Peter, *The Real Frank Zappa Book*, Picador, London, 1990.

index

For individual Midnight Oil songs, albums and video clips, see separate indexes at end of main index.

main index

A&M Records, London 89, 180, 214, 301
ABC *see* Australian Broadcasting Corporation
Aboriginal affairs *see* Indigenous issues
Abrahams, Chris 149, 237, 336
AC/DC 62, 80, 173, 214
   'Long Way to the Top' 62
ACE agency 88, 89, 118, 217
ACF *see* Australian Conservation Foundation
Adelaide Town Hall 97
Adolph, Constance (Connie, 'The Boogie Queen')
   88–91, 106–7, 116, 118, 130, 216–17, 219, 331
Advance Australia Where tour 107
Advisory Committee on Individual and Democratic
   Rights 44
Aerosmith 246
Age, The (Melbourne) 346
AIM (American Indian Movement) 163
Air Supply 78, 79
Airborne Studios, Sydney 78
Albert's studio, Sydney 80, 173
Allen, Craig 15
ALP *see* Australian Labor Party
Amphlett, Chrissie 126

Anderson, Nadya 119
Angels, The 76, 173
Annandale Hotel, Sydney 272
anti-nuclear *see* nuclear disarmament
Aoyama Studios, Tokyo 196, 362
apartheid 14
Apter, Jeff 218
Argall, Ray 147
ARIAs *see* Australian Record Industry Awards
Armatrading, Joan 177
Art of Noise, The 197
Artists United Against Apartheid 44
asbestos 282–3
ASIO *see* Australian Security and Intelligence
   Organisation
Australia Card campaign 44
Australian Broadcasting Corporation 38, 81, 147
Australian Conservation Foundation 17, 45–6, 48,
   52, 211
Australian Democrats 38
Australian Forest Action Network 42
Australian Independence Movement 27
Australian Labor Party 29, 38–41, 46–7, 211, 384

INDEX

Australian Record Industry Awards 170
Australian Security and Intelligence Organisation 37
Avalon RSL Club 69
Ayers Rock *see* Uluru

Baez, Joan 82
Barnes, Jimmy 184
Beatles, The 58, 59, 64, 77, 110, 162, 177, 214, 326, 377
   'I'm a Loser' 59
   'Let It Be' 177
   Revolver 326
Bercy Auditorium, Paris 221–2, 303
Best of Both Worlds (DVD) 111, 129
Biafra, Jello 138
Big Mountain, Oregon 163
Billy Graham Crusade 85, 300
Birmingham, UK 120, 214
Bjelke-Petersen, Joh 43
Black Fella White Fella tour 131, 146, 171, 346
Black Rain Falls (film) 23
BLF *see* Builders' Labourers Federation
Blue Murder (book) 205
BMG 370
Bondi Lifesaver (hotel) 74, 81, 89
Bonefetti, Sal 307–8
Bono 382
Bowie, David 173
Branson, Richard 89
Bray, Dorland 337
Brazil 232–4
Brittany festival 165
Brookes, Arlene 15
Brown, James 137
Bruce, Jack 60
Builders' Labourers Federation 26–7
Building Bridges project 167
Burn, Malcolm 334–5, 347–50
Bush, George 382
Butcher, Gordon 146, 149
Butcher, Sammy 146

CAA *see* Creative Artists Agency
Calgary Speedway, Canada 240

Campaign for Nuclear Disarmament (UK) 28, 128, 214
Capitol Theatre, Sydney 111, 121–2
Carey, Alex 34
Carey, Peter 40
Carter, Amy 47
Carter, Jimmy 47
Carter, Rosalynn 47
Castle, Claudia 232, 316
Caves Beach, NSW 87, 112
CBS 196, 327
Central Park gig 25
Channel 9 (TV) 38
Channel 7 (TV) 33, 78
Channel 10 (TV) 28
Chipp, Don 38
Civic Hotel, Sydney 74, 297
Clapton, Eric 187
Claringbold, David 149
Clash, The 23, 41, 129, 134, 165
Clayoquot Sound, Canada 49
Clear Channel 370
Clemenceau, George 12
Clinton, Bill 47
CND *see* Campaign for Nuclear Disarmament
Cold Chisel 76, 107, 184
Collins, Phil 186
Columbia Records 215, 228–9, 301, 307, 309, 311, 318
Connor, Abby 245
conscription *see* National Service
conservation movement 14
   see also environmental issues; green issues
Constable Care road safety campaign 17
Cooder, Ry 89–90, 236
Cook, Murray 65
Coombs, H. C. 'Nugget' 45
Coronation Hill 45–6
Costello, Elvis 88
Countdown (TV) 62, 81
Coverdale, David 160
Cramps, The 236
Creative Artists Agency 158
Cronulla Workers Club 114
Crosby Stills Nash and Young 64

crowd control 110–16
Crowded House 256, 336
Crystal Ballroom, Melbourne 360
Cure, The 236

Daintree Rainforests campaign 43
Daltrey, Roger 134, 135
Darling Harbour studio, Sydney 335, 347–8
Dauth, John 231
de Medici, eX 367
Denver, John 307
Depardieu, Gérard 165
Diesel and Dust to Big Mountain tour 218
Dingwalls, London 119
Dire Straits 42
Divinyls 126, 330
Do Re Mi 337
Dodson, Pat 147
Double Jay radio *see* 2JJ
Dragon 83
Draper, Simon 89
Dube, Lucky 325
Duigan, John 28, 34
Dusty, Slim 152, 366
    'Pub with No Beer' 366
Dylan, Bob 64, 82, 159, 215, 236, 276, 289, 307, 347

Eagles, The 177
Earth Day concert, Boston 48, 339
Earl's Court, UK 178
East Timor 365
Easybeats, The 80
Ebb Tide and the Shorebreakers 130
Eizik, Zev 85, 88–91, 93, 106–7, 109, 116, 118–19, 122, 216, 217, 300, 301, 304
Ellis Park, Johannesburg 238
Elysée Montmartre club, Paris 221
Emerson Lake and Palmer 59
EMI 89
environmental issues 16, 25, 26, 42, 46–50, 211, 282
    see also conservation movement; Exxon gig; green issues
Epic Records 317

European tours 129, 149, 162, 164, 211, 220–2, 236, 242–3, 354
Everleigh Railway Workshop 33
Exxon gig (New York, 1990) 17–24, 26, 215, 341, 374

Faith No More 236
Family Dog, The 336
Farm 56, 57, 60, 61, 69
    'Bus to Bondi' 61
    'Drought' 68
    'Section 5 Clause B' 61
Farrell, Perry 323, 324
Farriss Brothers 83
Festival Hall, Melbourne 162
Festival Studios, Sydney 287, 368
Field, Billy 200
    'Bad Habits' 200
Fillmore gig, Los Angeles 25
Film Australia 147
Finch 61
Finn, Neil 161, 335–6, 353
    Try Whistling This 336
Fisher, Gillian 35, 37, 41
Flood, Sean 34
Focus 59
Foley, Gary 45, 147, 163
4ZZZ (radio) 183
Foxboro Stadium, Boston 48
Frank, Chief Francis 49
Fraser, Malcolm 29–30
Freeman, Cathy 168
French's Tavern, Sydney 66, 69, 70, 74–5, 148, 297
Fricke, David 23, 25, 96–7, 134–6, 137, 153–4, 160, 161, 194–5, 243, 250, 272, 284, 310, 325, 327, 371
Fuzz Face 336
    'For Tomorrow' 336

Gabriel, Peter 138–9, 323, 324, 325
Gang of Four 119
Garrett, Andrew 65–6, 67
Garrett, Matt 65–6
Garrett, Peter 2, 3–4, 7–11, 13–17, 19–20, 25, 27, 32, 33, 24, 42, 43, 44–6, 49, 55, 57, 62–9,

INDEX

Garrett, Peter (cont.)
  70, 72–3, 77, 82, 86, 87, 89, 92, 98, 99, 101–5, 107–8, 111–18, 122, 123–7, 130, 132, 134, 140–1, 143, 147, 154, 155, 156, 163–4, 166–72, 176, 177, 179–85, 189–92, 194, 197–207, 208–9, 210, 211, 213, 216–17, 219, 223, 224, 231, 232, 235, 237, 238, 240–2, 246, 258–65, 267, 269, 271, 273, 276–7, 287–9, 294, 297–301, 304, 305–7, 315, 323–4, 328, 332, 333, 335, 337, 338–40, 342, 345–6, 348–50, 354–5, 359–64, 367, 368, 369, 371–6, 378, 383, 384
  ACF president 45–8, 52, 211–12
  1984 election campaign 30–41, 129, 196–7, 267
  Greenpeace International board 51–2, 274
  joining Midnight Oil 60–2, 333
  parents 65–7, 275
  political position 13, 209
  religion 363–4
  Rock Island Line 63, 129
  songwriting 252–4, 257, 275
  stage manner 7–9, 63, 70–1, 82, 91, 97–8, 134–8, 182
  view of the band 4–5, 67, 151
  see also Nuclear Disarmament Party
Geeves, Richard 128
Geldof, Bob 25
Ghostwriters 274, 336–8
  Second Skin 338
  'Someone's Singing New York, New York' 337
  'World Is Almost at Peace' 337
Gifford, Peter 'Giffo' 2, 4, 10, 31, 49, 57, 94, 99–104, 109, 116, 127–8, 130, 131–3, 139, 141, 149–50, 155, 161, 172, 177–8, 183, 184, 191, 192, 199, 200, 202, 206, 210, 260, 262, 266, 301, 304, 330, 340, 362
Gilding, Paul 15, 16, 26, 46, 51–2
Glastonbury Festival 130, 214
Globe Arena, Stockholm 221
Goat Island show (Sydney, 1985) 129
Gondwanaland 42
Good Morning America (TV) 382
Gordon, Herbie 317
Gow Brothers 325
Grafitti Man 25, 48, 163, 218
Grammy awards 45, 163, 302, 382

Grant, Peter 328
green issues 26, 30, 43, 52, 180, 209, 348
Greenpeace 15, 19, 46–8, 51–2, 82, 274, 284, 285
Grinspoon 356
Grossman, Rick 330, 337
grunge 273, 323–5, 327, 356
Guisot, François 12, 30, 53
Gunja 59

Hammersmith Odeon, London 129, 214
Handlin, Denis 45, 163, 215, 229, 302
Hanson, Pauline 355
Hard Report, The (TV) 229
Harding, Ken 78, 80
Harp Hotel, Sydney 352
Harris, Emmylou 347, 349–50
Harris, Rolf 214
Hawke, Bob 30, 32, 38, 46–7, 146
Hawley, Janet 346
Hayden, Bill 38–9
Hazat, Salomon 165, 222, 303
Helsham, Justice Michael 101
Hendrix, Jimi 135
Henry, Don 52
Herbert, Xavier 369
Hill, Ben 205
Hillman, Bones (Wayne Stevens) 2–4, 49, 57, 131, 139, 141, 161–2, 169, 172, 202, 206–7, 210, 212–13, 218, 219, 221, 224–5, 232, 234–5, 237–42, 274, 289, 324–5, 330, 332, 334–6, 341, 349, 357, 361, 364, 366, 368, 373, 379, 384
Hirst, Lesley 1
Hirst, Rob 1, 2–4, 8–10, 13, 18, 21, 27, 31, 41, 42, 48, 50, 54–7, 65, 66, 68, 69–71, 73–4, 77, 85, 87, 97, 99, 100, 103, 111, 118, 121, 132–3, 133–4, 135, 138, 141, 144, 149, 152, 154, 156–7, 161, 165–6, 169, 170, 172, 173, 177, 179, 181, 184, 186–7, 190, 193, 197–8, 200–3, 205, 206, 210, 213, 217, 221–3, 235, 238, 239, 242, 244, 256–9, 261–3, 265–67, 269–70, 274, 276–7, 282, 287–9, 293, 301, 304, 314, 315, 328, 330, 332–39, 342, 343, 344, 347–9, 354, 355, 356, 358, 359, 361, 364, 366, 368, 373, 380, 384
  early bands 58–61

INDEX

songwriting 251–4, 286
Willie's Bar & Grill 220
Hodgkinson, Chris 59
Hogan, Paul 168
Holding, Clyde 147
Hong, Colin Lee 86
Hoodoo Gurus 330, 337
Hordern Pavilion, Sydney 7, 129, 131, 161
Howard, John 47, 168–9, 289
Hummingbirds 236
Hunting Party, The 336
Hutchence, Michael 83

Ienner, Don 228–9, 280, 311–14, 316–22, 327
Indigenous issues 5, 24, 29, 45, 50, 141–53, 163–4, 167–70, 278, 332, 348
INXS 83, 85, 202, 203, 312, 367
Isle of Calf, Norway 211

Jackson, John 119
Jackson, Michael 160, 165, 240
Jagger, Mick 135, 276
Jam, The 119, 186
James, Andrew 'Bear' 2, 4, 54, 55–7, 63, 65, 68, 69, 80–7, 92–3, 99, 131, 132, 183, 256–7, 296, 300, 301, 330, 333, 340, 359
 early bands 57–60
James, Ron 'Wormy' 218
Japan 30–1, 129, 196–9, 263, 265–6, 362–3
Jeff Healey Band 236
Jefferson Airplane 64
Jervis Bay 14–16, 46
Jimmy and the Boys 75
JJJ FM (radio) 109–10, 117, 129, 199
Jobs – Every Home Should Have One gig (Sydney) 125
Johns, Daniel 189
Johns, Glyn 110, 116, 120, 176–81, 192, 261
Jones, Alan 44
Jones, Jeff 158
Just A Drummer 149

Karski, Les 83, 182–4
Keating, Paul 46

Kelly, Karina 33
Kelly, Paul 170
Kelpie X 336
Kerr, John 29
Kevorkian, François 200–1
KGFR radio, Texas 370
Killing Joke 119
King's Head, London 130
Kingsway Studio, New Orleans 334, 347
Kinks, The 340
Kravitz, Lenny 236

land rights *see* Indigenous issues
Lanois, Daniel 334, 347
Launay, Nick 119–20, 133, 153, 175–6, 186–99, 253–4, 263, 265–6, 272–3, 275–6, 278–9, 290, 293, 327, 336
Led Zeppelin 89, 328
Lennon, John 23, 184, 325
 'Instant Karma' 23, 366
Leumeah Inn, Sydney 73
Levin, Tony 325
Lewis, Stephanie 15, 127, 148–9
Liberal Party of Australia 29, 38, 40, 47
Liberdade (CD) 365
Lindsay, Diana 15
Lippold, Michael 105–6, 110–17, 122, 126, 127, 137, 152, 217–19, 233–7, 304, 378
Liquid 8 370
Little Feat 236
Little River Band 78
Live Aid 25
Livesey, Warne 138–9, 155–6, 173, 202, 203, 205–7, 338, 356, 368
Lloyd, Glenn 'Pig' 87
Lollapalooza 322–5, 382
London Forum 364
Long March for Justice, Freedom and Hope 45, 163
Lyceum, London 128, 214
Lydon, John 40, 119, 176
lyrics 8–9, 10–11, 27, 28–9

McBurney, Dave 170
MacInnes, Willie 21–2, 49, 91, 219–20
McLaren, Malcolm 88

401

INDEX

McMahon, Charlie 148, 152, 217
McMillan, Andrew 147–8
Macpherson, Elle 168
Machinations 109
Madison Square Garden 171
Madonna 246
Magoo 355–6
Majestic Hotel, Melbourne 81, 359
Management Three 294, 307, 309
Mandela, Nelson 50–1
Manly Pacific Hotel 128
Manly Reservoir 367
Manly Vale Hotel 115
Mann Center, Philadelphia 317
Markowitz, Rhonda 25, 136, 137, 294, 315, 381
Marquee Club, London 116, 214
Matt Finish 109, 330
Mayall, John 64
media 10, 13, 38, 332
Megaphon Studios, Sydney 272
Melbourne Entertainment Centre 308
Men At Work 255–6, 367
   'Down Under' 255
Mental As Anything 65
Meriwether Post, USA (venue) 98
Metallica 225
Milli Vanilli 280
Minogue, Kylie 141, 168, 214
Mi-Sex 83
Mitchell, Joni 240
Moginie, Jim 2–3, 10, 13–15, 21, 22, 27, 30, 48, 49, 54, 57, 62, 65, 66, 68, 69–71, 86, 90, 92, 99, 103, 113, 121, 126, 135, 137, 143, 144, 150, 176–82, 184–5, 190–3, 195, 198, 200, 202, 204–5, 210, 220, 235–9, 256–9, 261–9, 273–7, 286, 287–8, 292, 315, 326, 331, 333, 335–41, 343, 344–5, 347–51, 354–7, 359, 360, 361, 364, 366, 368–9, 373, 374, 384
   adoption 349–52
   early bands 57–61
   family 351–3, 358
   songwriting 251–4, 365
   style 187–9
Moman, Chips 230
Mondo Rock 83, 109

Mongrel Mob 86
Moomba Festival, Melbourne 122
Moon, Keith 60, 293
Morgan, Hugh 38
Morris, Amanda 367
Morris (Vasicek), Gary 2–3, 15–16, 18–19, 25, 45, 49, 65, 67, 72–6, 78–85, 87, 89, 109, 118–19, 122–8, 141, 147–8, 157–9, 162, 171, 201, 202, 212, 213, 214, 215, 217, 219, 226–30, 238, 240, 242, 247, 273, 280, 292–309, 311–22, 324, 327–9, 333, 339, 340–7, 354–5, 359, 361, 363, 366–7, 373, 376, 382, 383
Morris, Russell 365
Moss, Chris 19, 21–2, 24, 48, 157–8, 208–9, 243, 272, 301–3, 310–11, 313, 316–17, 341, 343, 381
Moss, Ian 184
Mottola, Tommy 21, 309, 311
Movement Against Uranium Mining 82
Moving Pictures 109
MTV 160, 230, 237, 245–6, 284, 295, 315, 317, 339
Mulawa Women's Detention Centre, Sydney 125–6
Munoz, Mason 18–21, 24, 98, 135–6, 215, 242, 245–6, 283, 311–13, 317–21, 343, 370, 382
Murphy, Chris 85
Murray, Neil 146, 150, 170, 351–3
   Going the Distance 351
Mururoa Atoll 166
Muse concerts 25
Music Farm studio, NSW 184
Musician magazine 96
Myer Music Bowl, Melbourne 28, 123

National Service 14, 29
Nature Nature 170
NDP *see* Nuclear Disarmament Party
Neale, Chris 78–9
Nelson, Doc 234–5
Neville Brothers 335, 347
New Zealand Labour Party 30
New Zealand tours 84–6, 92, 113, 116, 118, 129, 242, 300
New York Times 382
Nicholas, Dave 203
Nick Cave and the Bad Seeds 214, 236
Nirvana 272, 292, 393

No Fixed Address 145
No Nukes concerts, New York 25
Norman, Greg 168
North American tours 130, 133, 138, 148, 149, 157–8, 162–3, 211, 213, 216–19, 223–4, 239–40, 242–3, 317–18, 367, 369–70
North West Cape 30
Nothing's as Precious as a Hole in the Ground (painting) 367
nuclear disarmament 16, 25, 26, 27–30, 41–2, 166, 196, 264, 284
Nuclear Disarmament Party 7, 11, 30–40, 129, 196
    relations with SWP 37–8
Nucleus Agency 87, 297
Numbulwar 128–9, 145–6, 151–3
Nurungah 30

O'Connor, Sinead 236
O'Keefe, Johnny 368
Ol'55 77
Olympic Games, Sydney 140–2, 149, 167–9, 299, 367
Olympic Studios, London 176
One Night Stand (film) 28
Open Family Foundation 16, 17

Paddington Town Hall 75
Padgham, Hugh 119
Pambula Country Women's Association 56
Paradis, Vanessa 165
Paradise Studios, Sydney 42, 200
Parker Meridian Hotel 21
Parramatta Park 85, 109–10, 183
pay for play 159, 227
Pearl Jam 273, 292, 323, 383
Penrith Park, Sydney 125
People for Nuclear Disarmament 28
Philip, Duke of Edinburgh 45
Phineasa, Henry 170
Pickett, Pat, 152
Pier 84, New York 294
Pine Gap 30, 40, 44, 253
Pink Floyd 176, 178
Plant, Robert 135
Plimmer, Chris 87–8, 116, 119, 297

Poi Dog Pondering 228
Police, The 119
Political Blues (book) 44
political stance 13, 24–7
Pop, Iggy 138, 347
Porno for Pyros 323
Powderworkers 374
Powderworks Records 79–80, 297, 301
President Hotel, Tokyo 362
Presley, Elvis 377, 384
    'In the Ghetto' 384
    'Suspicious Minds' 384
Prince 137
privacy 2
Public Image Limited 41
Purple Link 58

Quiltman 163, 167

Radiators, The 109
Radio City Music Hall, New York 20, 211
Rage Against the Machine 323
Rainbow Warrior 268–9
Rainforest Action Network 42
Ramones, The 138
RCA 79
Reagan, Ronald 36, 285
reconciliation *see* Indigenous issues
Red Hot Chili Peppers 221, 236, 323, 393
Red Ochre 149
Reed, Glad 140, 148–9
Regent Hotel, Sydney 69–70
Regurgitator 356
REM 225, 378, 382
republic debate 278
Rex Hotel, Sydney 74
Rhinoceros Studios, Sydney 99, 174, 198, 202
Richards, Keith 189
Richardson, Graham 37, 41, 211–12
Riviera, Jake 88
Rock Against Racism 145
Rock Island Line 63, 129
Rock Theatre, Wellington 87
Rockefeller Center 18–19, 23, 382
Roger Smith Hotel, New York 231

INDEX

Rogers and Cowan 294
Rolling Stone magazine 23, 96, 136, 347
Rolling Stones, The 110–11, 165, 176. 177, 189
Rollins, Henry 138
Rose Tattoo 81, 173
Rose, Mitch 158
Roskilde, Denmark 211, 236
Rotsey, Martin 1, 2, 4, 9–10, 13–14, 21, 22, 48, 54, 65, 68, 69–71, 77, 87, 99, 103, 108–9, 135, 137, 170, 177, 179, 181, 184, 200, 210, 220, 236, 244, 251, 257, 258, 261, 263, 274, 315, 333, 335, 336, 344, 349, 359, 360–1, 364, 368, 373, 384
   early bands 59–60, 235
   style 187–9, 359
Rovenor, Jack 158
Royal Antler Hotel, Narrabeen 54–5, 71–3, 100–1, 130, 132, 296, 297
royalties 254–5, 314
Royle, John 59
RRR (radio) *see* 3RRR
Rundgren, Todd 59
Rurrambu, George 'Djilaynga' 146, 150
Russell, Michael 'Garfield' 149
Ruth the wallaby 127–8
Ryde Youth Centre 61

Sacks, Doug 180
St John, Ted 32, 34, 38
St Leonards Park, Sydney 76
Saints, The 214
Salvation Army 17
Santana 56
Saturday Night Live (TV) 313, 316
Save Jervis Bay campaign 14–15
Save the Lemonthyme Forest campaign 42
Save the Whales 82
Scales, Gisele 191
Schwampy Moose 59
Scobie, Johnny 164
Scorching of the Earth tour 107
Scott, Bon 62
Sebel Townhouse, Sydney 111
Seekers, The 214
Selinas, Sydney 34, 110, 116, 300, 362
September 11 *see* World Trade Center attacks

Seven Records 78–9
Sex Pistols 40, 88–9, 90
   Never Mind the Bollocks 89
Sharp, Martin 40
Shead, Gary 40
Sheraton Hotel, Rio de Janeiro 237
Sherbs, The 83
Shoalwater Bay 45
Silverchair 43, 189, 218–19, 336, 341, 378
   Neon Ballroom 189, 336
Simple Minds 119, 186
Sing Sing studios, Melbourne 356, 358
Skyhooks 83, 185
   Living in the 70s 185
Small Faces, The 177
Smashing Pumpkins 273
Smith, Steve 229
Socialist Workers Party 37–8
Solo Premier 75
Sony 18–20, 23, 45, 98, 126, 157–8, 162, 163, 196, 215, 228–30, 271, 277, 280, 283, 291, 301–2, 311, 322, 327, 329, 336, 343, 346, 355, 365, 366, 378
South Africa 50, 232, 235, 236
   see also apartheid
South America 232–6
South East Forests Coalition of NSW 42
Sparta 60, 69
Spivak, Arthur 307–8
Split Enz 83, 281
   'Six Months in a Leaky Boat' 281
Springsteen, Bruce 44, 135, 288
   'Born in the USA' 288
Sprint Music 68, 256
Stagedoor Tavern, Sydney 84, 101–6, 297
Stevens, Wayne *see* Hillman, Bones
Sting 51, 135
Stop the Drop gig, Melbourne 28, 123, 125
Strachan, Shirley 83
Strict Rules (book) 147–8
Studio 301, Sydney 153
Sun City, South Africa 44, 50
Sunnyboys, The 117
Supercharge 83
Swamp Jockeys 152

INDEX

Sweetwater Festival, New Zealand 118
Swingers, The 86
SWP *see* Socialist Workers Party
Sydney Entertainment Centre 27, 42, 43, 128
Sydney Morning Herald 151, 333
Sydney Town Hall 26
Symons, Red 83

Talking Heads, The 255
Tanelorn Festival, NSW 116–17
Tarthra School of Arts 56
Teller, Al 45, 229, 308–9
The The 236
3EON FM (radio) 28
3RRR (radio) 82, 109, 119, 183
Tibet benefit 272
Toad the Wet Sprocket 228
Tomorrow Never Knows (book) 219
Topaz 59
Town House studios, London 119, 175, 186–7
Townshend, Pete 284, 289
    'Lighthouse' 284
Toyne, Phillip 46–7
Trafalgar Studios, Sydney 84, 182
Triple J radio *see* JJJ
Trudell, John 163, 167
Turku, Finland 211
2JJ (radio) 38, 76, 79, 82, 99, 109, 129, 183
2XX (radio) 64–5, 183

UB40 130, 217
UK tours 116, 120, 128, 130, 162, 211, 242
Uluru 146, 152, 285
Uluru: An Anangu Story (film) 146–7
United Nations Media Peace Prize 28
Universal Amphitheatre, Los Angeles 211
US foreign policy 27
US tours *see* North American tours
U2 118, 165, 225, 377, 378, 379, 381–2

Valentine, Jo 38
Van Zandt, Steve 44
Vancouver Island, Canada 48
Vanda, Harry 80, 173
Vasicek, Gary Morris *see* Morris, Gary

Vault studios, Sydney 170
Vietnam War 14, 29, 288
Virgin Records 88, 89

Walker, Keith 76, 79, 181
Wanda Beach Youth Refuge gig 117
Warumpi Band 130–2, 145–7, 149–50, 152, 170
    'Blackfella/Whitefella' 149
    Go Bush 150
    'Island Home' 150
    'Jailangaru Pakarnu' 145
Waters, Muddy 64
Watson, Don 47
Watson, John 43, 343, 378, 382–3
Watson, Peter 70
Watts, Charlie 187
WDRE New York (radio) 22, 24
Weintraub, Gerry 294, 307–8
Wembley Arena, UK 214
Wemyss, Kathy 140
White Horse Tavern, Sydney 76
White, Patrick 34, 52
Whiteley, Brett 40
Whitlam, Gough 14, 29–30, 66, 145
Who, The 64, 77, 110–11, 120–1, 134, 138, 176, 214, 284, 288, 382
    Who's Next 284
    'Won't Get Fooled Again' 289
Wilcox, Murray 45
Willesee, Mike 38
Willis, Wayne 15
Wittenoom 205–6
Wizard 89
WOMAD (World of Music, Arts and Dance) 138, 322–6
Woodstock 56
Wootten, Hal 45
Works (record label) 329
World, The, New York 285
World Trade Center attacks 285, 369–70

XTC 119, 186

Yes 59, 61

Yothu Yindi 25, 152, 163, 167, 170, 218
   'Treaty' 170
Young, Angus 62
Young, George 80, 173
Young, Malcolm 62
Younger, Rob 138
Yunupingu, Mandawuy 170

Zappa, Frank 286, 287
   The Real Frank Zappa Book 286
Zenith Theatre, Paris 149, 221
Zig Zag Club, London 119–20, 122, 214

index of songs

Armistice Day 27, 116, 260, 290

Back on the Borderline 93, 182, 324
Bakerman 265
Barest Degree 348
Bedlam Bridge 230–1
Beds Are Burning 5, 25, 45, 140–1, 149, 154, 156–60, 163, 165, 167, 171, 221, 223, 230, 240, 270, 290, 295, 311, 327, 371
Bells and Horns in the Back of Beyond 264, 265
Best of Both Worlds, The 267, 287
Bicentennial 44
Black Skin White Heart 355
Blossom and Blood 201, 204, 269
Blot 68, 357
Blue Sky Mine 26, 68, 202–5, 208, 228, 230, 245, 270, 282, 364
Brave Faces 262
Bring on the Change 348, 349
Bullroarer 154, 156
Burnie 180, 262
Bus to Bondi 182
Bushfire 273, 275

Cold Cold Change 182, 183, 258
Common Ground 348–9

Dead Heart, The 25, 141, 147, 149, 153–4, 157, 160, 215, 259, 270, 311

Don't Wanna Be the One 7–9, 83, 116, 179, 185, 258, 261
Dreamworld 23, 154, 156, 268
Drought *see* Blue Sky Mine
Drums of Heaven 272, 336
Dust 182, 257

Earth and Sun and Moon 293
E-Beat 348
Eye Contact 84

Feeding Frenzy 278, 291
Forgotten Years 203, 204, 228, 230, 245, 270, 364

Golden Age 370–1, 374
Gunbarrel Highway 154

Harrisburg 264, 265
Head Injuries *see* Don't Wanna Be the One
Head Over Heels 182, 286
Hercules 201, 268
Home 348, 349

If Ned Kelly Was King 143, 179, 180, 262
I'm the Cure 184, 364
In the Rain 348–9
In the Valley 237, 275–8, 364
Is it Now? 258

Jacob's Ladder *see* Forgotten Years
Jimmy Sharman's Boxers 144, 259

King of the Mountain 204, 228, 230, 259, 270
Kiss That Girl 287–90, 368
Knife's Edge 184
Koala Sprint 84, 258, 348
Kosciuszko 27, 144, 197, 250, 267

Last of the Diggers, The 365, 366
Loves on Sale 179, 286
Lucky Country 116, 180, 185, 262, 286

Maralinga 27, 264
Minutes to Midnight 263–4
My Country 314, 316, 317, 322, 336

INDEX

Next Big Thing, The *see* US Forces
No Reaction 182, 258, 259
No Time for Games 184
Nothing Lost, Nothing Gained 182, 257

One Country 203, 204, 287
One Too Many Times 348
Only the Strong 137, 189, 194–5, 258, 259
Outbreak of Love 278, 286, 293, 314, 317–18, 322, 336

Pictures 201, 269
Powderworks 182, 259
Power and the Passion 27, 111, 186–7, 201, 250, 253–4, 285, 290, 367
Prayer for Peace *see* Forgotten Years
Profiteers 84
Progress 23, 200–1, 269
Pub with No Beer 366

Quinella Holiday 179

Read About It 10–11, 27, 123–4, 241, 258
Real Thing, The 365–6
Redneck Wonderland 356–7
Renaissance Man 364
River Runs Red 23, 228
Run by Night 99, 182

Say Your Prayers 365, 366
Sell My Soul 365
Shakers and Movers 286
Shipyards of New Zealand 263, 265
Short Memory 27, 191–2, 237, 258, 284
Sins of Omission 348
Sleep 265
Some Kids *see* No Time for Games
Somebody's Trying to Tell Me Something 191
Sometimes 23, 268
Soul Sacrifice 56
Stand in Line 27, 83, 148, 182, 183
Star of Hope 348
Surfing with a Spoon 182, 257, 348
Surf's Up Tonight 348

Time to Heal 334, 348
Truganini 272, 278–9, 283, 290, 293, 312, 316–17, 321, 322, 336

Underwater 329, 348
US Forces 27, 122, 125, 186, 188–91, 250, 284
Used and Abused 182

Warakurna 154
Wedding Cake Island 10, 109, 125, 184–5, 290
What Goes On 355
When the Generals Talk 250, 266, 267
Who Can Stand in the Way 264
Whoah 154
Written in the Heart 27, 116, 258

index of albums & eps

Bird Noises (EP) 109, 179, 184, 301, 364, 365
'Blue Meanie, The' *see* Midnight Oil
Blue Sky Mining 174, 202–7, 209, 211, 215, 223, 225–8, 230, 238–9, 244–5, 247–8, 269–73, 275, 277, 278, 279, 286, 287, 311–12, 327, 368
Breathe 209, 268, 329, 334–5, 338, 339, 347, 354, 356–8
Capricornia 207, 209, 290, 368–9, 371, 375, 382
Diesel and Dust 24, 44, 131, 133, 138, 154, 158–63, 165, 172, 173, 175, 182, 199, 202, 206, 207, 208, 209, 213, 218–21, 223, 227–8, 230, 238, 244, 247, 249, 268, 269, 272, 275, 278, 293, 294, 295, 307, 310, 327, 368, 369
Earth and Sun and Moon 176, 209, 237, 272–9, 286–7, 290–3, 312, 317, 319, 320, 322, 324, 327, 329, 336, 344
Head Injuries 84, 99, 182–5, 257, 258, 261
Midnight Oil 80, 181, 257, 258
Place Without a Postcard 116, 119, 120, 143, 176, 179, 181, 185, 186, 193, 214, 216, 258, 260, 261–2, 286, 287, 301
Powderworks see Midnight Oil
Real Thing, The 209, 365–6
Red Sails in the Sunset 31, 32, 129, 144, 157, 162, 176, 196–9, 209, 223, 263, 265, 268, 273, 310, 362

Redneck Wonderland 51, 209, 268, 354–8, 365
Scream in Blue 183, 209, 271–2
Species Deceases (EP) 42, 199–201, 268, 365, 367
10,9,8,7,6,5,4,3,2,1 27, 30, 32, 97, 120, 122, 125, 126, 129, 157, 152, 175–6, 186, 192, 193–5, 197, 209, 223, 229, 253, 258, 263, 264, 273, 301, 305, 306–7, 310, 331
20,000 Watt RSL 209, 354–5

index of video clips

Back on the Borderline 93
Bedlam Bridge 231–2
Beds are Burning 25, 160, 164, 245
Blue Sky Mine 208, 245
Dead Heart, The 25, 164, 245
Forgotten Years 211, 245
King of the Mountain 23
My Country 316
Truganini 283–4, 312–16, 321